THE OCCULT

A SOURCEBOOK OF ESOTERIC WISDOM

NEVILL DRURY AND GREGORY TILLETT

Grange
BOOKS

Above: An eclectic array of esoteric symbols, including elements of astrological and Qabalistic origin.

Published by Grange Books
An Imprint of Grange Books PLC
The Grange
Grange Yard
London SE1 3AG

This edition published 1997

Copyright © 1997 Saraband Inc.

Adapted and expanded from an original text, *The Occult Sourcebook,* © Nevill Drury and Gregory Tillett, 1978, by arrangement with the authors.

Design © Ziga Design
Editor: Clare Gibson

ISBN: 1-84013-069-5

ACKNOWLEDGEMENTS

The publisher would like to thank the following individuals for their assistance in the preparation of this book: Nicola J. Gillies, assistant editor and indexer; Wendy J. Ciaccia, graphic designer. Grateful acknowledgement is also made to the following individuals and institutions for permission to reproduce the illustrations used on the following pages:
© **Dave Bartruff/Corbis:** 51l; **BFI Stills, Posters and Designs:** 140; **Bibliothèque Nationale de France:** 36; **Corbis-Bettmann:** 4, 8, 15b, 16, 17t, 20b, 22, 25, 26, 31t, 34, 35t, 39, 44, 45, 50t, 52, 54, 55b, 58, 59b, 76, 87, 93, 95, 96b, 105b, 106t, 116, 128, 129, 130tl & tr, 132t, 136l, 147, 148; **CorelDraw:** 12b, 88t; **Fortean Picture Library:** 144t; **FPG International:** 106b (© Charly Franklin 1992), 107 (© James Porto 1992); **Hulton Deutsch Collection/Corbis:** 28t, 33b, 42, 43, 57, 63t, 66, 68, 79b, 80b, 100, 101, 114, 124, 141; © **Charles and Josette Lenars/Corbis:** 62; **Library of Congress, Prints and Photographs Division:** 12t, 29r, 30, 51r, 56, 63b, 64, 65, 67, 69, 81, 82, 83, 88b, 89b, 97t, 115, 135; **Library of Congress, Rare Books Division:** 10; **National Archives:** 143; **Peter Palmquist:** 123; **Penguin/ Corbis-Bettmann:** 138r; **Planet Art:** 17b, 21t, 28b, 29l; **Reuters/ Corbis-Bettmann:** 33t, 75b, 85, 96t, 121t, 125; **Saraband Image Library:** 13, 14–15t, 37t (hand colored by Northwind), 38b, 40, 49, 53, 55t, 61t, 71, 72, 73, 74, 77, 78, 79t, 80t, 89t, 90, 91, 94, 119, 136r, 137 (both), 139b, 149t; © **Michael A. Smith:** 48, 113; **Springer/Corbis-Bettmann:** 130b; © **Michael Tincher:** 32b; **UPI/Corbis-Bettmann:** 11, 24, 31b, 38t, 41, 46, 47, 60, 61b, 70, 75t, 84, 86, 92, 98, 102, 103, 104, 105t, 108, 109, 110, 111, 112, 117, 118, 120, 121b, 122, 126, 127, 131, 133, 134, 138l, 139t, 142 (both), 144b, 145 (both), 146; © **Michael S. Yamashita/Corbis:** 99; © **Charles J. Ziga:** 32t, 59t, 149b.

CONTENTS

Introduction

Below: Mystical traditions are, in large part, derived from ancient religions and mythology. The Hindu god Shiva (below) is known as the Destroyer. Osiris, right, symbolized perfection to the ancient Egyptians, while his sister goddess, Isis, was the Divine Mother.

Until quite recently, the term "occult" was reserved for the black arts alone. Today, the occult has a wider connotation: it encompasses the wisdom of the ancients and the many branches of esoteric thought adapted from their teachings down the ages. E.S.P., reincarnation, astrology, meditation, faith-healing, shamanism, Tarot and out-of-body experiences are just a few of the diverse subjects included, as well as New Age practices

and beliefs—whose origins are, in turn, rooted in the philosophies and faiths of the Eastern world. Once considered a dubious field of study, mystical beliefs are now embraced by millions around the world, and countless occult phenomena are scrutinized by scientists, who have come to acknowledge connections between the mind, body and spirit. In short, the occult has moved out of the realm of the sinister into the fascinating frontiers of human spiritual potential.

This sourcebook has been compiled primarily for those who are exploring new areas within the numerous and often confusing possibilities underlying the esoteric disciplines. It consists of a series of informative, straightforwardly written treatments of key areas

within the broad themes of magic; witchcraft; schools of mystical belief; divination systems; inner experience; and esoteric folklore and arts. Each section provides the reader with a clear, balanced description of the history and practices within its subject, accompanied by illustrations, as an orientation to the field or discipline. We hope that many of the chapters and sections in this book may be starting points for more detailed study of those areas the reader finds most interesting or useful. Each subject is keyed to the bibliographic section for further reference, and a "Who's Who"

appendix provides concise biographical sketches of the major figures in the history of esoteric and mystical thought.

Intended as a tool for discovery, we hope this sourcebook will add to each reader's personal understanding of what humans can become. It speaks to those who are concerned with expanding human consciousness and addressing the timeless, mysterious questions that have preoccupied our thinking from the dawn of history to today's millennial age.

—Nevill Drury and Gregory Tillett

MAGIC

In its simplest definition, magic can be described as the invocation of super-natural forces by magicians or witches in order to effect desired changes. Initially practiced by people attempting to control the frighteningly arbitrary forces of nature, over the millennia various magical traditions have developed, most elaborately in the Western world. This chapter examines the origins of magic; the magical cosmologies with which humans first attempted to explain the universe, and which came to influence Western magic; the beliefs, practices and aims of ritual magicians, as well as the equipment that they use; and the magical attacks that can be launched against magicians' adversaries.

THE ORIGINS OF MAGIC

The origins of magic lie at the very beginnings of history, from when humankind first appeared and was faced with a strange, often hostile environment and a mysterious, almost inexplicable existence. Vast forces moved around early humans, upon which they were totally dependent, and yet which were completely outside their control—the sun, the moon, the forces of nature, the movement of the animals and the growth of the plants. In their own lives people were faced with mysterious and powerful forces—birth, death, sickness and hunger. It was in search of an explanation for, and the ability to exercise some control over, these powers that humans developed magic. What they couldn't control physically—the movement of the seasons, or the fertility of the herds—they tried to manipulate symbolically in rituals. They developed myths to explain what things were and how

they came to be. In the course of these explorations they also stumbled onto some rudiments of science, and thereby began astronomy (at first as astrology), chemistry, medicine (in herbalism and later alchemy) and other disciplines. Most importantly, they began to explore their own natures, developing an elementary psychology. Indeed, one author has described magic as "a system of archaic psychology."

As their adaptation to, and control of, the environment increased, and their dependence on the forces of nature lessened, magic became more speculative and less concerned with the everyday needs of survival. Great controversy has raged over the differences between magic and religion, yet it seems certain that in the beginning there was no distinction and that it was only with the passage of time and the

Opposite: This nineteenth-century photograph is titled "Man Know Thy Destiny!" The monk's austere habit indicates his renunciation of material things, while the skull symbolizes human mortality, and the Christian crucifix and weighty tome illustrate the human spiritual quest.

Below: As demonstrated by his diagram of the solar system, Nicolaus Copernicus (1473-1543) challenged previously held astronomical beliefs by postulating that the Earth revolved around the Sun, not vice versa.

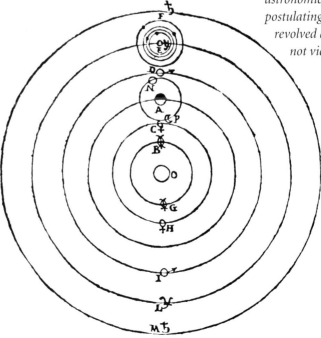

increasing specialization of activities within human communities that distinctions developed. A religious system developed to provide a mythology for the general populace, while magic remained the domain of a few, to whom the rest turned in times of need.

As science and technology relieved the more urgent human needs and made the world less hostile, magic turned inward to become a science of the mind and developed away from the search for control of the physical environment. In the West this development led to the emergence of an "intellectual" magic, while in other non-Western societies the original, so-called "primitive," tradition has continued.

MAGICAL COSMOLOGY

Cosmology is the study of the universe as an orderly whole, and for the mystic and the magician the cosmos is indeed an awesome and vast, ongoing process.

Since earliest times, humans have sought to rationalize their place in their environment. In Paleolithic times, they realized that they must do battle with the elements to survive and they conceived of gods in the wind, floods and storms. They imitated the animals they hunted in order to trick them into their lairs; and perhaps they considered that, by a similar method of imitation—in ritual or in special offerings—they could similarly ensnare the gods, or at least appease them in their wrath. Throughout recorded history, humans have structured their universe. There have been regional gods—of mountains, streams and the earth—and there have been ineffable, transcendent gods far beyond the sky.

Samuel Liddell MacGregor Mathers (1854–1918), one of the founders of the Hermetic Order of the Golden Dawn, was especially interested in cosmology and the study of ancient systems of mystical thought. He translated the medieval *Zohar*, the central books of the Qabalah, and other rare grimoires and magical writings. He was responsible too for writing some of the beautiful rituals of the higher Rosicrucian grades beyond the Golden Dawn, which were given only to advanced occultists. In writing these he assembled in a type of collage the sacred hymns, prayers and occult cosmologies of a number of ancient sources. Basically, he drew on those mystical religions that structured the universe. Magic basically asserts that the human psyche is a microcosm of the entire universe, and therefore the old religions with their hierarchies of gods are useful symbolic frameworks within which consciousness may expand.

Mathers believed, as do most occultists, that gods and deities are symbols of both the personality and aspiration. The gods of ancient Greece often seemed very human in their exploits; they were jealous and proud. In Egyptian mythology, Set successfully lured his brother Osiris to climb into a coffin, and he later scattered his body in pieces all over Egypt. Is this the way, we ask, in which gods should act? A careful analysis of comparative mythology shows that gods embody both negative and positive qualities, and it is up to us to emulate or neglect their example.

In the Golden Dawn, Mathers was using the meditative structure called the "tree of life" as his magical focus, because it enabled a detailed comparison of the gods of several major ancient religions to be made.

Magic seeks to enlarge the consciousness step by step, in a particular way. For magicians to

Opposite: *An allegorical image depicting such noted astronomers as Ptolemy, Copernicus and Galileo grouped around Urania, the Greek muse of astrology. The discoveries of these scientists helped humans to rationalize the workings of the cosmos rather than ascribing magical explanations to them.*

Below: *Aleister Crowley joined the Hermetic Order of the Golden Dawn in 1898, but by 1904 had become dissatisfied with its structure and rituals. He eventually founded his own magical order,* Argentinum Astrum, *in 1907.*

Above: *Aztec human sacrifice was performed to maintain cosmic order by appeasing the gods with human blood.*

gods. And since he wished his magical procedures to proceed step by step, in grades, he had to choose cosmologies in which the gods, or levels of consciousness, were *distinct*. The cosmologies chosen by Mathers as the basis of Western magic were the Egyptian, the Greek, and a neo-Platonic mystical system called "Chaldean."

The ancient Egyptians conceived of their world as being surrounded by a chain of mountains. The sun rose each day through a hole in the east, and sank each night in the west. The sun, whether he was Ra, Osiris or Khenti Amenti, was personified as a male deity who traveled during the hours of both day and night, so that half his time was spent traversing the sky by day and the other half in battling with the forces of the underworld—the twelve hours or "dungeons" of night. The underworld was a rather frightening place. Wallace Budge writes: "In all the books of the otherworld we find pits of fire, abysses of darkness, murderous knives, streams of boiling water, foul stenches, fiery serpents, hideous animal-headed monsters and creatures, and cruel death-dealing beings of various shapes."

meditate upon the figure of Mercury from the Roman pantheon, for example, would enhance their sense of lucidity and rational intellect. Luna and Diana, on the other hand, are changeable, emotional and instinctive, symbolizing a quite different facet of the personality. Mathers decided that, since he was dealing with the Western mind, he should use Western

The Egyptians noted to their satisfaction that the sun always rose with the new dawn, and so the sun became a symbol of the triumph of light over darkness and, by extension, of good over evil. The sun god entered and passed through the regions of the underworld (which was called the *Tuat*) by means of sacred words of power called *hekau*, which had been originally given by Thoth, the god of wisdom.

Two of the most important Egyptian sacred books were the *Am Tuat*, compiled by the priests of Amen-Ra at Thebes, and the *Book of Gates*, an Osirian work dating from the Middle Kingdom (*c.* 2000 BC). The latter is supplemented by the *Egyptian Book of the Dead*.

The Egyptian cosmologies stressed the rebirth of the sun-worshipper—both by reincarnation and resurrection. In the first case, the follower of the sun god entered his boat after death and rode with him through the underworld to be reborn with him each day. In the second case, the deceased person traveled down to Osiris's kingdom of the underworld, where the great god and his forty-two companion deities resided. To get there, the deceased person had to know the sacred names of power in the underworld and the names of the forty-two gods of the fields. The essence of the person (the heart) would be weighed against truth (symbolized by a feather) by Anubis in the hall of judgement, and Thoth would then give his verdict. If pure, the deceased would be allowed to stay. Meanwhile, a monster called Am-nut—a combination of crocodile, lion and hippopotamus—waited to devour the condemned.

Modern white magic can similarly offer its practitioners "rebirth" or initiation. In the Qabalistic rituals, the "sun-god" level of consciousness is represented by *Tiphareth*. The rituals of *Tiphareth*, the most important of all, were strongly influenced by the myths of Osiris, and magicians were dressed in ritual robes so that they could imagine they were Osiris reborn. There is also a strong emphasis on the names of power in modern magic. These are usually the sacred names of God in Hebrew, but the so-called "Ritual of the Hexagram," which can be used as a type of exorcism, has a strong Egyptian content. It should be remembered that the sacred name (invocation or "spell") reflects the universal belief in the power of sound. In the Bible we are told: "In the Beginning was the Word," and the same was true of the beliefs of the ancient Egyptians. In Hinduism and yoga, we find a similar emphasis on sacred mantras, which may be used in meditation, almost, as it were, to take the yogi back to the essence of creation.

While the Egyptian religion has had the greatest influence on modern magic, largely because of the diversity of its god images that

Right: In this detailed image from the Egyptian Book of the Dead, *the heart of the deceased is weighed against the feather of truth in Osiris's hall of judgement. The proceedings are presided over by the jackal-headed Anubis, god of embalming, while the ibis-headed Thoth, god of wisdom, stands ready to record the verdict. If the deceased's heart is deemed impure, it will be devoured by the terrible hybrid monster Am-nut (on the right).*

are useful for ritual, the Greek and Chaldean religions are also important.

One of the most influential concepts for modern magic was the idea, developed by the Greeks, of an underworld. The initiates of the Orphic mysteries were told that the body was like a tomb. On death (or in ecstasy) the spirit went into the heavenly regions and was then reborn, until it eventually emerged as a pure spirit living in an Olympian heaven far beyond the sky. (It was only in the early cosmology that Olympus was depicted as a mountain.) As in the Egyptian religion, the mysteries of Eleusis also dealt with cycles of nature, which were linked symbolically with the fate of humankind. The lessons of Eleusis were centered upon Persephone and Demeter, symbolizing the corn and "Mother Earth," respectively. Initiates were told the legend of Persephone's abduction into the underworld

at the hands of Aidoneus (Hades). Demeter, her mother and goddess of the harvest, sat in mourning and the crops failed, so Zeus sent Hermes to the underworld to give Persephone the seed of life—a pomegranate. This allowed Persephone to spend half her time in the world of the living, but for the other half she was obliged to continue as queen of the underworld. The Greeks (at Eleusis) were thus instructed that *life comes out of death* and rebirth is the natural order of things.

Modern magic regards the tree-of-life diagram as a symbol of the mind and its potential. In most people this potential is unrealized, so that the energies of the psyche are largely *unconscious*. The underworld thus becomes an excellent symbol for the unconscious thought processes of humans. It is interesting to note that the first path on the tree of life is that of the twenty-second Tarot card, *The World*, which

Below: In Greek legend, Demeter's daughter Persephone symbolized the corn that grows in the months of spring and summer, the period when she is allowed to leave the darkness of the underworld to bring renewed life to the world. In this relief she is depicted in dispute with Aphrodite over their rival claims to the beautiful Adonis.

shows Persephone dancing in a wreath of wheat. Just as she was taken down through the earth, the lowest sphere on the tree, *Malkuth* (normal consciousness), is represented by the four elements, Persephone, as a symbol of the wheat grain, is undoubtedly an earth deity. We see here the idea that mythology represents the symbols of the mind. Other references may be found in Plato's myth of Er (in *The Republic*) and the Roman *Aeneid* of Virgil, which both deal with journeys in the underworld.

Chaldean cosmology was the least important classical influence on the Golden Dawn magical society, but represented a vestige of Persian religion and Mithraism. The so-called "Chaldean Oracles" are believed to have been the work of three neo-Platonic philosophers: Julian the Chaldean; Julian the Magician (his son); and Iamblichus, who wrote the book *Concerning the Mysteries*.

The Chaldean system was similar to the concept of the tree of life. Its cosmology incorporated a trinity consisting of *Mystes*, the primordial fire; the Great Mother; and their

Right: *In this William
Blake painting of Hecate,
the Chaldean Daughter,
her lunar, terrible aspect is
emphasized by means of a
night owl, a predatory bat,
and a night-mare. Like
many powerful and
unpredictable goddesses,
she was simultaneously a
goddess of fertility,
witchcraft and death.*

Right: *In this William
Blake painting of Hecate,
the Chaldean Daughter,
her lunar, terrible aspect is
emphasized by means of a
night owl, a predatory bat,
and a night-mare. Like
many powerful and
unpredictable goddesses,
she was simultaneously a
goddess of fertility,
witchcraft and death.*

Divine Son. There was also a fourth deity, the Daughter, whom the Chaldeans called Hecate, who was the goddess of nature and the moon. Like Diana, she was pure and virginal, but she also had an unpredictable side to her nature; sometimes she is depicted with snakes for hair, like the Gorgons.

According to the Chaldean system, a person's body was intrinsically impure, and the spirit therefore had to be untainted to find its way back to its divine source. The initiates learned that they had to perform special rituals to rid themselves of the impurity of *Hyle* (earth), otherwise Hecate's demons would be unleashed upon them in revenge. Nevertheless, like the Egyptians, and also the Gnostics, who were contemporaries of Iamblichus, there was special emphasis on magical formulae. Illumination was said to result from *gnosis*, or divine knowledge. A person who knew the names of the cosmic rulers could call them forth and be uplifted by them.

From the Chaldean system more than any other source, some modern magicians acquired the idea that one could invoke the gods in ritual for specific spiritual illumination. A number of Persian/Mithraic passages, of considerable poetic beauty, were used in the magical ritual of *Taphthatharath*, which was supposed to conjure the spirit of *Hod* (intellect) into visible appearance.

RITUAL MAGIC

From the time of their earliest awareness of magic and religion, humans have employed ritual as a means of expressing their involvement in the powers of the universe, as a means of gaining contact with those powers, and of causing them to manifest themselves to people. The earliest evidence of religion in human history is that of the ancient cave-dwellers, who left remains of their rituals—essentially cults of the dead, the hunt and the "great mother." Ritual implements have been uncovered dating back to the very beginnings of humankind—statues of the earth mother; skeletons painted in red ochre to symbolize the blood of new life and buried in a fetal position within the womb of the earth; paintings of humans disguised as animals, performing rituals designed to ensure the success of the hunt; and evidence of offerings being made to the earth to ensure the fertility of the plants that provided food.

As they became decreasingly dependent on the hunt and the nomadic life of their early ancestors, so humans developed a different approach to magic and ritual. Early humans had been surrounded by a world of frightening phenomena, which they were largely powerless to control: flood, famine, darkness, death, sickness, fire. All the forces of the natural environment, on which their precarious existence was so dependent, had to be symbolized and controlled ritually, for their actual control was beyond limited human technology and understanding. When humans became cultivators of crops, their interest became even more centered on the cycles of nature, on which they were dependent for the success of the harvest. They were intimately involved in the cycle of life, death and rebirth, which is at the very heart of the cultivator—the seeds that contain the germ of life, yet appear dead, and are planted in the soil later to burst forth with life; the heavens that give rain and sunshine; and the earth, providing warmth and nourishment.

As their technology improved, humans became less dependent upon nature for their basic survival, and their approach to religion changed. But it remained a ritual involvement; there was only a limited amount of expressly theoretical teaching, for the masses could not read, nor did they have the time to devote themselves to speculative religion. In the rituals, however, which communicated the teachings contained in experiences that could not be put into words, they could both participate and learn.

Gradually, with the separation of magic and religion over the centuries, and with the establishment of the Catholic Church as the most powerful influence on the cultures of the Western world, ritual magic largely disappeared; certainly, it existed in small enclaves and among individuals, but the Church was most diligent in its persecution of those who participated in practices outside its scheme of belief. Among such groups as the alchemists, the Rosicrucians and, later, the Freemasons, some of the traditions of ritual magic were continued. Within the Church itself, the old methods of teaching by ritual involvement were continued—for those who could neither read nor write and had insufficient education to understand the basic concepts of the faith, let alone the sublime mysteries contained within the Catholic religion, the dramas of the Sacraments. The annual cycle of the Church year continued to communicate the doctrines of the Christian religion.

But at the same time, other traditions existed—some specifically non-Christian, and some within the Christian tradition—that employed ritual for magical purposes. Various

groups developed to perpetuate particular traditions of ritual magic and, with the declining power of the Church, these occasionally emerged into the open. Unlike the traditions of ritual magic in the distant past, these were specifically intended for the educated and the learned, who sought power, knowledge and experience through the techniques of ritual magic. Freemasons, Rosicrucians, alchemists, Templars—a whole range of traditions developed, and numerous individuals worked alone in the practice. Such names as Paracelsus (1493–1541) and John Dee (1527–1608) recall that these traditions continued, albeit often hidden from the world.

Above: The center of this southwestern Native American cave painting is illuminated by sunlight only during the winter solstice, demonstrating the reverence of its creators for nature's cycles.

Below: A Paleolithic cave painting at Lascaux, France. Cave paintings frequently reflect the importance of the hunt.

Right: *Eliphas Lévi, the author of such works as* The Dogma and Ritual of High Magic *(1856), did much to excite nineteenth-century interest in magic.*

Below: *Thomas Landseer's archetypal nineteenth-century image of the cloven-hooved devil, whose thigh is entwined with a snake bearing the legend "Honi soit" ("evil be"), in deliberate mockery of the motto of the English Order of the Garter.*

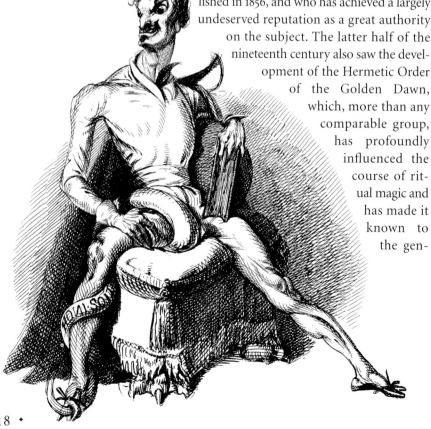

It was not until the nineteenth century that the traditions of ritual magic re-emerged to a significant degree. In 1801 Francis Barrett published *The Magus* (an almost unreadable and extremely complex volume), thereby beginning what has proved to be a long line of works on this subject. His influence was small compared to that of Eliphas Lévi, whose book *The Dogma and Ritual of High Magic* was published in 1856, and who has achieved a largely undeserved reputation as a great authority on the subject. The latter half of the nineteenth century also saw the development of the Hermetic Order of the Golden Dawn, which, more than any comparable group, has profoundly influenced the course of ritual magic and has made it known to the gen-

eral public. Deriving from this order, a number of other groups (including the Order of the Cubic Stone and the Fraternity of the Inner Light) have emerged to perpetuate, in varying forms, the traditions of magic. Today these traditions are continued by a variety of occult groups and by individual ritual magicians who work alone in the pursuit of this ancient path. Many of the schools that once followed the magical tradition have now ceased to do so, although they continue to exist in an altered form; foremost among this group are the Freemasons who, although once a genuine school of ritual occultism, now tend to de-emphasize this aspect of their work.

Ritual magic employs ritual, symbols and the ceremonial as a means of representing and communicating with the forces that underlie the universe and humankind. Ritual is a process of dramatizing what is being expressed, so that the whole aspect of humans—their bodies, emotions and minds—are employed in causing a total experience. Ritual makes use of all the senses—sight, hearing, smell, taste and touch—and uses all the methods of drama and all the techniques of religion. Ritual magic centers on symbols, those keys to the subconscious by which it is possible to communicate concepts and ideals beyond words or intellectual understanding. The aim of ritual magic is a transcendental experience—an experience beyond the limitations of the mind; an experience of the reality of being, of the realms of what might be called the "superconscious"; but an experience in a controlled, balanced and integrated way. Ritual magic thus aims toward the same end as many other techniques, such as those of the mystic or the taker of consciousness-enhancing substances. But unlike the mystic, the ritual magician works through action rather than contemplation, and through the externalization of inner realities, rather than introspection. And unlike takers of consciousness-enhancing substances, ritual magicians strive for a consciously controlled and directed journey inward, relying not upon synthetic or chemical experience, but upon the utilization of the natural faculties they possess, but rarely use. All the equipment of magic, its ceremony and ritual, and its words and symbols, are designed to focus and direct the will of the magicians, and to "turn them on" to inner realities. The ultimate end of ritual magic is not the causing of spectacular and apparently supernatural effects, but the transformation of the individual from a limited mortal into what is best described as a "superman," fully alive and totally free.

There are, as Eliphas Lévi noted, three basic laws of ritual magic, as follows:

The law of will—the power of the human will is a real power, which, when correctly stimulated and harnessed, is as potent as any physical force; but this will is quite different to the vague, ill-defined "wishing" with which most people confuse it. The will must be cultivated, disciplined and controlled.

The law of astral light—all things consist of one basic substance, which is known by various names, such as "astral light," but which, once understood, can be used by magicians and molded by their wills.

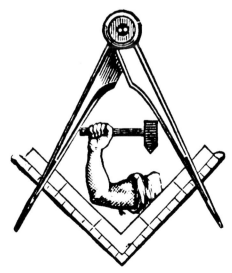

The law of correspondence—this is the ancient doctrine of the microcosm and the macrocosm, according to which "that which is above is like that which is below"; the human is a model of the universe, and the universe is a greater expression of those same principles embodied in the human. A knowledge of these correspondences between humans and the universe enables magicians to summon up within themselves any of the powers of the universe.

Although principles can be codified and expounded, the only method of reaching ritual magic stems from individual experience and involves disciplined self-development and the laborious transformation of the self through ritual consciousness.

Ritual Consciousness

A ritual is, in effect, an act of imitation. In tribal societies, shamans mirror in their actions the movements of the animals, birds and fish that they wish to ensnare. When rain is required, a ceremony may be conducted in which the falling of rain upon the earth is symbolized by the fluttering movement of the arms of the performers, or the pouring of liquids upon the ground, or some similar, appropriate action.

In the world of the occult, rituals similarly play a paramount role. Just as rituals of fertility beseech the gods to shower abundance upon the worshippers, so too can rituals incorporate the opposite intentions. There are, for example, certain occult rituals that practice a type of scapegoating. In Francis Barrett's famous compendium, *The Magus*, published in 1801, we see that certain witch rituals transferred illness and pain to an unfortunately victimized creature:

> *Take the eyes of a frog, which must be extracted before sunrise, and bind them to the breasts of a woman who be ill. Then let the frog go blind into the water again and as he goes so will the woman be rid of her pains…*

Removing the eyes of the frog clearly asserted human will over the frog, since it could no longer leap to freedom. The breasts, with their life-giving milk, were regarded as symbolic of health, and the casting of the frog into the

Left: Masonic and Rosicrucian symbols—the Masonic compasses, set-square and hammer, and the Rosy Cross. Both these secret societies developed complex magical rituals that were revealed only to initiates, who were usually educated men.

purifying waters was a ritual act of cleansing
the body of evil and pain.

In ritual, the contact between the ritual
object and the person who will benefit is usually crucial. A ritual similar to that quoted
above stated that, to cure a fever, a naked
woman should take the heart of any animal
and bind it to the patient. The disease would
then depart. In this instance the fever is
equated with the death of the sacrificed animal. The heart is the animal's very life force,
and this is virtually exchanged for the perilous
illness…at the animal's expense!

Witchcraft and tribal magic frequently dwell
on the afflictions imposed by nature, or by

enemies or hostile gods, upon humans.
Humans are subject to a barrage of external
forces—wind, fire, drought, flood and
storms—and their rituals provide a form of
protection. In earlier times and some indigenous cultures, the only way that humans knew
of protecting themselves was by imitating the
gods whose forces raged all around them.

In ancient Egypt, which saw the rise of one
of the most profound early cosmologies, it
became clear that one of the most enduring
phenomena in the observable universe is the
Sun. No one had ever seen it go out. No one
had ever seen it fail to rise with the new dawn
each day. It was appropriate, then, that the
Sun became a symbol of the Egyptians' destiny, for by imitating its motion and by identifying and following the sun god, a person
could find new life. It is from the Egyptians
that we have the earliest representation of resurrection as a doctrine, although this was
mirrored by other religious groups in reincarnation teaching. In some instances the two
went side by side.

Osiris, the god slain by his brother, Set, and
later miraculously reborn, symbolized resurrection. After their deaths, his followers would
travel down the river of the underworld to the
afterworld, passing through dungeons representing the hours of the night on the way. In
the afterworld they would be sustained ritually by eating barley cakes and by drinking ale,
symbolic of the body and the life of Osiris himself. On the other hand, followers of Amen-Ra
had noted that the Sun constantly reappeared
at the start of each day, and they assumed,
again in an act of ritual identification, that
humans, like the sun god, must be perpetually
reborn. In their after-death belief, it was said
that humans traveled in the train of the sun
god and took part in the continuing battle of
(sun)light over darkness.

We can see in these myths the beginnings of
rituals designed to transform humans themselves. Egyptian mythology had a major influence on the ritual magic practices of the
Hermetic Order of the Golden Dawn. The aim
of this order, which practiced white or beneficial magic rather than black or destructive
magic, was to use ritual to illuminate the mind.

Israel Regardie, an expert on the order, wrote
in his *Tree of Life*:

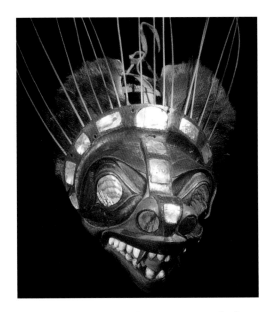

There are hierarchies of consciousness which are celestial and there are those which are terrestrial; some divine, others demonic, and still others including the highest Gods and Universal Essences…the whole Universe is permeated by One Life, and that Life in manifestation is represented by hosts of mighty Gods, divine beings, cosmic spirits or intelligences…

Unlike primitive societies, modern occult groups tend to regard the gods as symbols of the positive and negative energies of the mind. White magic thus entails enhancing the spiritual side of human nature, whereas black magic, or Satanism, tends to arouse the sexual or animal side of man.

In the Order of the Golden Dawn, the rituals were designed to provide the initiates with the feeling that they were traveling among the gods. These, of course, were represented by members of the order dressed in appropriately mythological regalia. However, for many the rituals were emotionally and intellectually inspiring. The poet W. B. Yeats, who at one time headed the Order of the Golden Dawn,

and who won the Nobel Prize for Literature in 1923, found ritual particularly illuminating: "There is traced within the evil triangle the rescuing symbol of the Golden Cross united to the Rose of seven times seven petals," he wrote, in describing one of the key rituals. For him, whose poetic imagination was inflamed by ritual, each petal seemed to be transformed "into the likeness of Living Beings of extraordinary beauty…"; when turning to the pillars of Horus in the ritual, it seemed that each one had become a "column of confused shapes, divinities… of the wind, who in a whirling dance of more than human vehemence, rose playing upon pipes and cymbals…"

According to modern occultism, the gods are alive in the minds of us all, and it is up to us to open the channels of inspiration. In this way, white magic is very similar to Kundalini yoga, for it too demonstrates the opening of channels of energy and illumination.

In ritual magic, it is essential that all the senses should be heightened, and so the ritual itself has to appeal to all of them, in unison. It does this as follows.

Sight: all of the ritual clothing and symbolic colors focus the consciousness in a certain way. For example, the colors of life are gold and yellow, in imitation of the sun. Red is the color of aggression, symbolizing blood spilled in war.

Sound: magic draws upon a vast repertoire of chants, mantras and invocations, which have a powerful effect on the mind and the creative imagination.

Taste: this may take the form of a sacrament like wine or, in some instances, as in the mysteries of Eleusis, a hallucinatory drink.

Smell: incense and perfumes are frequently used to provide a sensory atmosphere suitable for the ritual.

Left: The shaman who originally wore this mask believed that he would be imbued with the animal-like characteristics it represented, thus effecting his magical transformation and endowing him with supernatural powers.

Below: The winged sun disk, symbol of the Egyptian sun god, Amen-Ra. The solar disk is flanked by a pair of cobras, representing wisdom, rulership and protection, while the mighty pair of wings signify the god's mastery of the heavens. The symbols and regalia of ancient Egypt were particularly significant to the members of the Hermetic Order of the Golden Dawn.

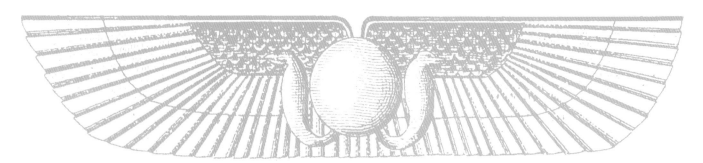

Above: This ancient magical wand was used by Egyptian magicians to battle against the venom of poisonous animals. It is decorated with symbols and images of creatures that were believed to symbolize life, fertility and regeneration, including the ankh, the tortoise, the scarab and the cobra.

Touch: throughout the ritual, initiates have contact with sacred objects. They can include the glass from which the life-giving fluid is drunk, or the sword that holds at bay the demons (of the mind) who are hostile to the initiates' task of enlarging their consciousness.

We can see from the above that ritual magic is especially designed to allow humans to transcend themselves. They do this by using symbols, mythology and magical equipment to help themselves to imagine that once again they walk among the gods and, in fact, have become gods themselves. In so doing they gain access to cosmic consciousness.

MAGICAL EQUIPMENT

Popular fiction, movies and television—from *Rosemary's Baby* to the various Dracula movies and Dennis Wheatley novels—have made the public familiar with the traditional equipment of the magician and the witch, often in a highly dramatic and not altogether accurate manner. Traditionally, magicians worked in a room set aside and consecrated for the purpose (a temple, or lodge), within a defined area usually marked on the floor (a magical circle), upon an altar, wearing robes specially prepared for the occasion, using specific tools (typically, a chalice, pentacle, sword and a wand). Additionally, they burned incense in a thurible (a censer), sometimes used daggers and staffs, and usually worked by candlelight. All this equipment was traditionally prepared very carefully according to the strictest traditions by magicians themselves and was solemnly consecrated for work. The old grimoirs (books of magical rituals) include elaborate directions for the making and use of magical equipment, although most of their instructions are beyond the abilities of contemporary magicians who have limited time and money to devote to their art. For example, to make a sword, iron had to

be mined by the magician, who refined and smelted it and then beat it to form the sword. If magicians are unable to make their equipment, then they should at least search carefully for the best possible and be prepared to pay high prices for the right things. All equipment is traditionally consecrated during a special ritual and thereafter kept from all common usage and away from other people. It is never used for any purpose other than magical work, otherwise its potency would be lost. The equipment should always be kept clean, wrapped in silk and treated with reverence; the psychological power of the objects derives from the devotion with which they are treated.

The temple (lodge, chapel, oratory, shrine or laboratory) should be a room in which only magical working is carried out and to which outsiders have no access. After being scrupulously cleansed, it is consecrated for use and the ritual objects are placed within it. Traditionally it should lie east-west. At the door are two pillars, symbolizing the doorway to the inner world, through which magicians pass when entering their temples. In the center is the altar, surrounded by the circle within which the magician works. In some workings, the altar is placed at the east of the temple, the symbolic direction of the rising sun. At each of the four cardinal points (north, south, east and west) are placed objects or symbols representing the four elements (earth, air, fire and water) and the four archangels (Michael, Gabriel, Auriel and Raphael).

The circle represents the actual working space of magicians, who should never step outside it during a ritual. Traditionally, to do so was believed to place them in terrible danger, since the powers that they had summoned would destroy them if they left the protection of the circle. The circle is usually traced in chalk on the floor, or laid out in pieces of material, with symbols inscribed around its circumference.

The altar is usually a double cube, black on the bottom half (symbolizing earth) and white on the top half (symbolizing the spirit). Only magical equipment is ever placed upon the altar, which usually has one or more white cloths placed upon it and in some cases a perpetually burning lamp, symbolizing the divine presence. All magical working is done within the circle upon the altar.

The robes include the outer and inner robes, sandals and, in some traditions, a stole and a headdress. The inner robe is usually a monastic-style garment in white (although some traditions employ black to symbolize the unregenerated human— not darkness), with a hood. The outer garment varies in color and is usually a sleeveless, cloak-style coat. While sandals are generally worn, some traditions advocate that the feet should be bare. The stole symbolizes the power of magicians and is simply a strip of material, usually decorated with symbols, hanging around the neck, down to the knees. Headdresses vary in form, from elaborate ones that resemble bishops' miters, to Egyptian styles, or simply skullcaps. They are usually worn because tradition (deriving from the Old Testament) taught that humans' heads should be respectfully covered when approaching the divine.

The tools each represent a natural element: the cup (water), the pentacle or plate (earth), the sword (air) and the wand (fire). Additionally, candles are burned upon the altar, and sometimes other vessels are also used (for example, for storing oil or water). The tools are usually fashioned of metal, engraved with sacred symbols and specially consecrated by the magician for the work.

Incense is burned both to purify the air and to drive away evil spirits, as well as to create a pleasant atmosphere with which to attract good spirits. A thurible (an incense container on a chain) can be used

to hold burning charcoal, upon which granulated gum (often derived from Arabia, taken from trees and usually consisting of olibanum and benzoin mixed together) is placed. Sometimes extra herbs are added (*e.g.* rosemary or cinnamon) to increase the fragrance, or consciousness-enhancing substances to affect the mind. Incense sticks and cones are often considered unacceptable because they derive

Above: A seventeenth-century woodcut representing Faust successfully conjuring up the devil. Faust stands within a magic circle that has been inscribed with signs of the zodiac and the planets; he must remain within the circle for his own protection.

Left: Arthur Rackham's interpretation of the powerful witch Morgan le Fay, sister of King Arthur and opponent of Merlin, stealing the magical sword, Excalibur. The sword is an important tool in ritual magic.

Right: *Rose Kelly, Aleister Crowley's first wife, claimed to have witnessed the appearance of Beelzebub and his forty-nine demonic minions whom Crowley sent from Loch Ness to attack his rival, Mathers, in Paris. Mathers survived this magical attack.*

Right: *Rose Kelly, Aleister Crowley's first wife, claimed to have witnessed the appearance of Beelzebub and his forty-nine demonic minions whom Crowley sent from Loch Ness to attack his rival, Mathers, in Paris. Mathers survived this magical attack.*

from virtually unknown origins and may contain all manner of inappropriate substances. Pure gum with sandalwood dust, natural herbs, spices and oils make the best ingredients. They should be blessed when placed upon the charcoal.

The equipment was obviously modified according to the needs of magicians and the ritual each performed. Egyptian-style equipment would not be used in a ceremony invoking Roman gods, for example, nor would statues of Buddha stay in a room devoted to the Christian tradition. Magicians had to be interior decorators in part, co-ordinating and integrating their material resources to create the most conducive atmosphere for their work. They did not collect odds and ends, but were specialist craftsmen.

With the contemporary revival of interest in magic, a large-scale business has been established in the selling of allegedly genuine magical equipment—robes, tools, incense and oils. This is completely contrary to the traditions of magic, and the burning of mail-order incense and oils is considered especially unwise: their constituents are unknown, their makers are of dubious intent and their effects are unpredictable.

MAGICAL ATTACK

If magicians have supernatural powers, can they be used to attack their enemies? Certainly there is a widespread tradition throughout history of spells and curses being used to injure or even kill people, either enemies of magicians or conjurers, or enemies of the clients who pay them to make the attack. Examples of alleged "magical attacks" include the ancient and universal theory of victims' lives being blighted by the "evil eye"; "the hag syndrome," in which "hags" sit on the chests of their sleeping victims, crushing, sometimes paralysing and always terrifying them; and the debilitating "psychic vampirism" described by Dion Fortune. But the concept of a magical attack has come to have a special meaning drawn from the traditions of Western magic. Occasionally ritual magicians have come into conflict and have engaged in "psychic warfare," each performing rituals designed to cause harm to the other. Sometimes such rituals are intended to do actual physical injury to the victim, causing him or her to become ill or to suffer pain. On other occasions the rituals are intended to invoke supernatural beings who will attack or terrorize the victim.

When carrying out such an attack, magicians are traditionally required to take precautions to protect themselves, especially in cases when they invoke entities that may not only attack the victim, but may also turn and attack the magician.

In general cases of magical attack, when there is no actual battle underway, the victim may be completely unaware of what is happening and may merely feel unwell and restless, exhibit a variety of physiological and psychological symptoms or suffer various psychic manifestations. The outward symptoms will be very much the same as in the case of an individual who is suffering from some form of influence or obsession. The attack may be launched for a variety of reasons, but is usually either intended to cause suffering to an enemy or to force a person to conform to the will of the magician.

The treatment of such an attack varies according to the symptoms and the source; usually the physical symptoms will have been treated medically, without success, before it is realized that they have a psychic origin. However, it must be emphasized that psychic or magical attacks are comparatively rare (most would-be magicians have neither the knowledge nor the skill required with which to initiate one).

While there are very few accounts of magical attacks written from a serious occult point of view, two rather outstanding instances have been documented. The first, and probably the best known, is that related by Dion Fortune in her book *Psychic Self Defence*, in which she tells of an attack upon her by the leader of a magical fraternity. The symptoms were extremely unusual—innumerable large cats began appearing in the neighborhood and, eventually, an enormous phantom cat manifested itself. Fortune was also attacked astrally when she left her body to undertake some occult work, and it was there that the real battle took place, with the attacker and the victim engaged in combat while out of the body. When she returned to her physical body, Fortune found that she was badly scratched, as if by a cat—a physical symptom of the astral battle. However, having triumphed over the attacker, the cats disappeared and all symptoms vanished.

The second account of a magical attack was given by the French novelist J.K. Huysmans, who was involved with an occult fraternity in Paris at the end of the nineteenth century, and who claimed to be the victim of magical attack by Stanislas de Guaita, the leader of a rival magical group. An account of this story is given by James Webb in his book *The Flight from Reason*. The outcome of Huysmans's claims led to a more physical attack, with the author being challenged to a duel by de Guaita.

Left: *Circe and her attendants enchant the sea in order to be rid of Scylla. Circe was a dangerous Greek sorceress, who lived on a magical island guarded by the unfortunate humans whom she had transformed into lions and wolves. Further victims of her magical attacks include members of Odysseus's crew, whom she turned into pigs.*

FORMS OF WITCHCRAFT

This chapter examines the most prevalent forms of witchcraft worldwide, including those of ancient origins and diverse present-day traditions. The so-called "primitive" traditions of shamanism and tribal magic have endured over millennia, while the principles of voodoo, which evolved into a distinctive and syncretic tradition of its own, were imported by West African slaves to the New World. All forms of witchcraft—in its widest definition as the use of supernatural forces for good or evil purposes— are attracting increasing interest today. The history and practices of European witchcraft and Satanism, both of which occasioned so much fear in Christian Europe in earlier centuries, are also extensively discussed, along with the role of such individuals as Aleister Crowley in their late-twentieth-century revival.

SHAMANISTIC MAGIC

Shamanism is the magic of ecstasy, of leaving the body and soaring to great heights of mystical illumination. Mircea Eliade, the famous scholar of comparative religion, described the shaman as "the technician of the sacred." Shamans are able to move by an act of will from one plane of existence to another.

In the strict anthropological sense, shamanism is best represented in Siberia and in South and Central America among the indigenous peoples, although it also exists in Central Asia, Oceania and Indonesia. Usually shamans are magicians or healers who claim to be able to contact the deities and spirits sacred to their people. The shamanistic world is alive with awe-inspiring and often terrifying supernat-

ural beings, and it is up to the shaman to encounter these entities and to learn their mysterious secrets. These will, in turn, confer upon the shaman a profound respect for the "sacred things," and in the case of healing, a divinely revealed remedy for sickness or disease.

Shamans frequently use natural hallucinogenic substances like datura and peyote (plants) or psilocybin (a fungus) to gain special access to magical territory. According to anthropological accounts, when under the influence of such substances, shamans feel that their universe has become sacred and throngs with awesome beings and presences. Perhaps their "souls" soar away from their bodies and they converse with the ancestors of the first dawn. Perhaps their hallucinatory states allow them to see another person as a collection of "luminous fibers." In such states of altered consciousness, shamans claim to perceive the vital

Opposite: *The typical "Halloween" witch,* Punch *magazine, 1911. Her pointed hat, broomstick and black cat are familiar features.*

Below: *Native Americans of the Plains region. The calumet, or peace pipe, is regarded as a means of attaining spiritual communion with the Great Spirit. Some researchers believe that it may have been derived from the shaman's sucking pipe, used to suck out venom from the body of an afflicted victim.*

Above: *An African witch doctor. Like the shaman, the witch doctor, or medicine man, has an important position within his tribe, for he possesses special powers of healing, benevolent witchcraft and the ability to converse with the tribe's totemic spirits.*

Right: *The shaman uses the repetitive and rhythmic sound of his rattle to induce the ecstatic, trancelike state within which he makes his out-of-body journeys.*

processes, or energy, in the body of the person whom they are treating. Sometimes in shamanistic accounts, magicians claim that the body seems to become transparent, allowing them to look inside it. If a magical object —a power stone or dart—has been sent by a sorcerer to cause illness in the body of the victim, it is the shaman's function to discover and suck forth the offensive object from its harmful position. And if the patient has lost his or her "soul," the shaman must follow it on a visionary journey, locate it, and then bring it back to a place of safety where it cannot be endangered.

Perhaps the most impressive acts of shamans, however, are their ecstatic flights into the world of their native mythology. They are lifted up, perhaps on a winged horse or eagle, and journey to the lands of their ancestors, who live in the heights of the universe. For shamans, their gods are entities whom they can visit and converse with, and they in turn can bestow supernatural powers upon the shamans.

In the remarkable writings of Carlos Castaneda, we find one of the best contemporary accounts of the world of the shaman. Castaneda spent ten years attempting to grasp

the magical concepts of the Mexican shaman Don Juan Matus, whom he had originally met on an anthropological field trip to Arizona. Don Juan used a number of hallucinogens to help him to encounter his supernatural allies, and such a spirit helper was one with "a power capable of carrying a man beyond the boundaries of himself." Don Juan reserved special reverence for peyote and, in particular, for its associated deity, Mescalito. Castaneda was to describe his mystical encounter with this being of nature: "His eyes were of the water I had just seen. They had the same enormous volume, the sparkling of gold and black… Except for the pointed shape, his head was exactly like the surface of the peyote plant."

Another anthropologist, Michael Harner, studied the indigenous Jivaro of eastern Ecuador. When he partook of their hallucinogenic drink, *natema*, he found himself encountering their tribal gods: "I met bird-headed people as well as dragonlike creatures, who explained that they were the true gods of the World. I enlisted the services of other spirit helpers in attempting to fly through the far reaches of the Galaxy."

Superficially, the world of the native shaman may seem to be of little relevance to the modern Western magician, but this is not the case. It is an interesting coincidence that the shamans of Siberia refer to the cosmic tree in which all the deities live. The Qabalah, which is the main point of reference of all modern magicians, also has its tree—the tree of life. And just as shamans journey upward to meet their gods, so too occultists perform rituals and meditative trance exercises, which help them to scale the "heavens" of inner space.

In the Hermetic Order of the Golden Dawn, most of the practical magical work was of a ritual nature, in which the members dressed and performed like gods, mostly those of ancient Egypt, and tried to become inspired imaginatively by acting in their place. But there was also a shamanistic type of magic, which, like the native variety, involved leaving the body in a trance and encountering the spirits and deities of the tree of life.

One of the most impressive accounts of modern "astral journeys" is that of Aleister Crowley's vision of Jupiter, which was first published in his occult magazine, *The Equinox*.

I perceived other suns rising around me, one in the North, and one in the South, and one in the West. And the one in the North was as a great bull blowing blood and flame from its nostrils; and the one in the South was as an eagle plucking forth the entrails of a Nubian slave; and the one in the West was as a man swallowing an ocean.

And whilst I watched these suns rising around me, behold, though I knew it not, a fifth sun had risen beneath where I was standing, and it was as a great wheel of revolving lightnings. And gazing at the Wonder that flamed at my feet, I partook of the glory and became brilliantly golden, and great wings of flame descended upon me, and as they enrolled me I grew thirty cubits in height—perhaps more.

Then the sun upon which I was standing rose above the four other suns, and as it did so, I found myself standing before an ancient man with a snow-white beard, whose countenance was afired with benevolence. And as I looked upon him, a great desire possessed me to stretch forth my hand and touch his beard; and as the desire grew strong, a voice said unto me: "Touch, it is granted thee."

I would have lingered, but I was dismissed, for the four other suns had risen to a height equal to mine own. And seeing this I stretched out my wings and flew, sinking through innumerable sheets of binding silver. And presently I opened my eyes, and all around me was as a dense fog; thus I returned to my body.

Above: The prophet Ezekiel's fiery vision of God and four cherubim, from a seventeenth-century Bible.

Above, left: The shaman's mask helps him attain magical visions.

Left: Such symbols as those of the planets Mecury, Venus, Jupiter and Neptune can act as "doorways" to inner consciousness.

Occultists and shamans use a variety of methods to attain such visions. Usually they relax their bodies and enter a state of trance. At the same time, they *will* themselves to enter their minds through different pathways. One of the most appropriate means is to use the Tarot cards as doorways, since these lead to different levels of consciousness on the tree of life. It was also common in the Golden Dawn for magicians to use the Tattvas, or symbols of the elements.

The basic assertion of shamans or trance magicians is that by encountering the gods of our minds in this way, we in fact discover ourselves. All of us have a vast, cosmic potential, which is, for the most part, untapped. The shaman offers a technique for discovering this sacred inner knowledge, and the gods once again come to life.

TRIBAL MAGIC

Although they demonstrate a huge diversity of tradition and practice, most tribal cultures use magic either to counter malevolent sorcery, or to try to influence the spirits with which a particular tribe identifies. Most tribes believe in the protective power of their totemic guardian spirits, and the ability to invoke these spirits is sometimes invested in an intermediary between tribe and spirits; shamans are important tribal magicians, as are the "witch doctors," or "medicine men," of Africa and Australia. However, the tribe can also collectively call on their spirits.

In certain Native American tribes, the young male's vision quest reveals his own, personal, guardian spirit, which may endow him with a medicine bundle containing sacred items representative of the spirit. Animals are often associated with such totemic spirits, and harming them is taboo; totempoles are collective, and frequently protective, images of tribal totemic spirits. Masks and ritual garments can also represent guardian spirits, and are sometimes believed to imbue the wearer with the specific powers of the spirits they stand for. Direct communion with the spirits can be achieved by the smoking of the Native American calumet, or the sacred pipe. Further Native

American rituals include the self-sacrificial Sun Dance of the Plains, in which a lodge is constructed and the dancers are attached to its central pole by pegs inserted under their skin, after which they dance—often for days—until the pegs are ripped from their flesh.

In Africa and parts of Melanesia and Australia, where witchcraft is usually considered harmful, and is practiced—sometimes unconsciously—by those in whom such powers are inherent, and where sorcery is regarded as being intentionally evil and can be practiced by anyone, the witch doctor, or medicine man, holds a special tribal position. In the Zande religion of the Azande people of northeastern Zaire and southwestern Sudan, for example, witch doctors detect and combat the negative effects of witchcraft (*mangu*) and sorcery (*gbegbere ngua*) with various plants, herbs, and fetishes. (In many tribal cultures, protective spirits are either represented by fetishes—types of amulets or talismans— or are believed to inhabit them. Also termed *gris-gris* in voodoo, perhaps the best-known fetishes are those of the North American Zuñi, which are regarded as petrified creation spirits. The spirits of the Hopi tradition are the *kachina*, whose power is invoked by the wearing of sacred masks; *kachina* dolls representing the spirits are not sacred, however, but are used solely for educational purposes.) In the tribes of Bantu Africa, too, the *nganga* may be a mere herbalist, a witch doctor, or a powerful countersorcerer. The medicine man performs a similar function in Australia, where he is also a diviner.

Some medicine men receive their powers through study; others are "chosen" by the spirits. Aboriginal medicine men derive their powers from their totemic ancestors, who insert quartz crystals into their bodies, and additionally impart their visionary experiences to these mortals. Black Elk (1863–1950), the famous Oglala Sioux medicine man, received a "great vision" from his totemic spirits, which, when reenacted according to tradition, released his powers of healing. The visions sent by the spirits are extremely

Right: Many tribal societies represent their totemic spirits collectively, stacked one on top of the other to form a totem pole. The totem pole is thus both a symbol of supernatural protection and an affirmation of tribal identity.

important in Native American culture, and thus much importance is attached to dreams; the webbed dream-catcher is the physical expression of this desire to receive messages from the spirits.

By contrast with such empowered individuals, the chantways of the southwestern Native American tribes are lengthy curing ceremonies, in which the tribe participates collectively. During the chantway, healing chants calling on the supernaturals, accompanied by dancing and purification ceremonies, are used to restore the proper balance to any harmful imbalance caused by human agents. The famous sand paintings of the Navajo, on which the afflicted victim sits, herald the arrival of the supernaturals. The painted sand is then rubbed on the victim, uniting him or her with the supernaturals, and thus removing the affliction. Further collective Native American healing bodies include the medicine lodges, which possess all the secret knowledge of the tribe, including that of healing. Perhaps the most famous is the Iroquois False Face Society, whose members wear masks that are believed to be inhabited by the spirits.

Left: A New Zealand Maori shaman stands before his tribe's totem pole. The club that he is holding mirrors the one carved in the center of the totem pole, thus reinforcing the close connection between the tribe and its totemic spirits.

Left: An African witch doctor's assistants prepare the ingredients necessary for a ritual invocation of rain.

Right: *A* kachina *doll, representing one of the many* kachinas, *or totemic spirits, upon which the Hopi depend for the tribe's well-being. The* kachinas *are believed to spend half the year in the otherworld and the other half with the tribe. Their presence is celebrated with ritual dances.*

Below: *The Navajo* Yeis, *or totemic spirits, are believed to enter the sand paintings that are created during chantways, bringing with them their supernatural healing powers. Each sand painting is created for a specific ritual and is then destroyed, thus symbolically removing the affliction.*

All tribal cultures regard mystical communication with their totemic spirits as being of paramount importance to the fortunes of both the individual and the tribe. Reinforced by sacred ritual, total and perfect communion with the spirits is constantly striven for, in order to evoke their power and knowledge. Such beliefs and practices share much in common with those of the occult.

VOODOO

Voodoo refers to the native religion of Haiti in the West Indies, which stems from the traditional West African religions brought to the West Indies by the slave trade, and which centers on an extensive pantheon of gods and goddesses who take possession of devotees during religious ceremonies. This religion also spread with slavery to some of the Southern states of the USA, to other parts of the Caribbean, and to Brazil. Wherever slaves went, they merged their traditional African religious beliefs with elements of the local religion. Voodoo therefore consists of both traditional West African beliefs blended with local variations, and also of various magical techniques employed to achieve certain ends, including the descent of the gods into individual worshippers to give oracles and to provide protection. These magical techniques are known as *obeah*.

Voodoo has been popularly regarded as a mass of frightening superstitions and black-magical practices. Certainly, to the outsider, it may appear as such, depending for much of its power upon the inculcation of fear into its adherents. However, voodoo has an elaborate and complicated theology and constitutes a complex metaphysical system of explanations regarding the relationship between humans and the universe. Only the priests of voodoo know this belief system in full, receiving it during their training and through a series of initiations. They are the agents of the "invisibles," or gods (*loa*), who can, to some extent, control and direct the *loa* and, when possessed by them, act as oracles. The priests are expected to be able to use black and white magic equally, according to the needs of the occasion, and must be ever aware that the *loa* are both powerful and jealous, quite capable of destroying those who serve them. In order to possess the crucial supernatural powers of voodoo, priests must take the ultimate risk of becoming involved with forces that are not necessarily benevolent, and which can change their attitudes to their people with surprising frequency. The pantheon of the gods of voodoo includes many of the traditional West African tribal deities, together with some unexpected additions—for example, many Catholic saints have been incorporated into the voodoo pantheon in areas where Catholicism is the dominant religion (or at least the religion of the respectable). Voodoo has never been an exclusive religion and its method of dealing with other belief systems has been to fuse them into its own, so that a voodoo devotee can attend a Catholic mass without any sense of alienation, simply interpreting the mass in a different way to that of other worshippers.

The typical rituals of voodoo, such as the Rada and Petro rites, include an emphasis on music, especially the beating of drums, which has an hypnotic effect on the worshippers; and energetic and rhythmic dancing, which leads to ecstasy and often to collapse or to possession by one of the gods. Some of the ceremonies are open only to initiated members, who have been through complicated ritual processes during which they have been taught the philosophy of voodoo, the names of the gods and the ritual techniques. As with all initiations, in voodoo this involves a ritual "death" and "rebirth."

Left: A voodoo doll, or fetish. Fetishes represent supernatural spirits, and are believed to have a variety of powers, ranging from the ability to bring luck to the cursing of enemies; in the Santerían religion a black rag doll is a protective agent.

Left: A Haitian voodoo ceremony. The participants have been hypnotized by a drumbeat and dance in ecstasy on the symbols marked on the floor, oblivious even to pain.

Right: As in Haiti,
hypnotic drum beating is a
feature of African voodoo
ceremonies. Here, face
painting and body
adornment are additional
elements in the ritual.

Right: As in Haiti,
hypnotic drum beating is a
feature of African voodoo
ceremonies. Here, face
painting and body
adornment are additional
elements in the ritual.

Although voodoo was originally the religion held by slaves, it has not died out with the disappearance of slavery: it continues to constitute a major religious movement in the Caribbean in particular, especially in Haiti and the Dominican Republic. In Brazil, Macumba is a popular form of voodoo, comprising the Candomblé religion, which was established in the first half of the nineteenth century; the Umbanda cult, which was founded in 1904; and the black-magic practices of Quimbanda. The related religion of Santería, too, was brought by Hispanic immigrants to U.S. cities, while South American spiritism has also been influenced by voodoo. With the popular revival of interest in the occult, there has been a corresponding revival of interest in voodoo, especially in the Southern states of the USA, where a number of voodoo groups (of varying degrees of authenticity) have been established and shops sell the necessary ingredients for the practice of voodoo.

TRADITIONAL WITCHCRAFT IN THE WEST

Tales of famous witches and sorcerers abound throughout history: in ancient Greek legend, for example, Hecate was the terrifying goddess of magic, the dead and witchcraft, while Jason's wife, Medea, was a priestess of Hecate and a powerful sorceress. Merlin, the necromancer of Arthurian legend, is perhaps the archetypal wizard. Despite the respect accorded by the ancients to people who openly practiced witchcraft, it is now often assumed that witchcraft traditionally constituted some sort of underground religion, usually identified with the worship of the devil and a cult of evil, which existed throughout Europe in the sixteenth and seventeenth centuries. This popular view identifies the witch with the old crone of legend, possessed of certain psychic powers, with a knowledge of herbalism, and of an evil disposition, who met with other witches on dark nights to worship the devil. This view has been perpetuated by literature and movies and has been given support by several academics, notably the British anthropologist Dr. Margaret Murray. But the reality of history is far less exotic than the popular myth: there is no decisive evidence to prove the existence of any European religious movement during this period that either existed underground or involved worship of the devil. Theorists like Gerald Gardner (1884–1964), who believe that witchcraft existed as the continuation of a Stone-Age fertility religion, have not substantiated their claims.

There are several principal theories regarding European witchcraft in the sixteenth and seventeenth centuries. According to one theory, witchcraft as a religion of devil worship actually existed, and the Church undertook to oppose it through the witchcraft persecutions of the sixteenth and seventeenth centuries. This theory assumes the existence of both a devil and the possibility of men and women worshipping him and entering into agreements (the traditional pacts) with him. The principal exponent of this view was Montague Summers (1880–1948), who wrote extensively on the subject.

Another theory holds that witchcraft was a continuation of an ancient fertility religion, which had once been the original religion of humankind, forced underground by the growing influence of established Christianity. This theory, which bases its conclusions largely on the evidence of witch trials and the documentation of the Church, accepts that this religion was widespread, organized and fairly consistent in its beliefs and practices. The principal exponent of this line of argument was Margaret Murray, who wrote several textbooks expounding it. Many modern witches advocate her view of witchcraft, and many have written in support of it, using the evidence that she presented to reinforce their claims.

Some believe that witchcraft was merely an illusion born of hysteria and madness and that the trials and persecution of witches were simply a reflection of widespread social delusion. This theory was first put forward in the sixteenth century by Reginald Scot, in his *Discovery of Witchcraft.*

The theory accepted by most modern authorities is that postmedieval witchcraft, while not constituting an organized cult of the devil, was an amalgam of the various surviving strands of traditional folk religion and mythology, practiced by individuals within societies throughout Europe, both in isolation and collectively. It included such elements as herbalism, fortune-telling, simple folk superstitions, myths, legends and remnants of older pagan religions that had been passed down through the generations, becoming progressively less clear and more distorted with the passage of time.

In the age of superstition and fear of the devil, anything outside the strict confines of orthodox Christianity was viewed as supernatural and evil, and thus to be destroyed. Older women, herbalists, epileptics, those gifted with psychic powers or who deviated in any way from the norm—all these people were in real danger of being viewed as agents of the

Above: *Eugène Delacroix's painting of the Greek witch and priestess of Hecate, Medea, killing her children by Jason after he abandoned her.*

Left: *A woodcut after Holbein depicting a woman spinning yarn under the light of the moon. During the sixteenth and seventeenth centuries she would almost certainly have been suspected of being a witch because of her knowledge of nature.*

Below: *This image from a medieval Catholic illuminated manuscript unequivocally equates the French Waldensian "heretics" with devil worship and witchcraft. The movement was founded in 1170 and, despite its savage persecution by the Church, still survives in Piedmont to this day.*

devil, or witches. In such cases, they were consigned to inquisitors and, ultimately, execution. The witchcraft persecutions of the repressive sixteenth and seventeenth centuries were also based on accusations of sexual behavior associated with devil worship. Naked dancing, "abnormal" sexual behavior, intercourse with the devil, the use of stimulating substances—these were characteristic of the "evidence" given against the accused.

In practice, accusing someone of witchcraft during this period was often a simple scapegoating device, by which misfortune could be explained and (the accusers hoped) eliminated. The "evidence" of evildoing could be occurrences of sickness, drought, infertility or

death—all of which could be the results of curses. In many communities, including Salem, Massachusetts, the scene of infamous witch trials of the 1690s, it was virtually impossible for the accused to prove their innocence. In the Salem trials, an alibi was taken as proof of guilt, because it "proved" that the accused could be in two places at once. In other cases, heretics were victimized as witches. Countless innocent people were killed during this holocaust. Nevertheless, among those accused by the witch-hunters were self-proclaimed witches, psychics and people who adhered to the "old religion."

Witchcraft is often totally identified with the popular view of the European phenomenon of earlier centuries, but it is spread widely throughout history and in most societies. In primitive societies, it was generally a system of magical practices and beliefs held by a few individuals within a group. Often it was seen as evil and dangerous (when it was generally known as "sorcery"), although many cultures have viewed it merely as an alternative to the orthodox religious system or, indeed, as an integral part of that system. Thus, for example, in many African societies witch doctors perform important functions in casting spells, healing and divination. Their activities are part of the overall religious system and, while it is recognized that they possess the power to do evil, their work is usually believed to be good. But some individuals who possess similar powers are regarded as evil, and are known as sorcerers.

In all societies some individuals have been recognized as constituting some sort of link between this world and another dimension, who are perhaps able to influence the present and foretell the future, or are capable of healing or casting curses. In many societies such gifts are believed to be hereditary, so the function of the witch passes down from generation to generation. Those accused of witchcraft in Europe were mostly women (although men were sometimes involved in their practices), but in many countries the witch is almost invariably male. Such factors as homosexuality, epilepsy and mental illness have often been sufficient to condemn people as witches in some societies.

Across all cultures, from Western through to African, Asian and South American, the practice of witchcraft can be divided into three

Left: The Caribbean slave Tituba acts out tales of witchcraft to entertain children in Salem. Although she admitted doing the devil's bidding during the subsequent witch trials, Tituba saved her skin by accusing Sarah Good and Sarah Osborn of afflicting the children. She was later sold to a new master.

areas. The first of these is the philosophy, or the beliefs behind the practice of witchcraft, the explanations given for how things came to be and the mythology of how witches are able to fulfill their functions. This belief system is usually linked to some type of fertility religion, based on the cycles of nature and on a variety of myths that have been handed down orally. It constitutes the world view of the witch and the view of witches held by members of the cultures in which they live. For example, in sixteenth- and seventeenth-century Europe, the world view was largely Christian, hence the witch was defined within that system as being a devil worshipper; witches themselves, on the other hand, interpreted their position as adapting the traditional myths of the pre-Christian era to fit into the Christian system.

The second area concerns the methods and activities, as opposed to beliefs, of the witch: the casting of spells, the rituals of healing and the art of herbalism. Such techniques are usually passed down, often in secret, from one generation to another. Various tools can be used; substances can be employed (both those with curative properties and hallucinogenic substances that stimulate visions of a super-natural dimension); and rituals are followed.

The explanation of how the technology of witchcraft works, within the framework of the witches' philosophy, forms the third area, sometimes described as the "science." While scientists reject the use of the term "science" when applied to witchcraft, nevertheless most systems of magical practice are internally consistent and, given the basic premises upon which they work, logical. It is the basic premises, not the logic, that science should challenge. For example, the method may prescribe the rubbing of red ochre over the body of a dying child; the "science" explains this practice by invoking the laws of similarity: blood is red and blood gives life; ochre is red, therefore ochre will communicate the same life as blood.

Witchcraft, in the traditional sense, continues to be practiced today—both in indigenous cultures around the world, where it remains relatively unchanged, and in modern societies, where witches often operate as professional consultants, thereby meeting the old needs in a new context.

Left: The execution of the English witches of Chelmsford in 1589 was a common conclusion to the antiwitch hysteria that was so prevalent in the sixteenth and seventeenth centuries. Their animal familiars—regarded as a sure sign of being a witch—cavort around the hanged women's feet.

Above: When photographed in the 1970s, American witch Morgan McFarland subscribed to the belief that the "old religion" was a benevolent and ancient one.

Right: The ancient Celts practiced human sacrifice to appease their gods and ensure a good harvest. One of the methods used was the construction of a giant wicker figure, into which victims were loaded and burned to death. Although natural fertility is crucial to modern witches, human sacrifice is not a part of their rituals.

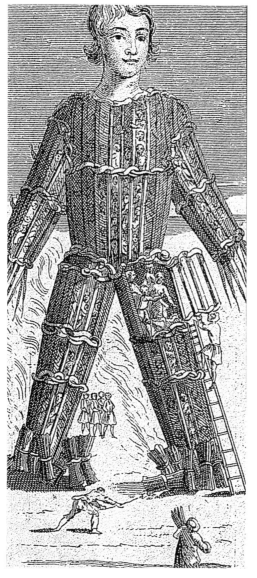

MODERN FORMS OF WITCHCRAFT

The contemporary Western witchcraft movement constitutes one of the most widespread and active forces within the modern occult revival, with the development of the neo-pagan, Wiccan and Dianic traditions being especially noteworthy. Throughout the United States, Europe, South America and Australia, increasing numbers of people are becoming involved in various forms of witchcraft, from the ritual magic of ceremonial robes and quite suburban ritual healings, to more extreme practices. Since many of these witchcraft groups are closed to outsiders, estimates of the size of the movement vary, from hundreds to hundreds of thousands. There are certainly many thousands of self-proclaimed witches in Europe and the United States; indeed, there are few cities in the world today without witchcraft groups, and the movement continues to grow as it is increasingly publicized and as it becomes more "respectable." Members of witchcraft groups, far from fitting the stereotypes of literature and mythology, range through all age groups and include manual workers, students, academics, doctors, lawyers, homemakers and teachers—in fact, all manner of ordinary people.

Although there is considerable variety in the beliefs of those calling themselves witches (and today that term is used for both men and women; the traditional term "warlock," once used to described a male witch, is now rarely used), most subscribe to certain fundamental beliefs about the origins and nature of their faith. (While adherents of Wiccanism prefer to be called Wiccans, and witchcraft "the Craft," since many types of traditions are included in our discussion, the more general words, "witch" and "witchcraft," are used here to include all such beliefs.)

Witches believe that their religion is a continuation of the original "old religion" of humankind, a fertility cult centering on the worship of the forces of nature, usually personified by both a female (the earth mother, the great goddess, the fertility deity) and a male (the horned god) deity, along with numerous lesser entities, including elementals, or spirits of nature. This religion is claimed to derive from ancient times, generally said to be the Stone Age—some even trace its origins to the lost continent of Atlantis—when humans were closer to nature and more aware of their environment and the powers hidden within it.

This primal religion, witches believe, continued unchanged throughout the centuries. With the coming of Christianity and its enforcement as the official Western religion, the "old religion," as witchcraft is often called, was forced underground and obliged to continue as a secret tradition, usually practiced within families. Modern witches cite the evidence of the witchcraft persecutions and trials of the sixteenth and seventeenth centuries as proof of the existence of this underground tradition.

The teachings and practices of the "old religion," including an elementary knowledge of medicine, herbalism, healing, a traditional ritual calendar and the secret, sacred names of the gods and goddesses, was, according to witches, perpetuated by this underground tradition. Some believe that their traditional knowledge, together with initiation into the religion, was transmitted in a succession passing from male to female and vice versa.

With the general decline in the influence of Christianity and the power of the Church (symbolized for many in Britain by the repeal of the laws against witchcraft in 1951), witches see the opportunity for the "old religion" re-emerging from its previous secrecy to become a more or less open practice. Their present-day religion is a continuation of witches' historic tradition and represents for them a modern version of the faith.

Such beliefs are unsubstantiated by historical or anthropological evidence; however, witches generally argue that their secret teachings, rituals and words "prove" their authenticity—and as these things are secret, they cannot be made available to satisfy the skepticism of scientists.

Contemporary Western witchcraft is largely credited to the work of three people. Margaret Murray, a British Egyptologist and scholar, advanced the theory that a secret tradition of witchcraft had always existed and was continued in contemporary Britain. In her writings, the first of which was published in 1921, she "reconstructed" the "old religion," and her books have become valuable sources for many followers of Wiccanism, despite having been disparaged by scholars.

Gerald Gardner, a Briton who traveled widely in the Far East and was interested in folklore, was the second influence on modern witchcraft. He claimed that he had been initiated into a traditional witches' coven in southern England's New Forest in 1939 and was authorized to revive the "old religion." He established a number of covens in Britain, wrote several books on witchcraft and received wide publicity. He is sometimes referred to as the "father" of modern witchcraft, and his tradition is termed "Gardnerian."

Alexander Sanders, another Briton, claimed to have been initiated into witchcraft as a young boy by his grandmother, thereby perpetuating an ancient family tradition. He went on to establish numerous covens throughout

Above: The Roman goddess Diana, pictured in the guise of a Druidess by Rover Lionel. She is garlanded with a wreath of mistletoe and bears a crescent-shaped sickle— both important Druidic symbols. Diana was a focus of pagan goddess cults, and her worship has been revived during the twentieth century.

Right: An illustration from an early twentieth-century Wiccan book of spells. The usual witches' accouterments of broom, familiars and fire are depicted here, but the witch herself has assumed a supernatural form.

Britain, attracting considerable publicity, and proclaimed himself "king of the witches." His tradition is called "Alexandrian."

Despite some claims to independence, such as those who adhere to the Dianic tradition, which combines witchcraft with a feminist world view, all modern Western witchcraft groups derive at least some of their teachings, rituals and traditions from these three sources.

Since the 1960s both neo-paganism and Wiccanism have spread widely in the United States and Britain. Polytheistic and pantheistic, adherents of these movements regard life and nature as sacred and believe that magic should be used for purposes of good. Drawing on diverse traditions, including the Druidic, Celtic and shamanistic, modern witches attempt to develop their magical skills both in order to channel spiritual power and to commune with the "divine force" that binds all people and nature together.

Modern witches meet regularly in groups, known as covens, usually consisting of between six and twenty members (the traditional number being thirteen). The meetings are open only to initiated members and are regularly held for worship, usually on nights of the full moon, when healing work is undertaken, spells are cast and new candidates are initiated. They also occur on the special festivals of the year relating to the cycles of nature in the northern hemisphere (for example, the summer solstice, the equinoxes, or May Eve). On these special occasions, rituals relating to the festivals are performed. Some coven members undertake their work in ceremonial robes, others in the nude; some employ techniques of sexual magic in their work, while others are highly puritanical in such matters. Sexual magic is based upon a number of principles:

1: Humans possess hidden powers (often identified with the subconscious mind), which give them greater perception, raise them to states of ecstasy, expand their consciousness and stimulate increased physical, emotional and mental powers.

2: These powers lie "buried" beneath some "barrier," which conscious control cannot penetrate, but which can be overcome through a variety of techniques, including by taking consciousness-enhancing substances and alcohol.

3: This mental "barrier" can be penetrated through heightening the physical, emotional and intellectual focus of the body by sexual stimulation, leading up to a "breakthrough" at the point of orgasm, at which point energy is released.

4: This release of energy can be used for many purposes, including magical (for example, in the casting of a spell).

5: This energy can be focused and contained to some extent in various objects and substances: for example, in talismans upon which sexual fluids have been poured, or in objects that are consecrated or "charged" at the moment of orgasm.

While the majority of witchcraft groups would describe themselves as "white" (that is, as using their knowledge for good), in accordance with the Wiccan Rede "An' [if] it harm none, do what ye will," some groups are explicitly "black" (using their knowledge for evil purposes—for example, for curses or destroying enemies). There are also, naturally, some pseudowitchcraft groups in which the "old religion" is used as a front to entice subjects for such exploitative and destructive purposes as sexual abuse, substance abuse and blackmail.

ALEISTER CROWLEY: LORD OF THE NEW AEON

Aleister Crowley, variously known as the "Laird of Boleskine," "The Great Beast 666," and "the wickedest man who ever lived," is probably one of the most maligned figures in the history of the occult. It is true that Crowley had sadistic tendencies in his childhood and suffered from megalomania, as was shown by his efforts to surpass all his rivals in the Hermetic Order of the Golden Dawn. But he was also a magician of considerable style and originality, and some of his concepts may even prove to be significant in the history of psychology. As early as 1929, Crowley published his work *Magick in Theory and Practice*, one part of which was devoted to a systematic tabling of subconscious imagery in the mind.

From the very beginning, Crowley's life was full of contrasts. Born in 1875, he was raised in a strict Plymouth Brethren home, studied at Cambridge University and pursued interests as varied as mountain-climbing, rowing and chess. He became a friend of Alan Bennett, a member of the Golden Dawn, and embroiled himself in a deep study of magic and mysticism. Evicted in 1923 from Cefalu in Sicily by Mussolini, where he had established an abbey for the practice of ritual magic; constantly involved in legal disputes over the publication of Hermetic secrets; and infamous for his escapades with women, Crowley first became notorious when he proclaimed himself the "Anti-Christ" in 1904. He was to become one of the most spectacular figures in the history of contemporary magic.

Prior to his pronouncement, Crowley had pursued an orthodox training in the magical arts in the Golden Dawn. Introduced to the order in 1898, he soon grasped that those with the loftiest grades were able to wield profound spiritual authority over their minions, while claiming a rapport with "secret chiefs" who emanated from higher planes of being. In *Magick* he wrote: "Every man is more or less aware that his individuality comprises several orders of existence." "Magick" (which Crowley spelled with an additional "k") was a means of transforming the consciousness by will to allow union with the supreme spiritual forces in the cosmos.

Crowley was initiated as a neophyte in the Golden Dawn on November 18, 1898. In December of that year, he took the grade of "Zelator," and those of "Theoricus" and "Practicus" in the following two months; he was keen to ascend the occult grades of the tree of life as quickly as possible. Crowley was also the first magician to attempt the six-month Abramelin ritual, which had been translated from the French by Mathers, the co-founder of the Golden Dawn. During the rituals, Crowley had visions of Christ, and then saw himself crucified. John Symonds writes:

He stood within the Divine Light with a crown of twelve stars upon his head; the earth opened for him to enter into its very center, where he climbed the peak of a high mountain. Many dragons sprang upon him as he approached the Secret Sanctuary, but he overcame all

Left: Aleister Crowley in the Egyptian-influenced robes of a hierophant of the Hermetic Order of the Golden Dawn. Crowley joined the order in 1898 and progressed quickly through its grades.

Right: *Aleister Crowley pictured with Rose Kelly, whom he married in 1903, and their daughter. It was Rose, rather than her husband, who received the message from Horus that would change Crowley's life. Unsurprisingly, Rose eventually became insane, whereupon Crowley divorced her and took solace in a string of mistresses whom he dubbed "Scarlet Women."*

with a word. This was an alchemical vision of his success in the Great Work. Crowley realized that he was born with all the talents required for a great magician.

Crowley claimed that certain incidents occurred in 1904 that suggested to him that his genius, and his role in the world, reached farther than Britain. Having failed to dislodge W.B. Yeats as head of the Golden Dawn, Crowley suddenly and impetuously embarked upon a series of travels through Mexico, the United States, Ceylon (now Sri Lanka) and India. He finally arrived in Cairo, which was to be a major milestone in the building of his new, magical universe.

On March 14, 1904, in his room near the Boulak Museum in Cairo, Crowley performed a magical ceremony invoking the Egyptian deity Thoth, god of wisdom. According to Crowley's account, his wife appeared to be in a dazed state of mind and, four days later, while in a state of drowsiness, announced that Horus was "waiting" for her husband. Crowley was not expecting any such announcement; he was even more surprised when she led him to a museum he had not previously visited. When she pointed to a statue of Horus in the form of Ra-Hoor-Khuit, he was amazed to find that the exhibit was number 666, the number of the "Great Beast" in the biblical Book of Revelations. Crowley regarded this as a portent and returned to his hotel, where he performed a ritual for Horus. His wife again fell into a trance and began to dictate a series of statements emanating from a semi-invisible Egyptian spirit named Aiwass. In the communication, later published as *The Book of the Law*, Crowley claimed he was instructed to abandon the ceremonial magic that he had been taught in the Golden Dawn and to pursue sexual magic instead. In so doing, he had to discover the whereabouts of the Scarlet Whore of Babylon, as mentioned in the Book of Revelations, for it had been confirmed that Crowley was indeed the Anti-Christ who would succeed Jesus. He was to be the Lord of the New Aeon, he believed: "Now ye shall know that the chosen priest and apostle of infinite space is the prince-priest the Beast," proclaimed Aiwass, "and in his woman called the Scarlet Woman is all power given." It seemed to be a curious parody on Christ and the Virgin Mary.

Crowley realized that an event of the magnitude of his cosmic initiation only occurred every 2,000 years, and that it constituted a new phase in the evolution of humankind. He would incarnate in the world the mystery of the sexual union of the great Egyptian gods Nuit and Hadit; he would be the "god-child." He was furthermore the successor of Osiris, Christ and Mohammed: "With my Hawk's head [i.e., Horus's] I peck at the eyes of Jesus...I flap my wings in the face of Mohammed."

This "illumination" by Aiwass conferred upon Crowley a new sense of his own authority; he had tapped the highest spiritual energies of the universe—and he had done so in Egypt, the legendary home of magic. He wrote to Mathers to inform him that *his* ritual formulae were now obsolete; Crowley notes, "I did not expect, or receive, a reply."

Always fond of structure and authority, Crowley decided to form his own occult order, calling it the *Argentinum Astrum,* or "Silver Star." To begin with, its structure imitated that of the Golden Dawn, although after his contact with the German *Ordo Templi Orientis,* he did include some sexual magic in his rites. The O.T.O., as it was known, was an occult fraternity based on sexual magic and had been founded in Germany in 1906 by Theodor Reuss. Crowley derived his sexual-magic teach-

ings from both his own research and experimentation and from the O.T.O. His sexual-magic techniques were, he claimed, expressly for the purpose of obtaining magical power and experience, encompassing a wide variety of supposedly spritual practices.

The A.A., as Crowley's society was known, initiated nearly a hundred people. Among the most noteworthy were Norman Mudd, professor of mathematics at Bloemfontain University in South Africa; Victor Neuburg, who was a "father-poet" to Dylan Thomas and Pamela Hansford-Johnson; and the visionary artist Austin Spare. Crowley also inspired a number of sexual-magic societies in the USA, namely the Choronzon Club (named after the demon of chaos); Louis T. Culling's Great Brotherhood of God; the Californian O.T.O. (one of whose members was L. Ron Hubbard, the founder of Scientology); and the Fellowship of Ma Ion, which was based on an idiosyncratic blend of Catholicism and Crowley.

Aleister Crowley died a confused man in December 1947. He had failed to locate the Scarlet Whore of Babylon. He did, however, leave behind him a large output of magical writing, including works on the Tarot, the Qabalah, the *I Ching,* yoga, the Enochian calls of Dr. Dee and the symbolic meaning of ritual. He remains one of the most influential occultists of the twentieth century, and his works continue to be republished at a prodigious rate long after his death.

Below: Aleister Crowley in old age. He died an inglorious death in 1947 in a boarding house in the English seaside resort of Hastings, but is still remembered today as one of the most notorious magicians of the twentieth century.

Below: A deathbed struggle for a human soul depicted by Hieronymus Bosch. As death enters the room, an angel indicates the divine light that emanates from the crucifix, appealing to the dying man to choose eternal salvation rather than the damnation that awaits him if he is tempted by the devil's bags of gold. The relationship between Christianity and Satanism is one of inversion and opposition.

Traditional Satanism

Traditionally, Satanism has been interpreted as the worship of the devil, the figurehead of evil, a "religion" founded upon the very principles Christianity rejects. Satanism therefore exists only where Christianity exists and can be understood only in the context of the Christian world view. In Satanism things are, so to speak, reversed—the Christian devil becomes the Satanist's god, Christian virtues become vices, while vices are turned into virtues. Life is interpreted as a constant battle between the powers of light and darkness, and the Satanist fights on the side of darkness, believing that the dark powers will ultimately achieve victory.

By this definition, there have been very few Satanists throughout history. The Christian Church has often interpreted a wide range of non-Christian religions as Satanic, and the activities of its own heretics as indicating adherence to Satanism. This was especially true of the early Gnostics, whom many churchmen believed to be Satanists, although they clearly were not. Nevertheless, the idea and principles of the Gnostics have profoundly influenced later Satanists, especially the dualistic philosophy (that is, their belief in two opposing forces—light and darkness—interlocked in constant battle).

In its persecution of heretics and others who refused to conform to its rigid doctrinal confines, the Church created a synthetic image of supposedly typical Satanists: Christians who formally renounced the vows of baptism, rejected the Church and dedicated themselves to those things Christ forbade; they did not reject the Christian world view, since their own philosophy had meaning only within that context. The Church pictured exotic and sacrilegious rituals in which men and women rejected their faith, entered into pacts with the devil and engaged in all manner of abominable and immoral acts. Central to such behavior was the black mass, an inverted celebration of the central ritual of Christianity, in which the Host (which Christians believe to be the body of Christ), stolen from a church, or consecrated by an defrocked priest, was desecrated. In this ceremony, every action the Church forbade was believed to occur—from a whole range of sexual "perversions" to the sacrifice of infants (often unbaptized) and the recitation of the Lord's Prayer backward. The whole ceremony was directed toward inverting the Christian symbolism (centered on the inverted cross that stood upon the Satanist's altar) and raising up the Devil.

Although such images of Satanism were largely the creation of the vividly imaginative Church inquisitors, their practice actually developed, especially in France during the seventeenth and eighteenth centuries, when certain aristocrats participated in an underground movement of Satanism as a way of rejecting the values of society—and doubtless as an excuse for engaging in unusually exciting forms of self-indulgence. Generally, however, Satanist groups have remained hidden—they have little to gain from publicity and much to lose, especially since many of the traditional ingredients of their worship are intrinsically illegal (including drugs, murder and violence) and are unacceptable even in liberal societies. Thus very little is known of the groups that have, throughout history, followed this path. Various accounts have been given of a widespread "cult" of evil by such authors as Montague Summers, but these tend not to be grounded in fact. Groups have indeed existed, but most of them have simply used the trappings of an anti-Christian religion as a pretext for extreme indulgence in hedonism—for example, the infamous English "Hell-Fire Club," founded by Sir Francis Dashwood (1708–81).

Throughout history, individuals and groups have employed the rituals of Satanism either as a means of searching for worldly power or as a symbolic rejection of the established values of their society. It was members of this latter category, rather than true Satanists (in the sense of those who literally worship the Devil as Christians worship their God), who left their mark on history. And many groups (including, for example, Freemasons) were labeled Satanic by the Church in its attempts to suppress them. Since Satanism is essentially a reaction against Christianity, it is not known in any real sense outside the Christian world, although it was once popularly (and erroneously) assumed that some oriental religions (for example, the Hindus' worship of Shiva in India) represented Satanism. However, in any naturally dualistic religion, the worship of either the creative or the destructive aspects of a deity is acceptable to believers and cannot be equated with the mutual opposition of Christianity and Satanism.

Many Western magicians (another category of people indiscriminately labeled by the Church as Satanists) approached the devil in this dualistic way, or saw Satan as a source of power that could be controlled and utilized for their own purposes without any attendant connotation of devil worship. Such people were regarded as practitioners of "black magic," or the "black arts." Since the Church condemned all magical and occult practices, these phrases had little meaning and tended to include Satanism and devil worship.

Strictly, the term "Satanism" should be reserved for those who deliberately choose to worship and work with the power of evil, gen-

erally personified by an individual devil, usually known either as Satan or Lucifer, under whom many subordinate entities (paralleling the angelic hosts of heaven) work. The few people who actually fitted within this definition evolved elaborate theologies of the Devil to match the theologies of the Church, concentrating especially on the names and natures of lesser devils over whom they could gain control and through whom they could achieve their ends. It is inappropriate to refer to the medieval magicians, whose grimoires were popularly believed to contain the secrets of black magic, as Satanists, for they were not concerned with the Devil so much as with forces of various kinds, personified by individual entities, with whom they conducted what virtually amounted to business relationships.

Modern Satanism

Parallel with the general decline in the influence and authority of Christianity, traditional Satanism—which had developed in opposition to that religion—also declined. But with the occult revival of the twentieth century there has been an upsurge of interest and involvement in Satanism as well as an increasing number of books and articles on the subject. Generally, however, contemporary Satanists do not follow the traditional pattern of worshipping Satan instead of the God of the Christian religion. Traditional Satanism only

Above: One of the ways in which the Church sought to repress "heretical" beliefs was by burning the books that propagated them, as illustrated in this thirteenth-century illuminated manuscript. Magician's grimoirs would certainly have been burned, along with those who used them. The Church suppressed all literature it deemed to be unsuitable, or that questioned any aspect of Church authority.

Above: Anton Szandor La Vey, the founder of the First Church of Satan, pictured with his acolyte wife during a black mass. The use of the clerical garb, candles and chalice in this context are symbols of the Satanists' inversion of Christianity.

holds power where the Christian, and most often the Catholic, religion is accepted, and it is difficult to blaspheme against God or to violate the sacraments of a religion in which one never believed in the first place. Modern Satanists fit into several categories, some of which overlap, as well as a few groups whose members would claim to be outside any of these categories.

The traditional, anti-Christian, Satanists, who worship the devil of orthodox Christian belief, celebrate the black mass, profane the Sacrament, desecrate churches and graveyards and believe that the devil will ultimately triumph over the God of Christianity. (Examples of this group include the Order of Satanic Templars in Britain). Another category is a secular, humanistic, Satanism, which has neither a personal devil nor a personal god. These modern Satanists devote themselves to humanity and oppose the restrictions and inhibitions Christian culture has imposed upon humans. They advocate, for example, the seven deadly sins as virtues and use traditional Satanic rituals as processes for liberating individuals from their inhibitions. The First Church of Satan in California is an example of this category.

A paganistic Satanism, which worships the "forces of darkness" in contrast to the "forces of light," is a third category, interpreting its worship in terms of old mythologies and religions (for example, the Greek, Egyptian and Roman), but with a special interest in Christianity. These groups generally call themselves "pagan" and view their activities as constituting a new religion, rather than as the continuation of a traditional one (for example, *Ophitic Gnostic Cultus*).

Satanic witchcraft, which uses the traditions and rituals of modern witchcraft as a basis for modified witchcraft practices, views the "horned god" as the equivalent of the devil of Christianity and a more powerful and worthwhile god to worship. This group uses the techniques of witchcraft (for example, cursing and casting spells) in the context of a traditional, historic religion. Members of the Satanic Brotherhood are Satanic witches.

In hedonistic Satanism, rituals, consciousness-enhancing substances and sexual techniques are used to gratify the senses; the morality they proclaim is founded on pleasure. Although there are some loosely religious overtones, such groups are not philosophical. They view their activities as concerning gratification (all the more so because they are "evil" in the eyes of society) rather than worship. Hedonistic Satanist groups tend to be small, privately organized and rarely publicized; they are increasingly associated with pornography.

Satanists of all these types recognize the existence of two forces in the world, traditionally referred to as "black" and "white" (in Christian terms as "good" and "evil"). Viewing "white" as the religion of the establishment, the Satanists reject it in favor of its opposite—for example, preaching gratification of the senses rather than abstinence, or self-centeredness rather than self-sacrifice. They believe that the "powers of darkness" (whether they are personified or not) are life-giving forces, of which the "white" religion is afraid. Sex is important to them because of its "repression," or limitation, by Christianity and because of the power, gratification and pleasure it provides. Satanists believe that the powers of darkness will ultimately triumph and they view themselves as powerful, virile, strong individuals, in contrast to the weak, inhibited and frightened masses. They believe that if humans have the power to heal and bless, then they also possess the power to kill and curse and should use this for their own advantage. They reject morality in any conventional sense, believing that survival and self-fulfillment is the individual's most important aim, regardless of the cost to other people. Some Satanic groups have evolved mythologies explaining their teachings, usually relating to the legendary fall of Lucifer from heaven, his subsequent battle with God for the domination of the world and his future triumph and return to heaven to reign. They believe that his power is gradually increasing and work with him in the hope of reward, both in the material sense here and now, and in some future life.

Rejecting the essential values and norms of acceptable behavior in society, Satanists have always been obliged to maintain some degree of secrecy: the law is against them and social sanction denied them. Groups of Satanists have tended to be small and secret, so their history is poorly documented, except in cases involving conflicts with the law. In modern times, groups have emerged in Europe and particularly in the United States, where they have taken advantage of the relative permissiveness of modern society and encouraged some publicity. Perhaps the most famous of these is the First Church of Satan, founded in Los Angeles in 1966 by Anton Szandor La Vey and established as a church throughout the United States. Several other groups have imitated La Vey's; some have also been established as "black witchcraft" covens. The murderous Manson gang, which practiced a bizarre mixture of Satanism and occultism, exposed the practice of Satanism in America, while increasing public interest in the subject. As more people reject the traditional values, religion and morality of their society, the Satanist movement will inevitably have greater appeal.

Traditional Satanists use inverted forms of orthodox Christian worship (for example, reciting the Lord's Prayer backward, or celebrating the black mass) to symbolize and focus their rejection of Christianity and to invoke the powers of darkness. Other Satanist rituals are based upon ancient mythology (usually Egyptian, Greek or Roman), while secular, humanistic, Satanists view their rituals as psychological techniques for liberating individuals from their repression, thus enabling them to find freedom and pleasure.

Satanists have traditionally used rituals to curse enemies and in the hope of gaining material rewards and acquiring power. Such rituals are invariably composed of words, symbols and actions that invert the general values of their society—for example, indulging in "perverted" sexual behavior, using excrement, displaying inverted crosses and using black vestments or black candles to symbolize the darkness they worship. To stimulate the senses, consciousness-enhancing substances and sexual activities are employed, often incorporating some degree of sado-masochistic behavior. The notorious "black mass" of traditional Satanism was largely a sexual rite, during which the celebrant had sexual relations with a prostitute who served as an "altar," and in which a variety of forms of sexual stimulation were employed to arouse the congregation.

Satanic groups, usually called "covens" or "lodges," are strictly secret (with the notable exception of the First Church of Satan, in which they are semisecret). They admit only those initiates who have been prepared over a long period of time. Some Satanic groups follow traditional occult patterns in their ritual, holding ceremonies on nights of the full moon and on the major festivals of the witches' calendar.

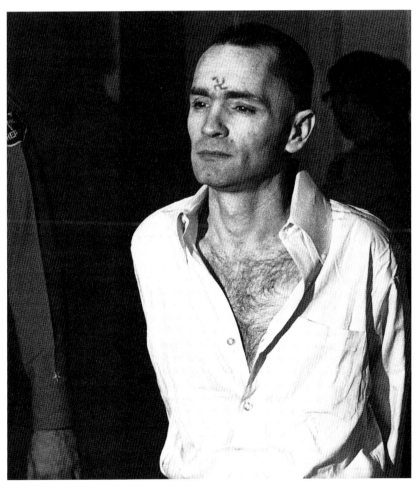

Below: Charles Manson at his trial in 1971. He claimed that the murderous activities of his gang, including the killing of the actress Sharon Tate, were directly inspired by Satan.

SCHOOLS OF MYSTICAL BELIEF

Occult and mystical beliefs have a rich and varied history. Although many schools of mystical belief were not formally established until medieval times, their traditions are said to stretch back to the days of ancient Egypt and beyond. Strongly influenced by such systems of esoteric thought as Hermeticism and the Qabalah, alchemy, Rosicrucianism and Freemasonry all developed into leading schools of mystical belief, elements of which were in turn applied to twentieth-century occult societies such as the Hermetic Order of the Golden Dawn. And when the concepts and practices of Eastern religious traditions, such as the Tattvas and reincarnation, became better understood in the West, they too were enthusiastically adopted by groups interested in mysticism, including the Theosophical Society. Other mystical schools of belief, such as Spiritualism, developed relatively independently. Although most schools of occult and mystical belief have been characterized by a certain amount of synthesis and cross-fertilization, the modern New Age movement has developed this eclecticism to a remarkable extent. This chapter gives an introduction to the most influential schools of mystical belief, detailing their credos and history as well as their enduring effect on the occult.

THE *HERMETICA*

Along with the Qabalah, the *Hermetica* is one of the foundation stones on which the modern occult traditions are based; indeed, the *Hermetica* and Hermeticism were so significant in informing the principles of early eso-

teric scientific disciplines that they can be collectively termed the "Hermetic arts."

In traditional belief, the *Hermetica* was a collection of forty-two books of Egyptian magical wisdom that were believed to have been written by Hermes Trismegistus (the Greek for "Hermes thrice-greatest")—a name with which Greek settlers in Egypt unified the Greek god Hermes and the Egyptian god Thoth (whom they actually identified with each other, since both were associated with the dead, healing and magical knowledge) to create a new entity. In Hermetic legend, Hermes Trismegistus ruled for 3,226 years, and during his rein he conquered the monstrous Typhon, the symbol of ignorance. According to his followers, this most powerful philosopher-magician-king-priest carried a caduceus, representing illumination, as well as a great emerald tablet, on which he recorded his philosophy.

The emerald tablet was said to have been found in the cave in which Hermes Trismegistus was entombed (although he was also believed to have been mummified and entombed within the Great Pyramid of Giza), and transcriptions were made of it (of which no two are identical). One translation of the emerald tablet was especially relevant to alchemists in their attempts to achieve the perfect transmutation:

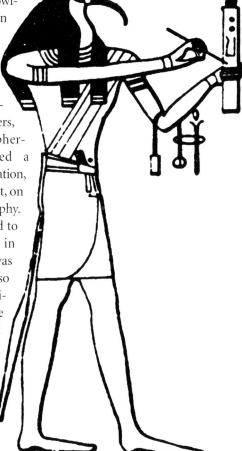

Opposite: A Buddhist mandala, a symbol of the universe and a valuable aid to meditation.

Below: Thoth, the Egyptian god of wisdom. Hermes Trismegistus was an amalgamation of Thoth and the Greek god Hermes.

It was thought that the papyrus books of the *Hermetica*, supposedly dictated by Hermes Trismegistus, were lost when the library in Alexandria in which they were stored was burned to the ground (in AD 646). The eighteen treatises that survived were said to have been secretly buried in the desert; they include *The Divine Pymander* and *The Vision*.

With its emphasis on repentance, the search for wisdom, and unity both with the supreme being and all living things, the *Hermetica* had a profound effect on Western mystical belief when it first reached Europe in the late fifteenth century—and even on Christianity, for it appeared to predict the birth of Christ. Although the French scholar Isaac Casaubon (1559–1614) discredited the legend on which the *Hermetica* was based, claiming to prove that it was written by second- or third-century Christians who had a knowledge of Platonism, Stoicism and the Qabalah, it nevertheless remained an important element in occult philosophy, particularly in alchemy, and is still credited with relevance today.

THE QABALAH

Probably more than any other mystical philosophy apart from the *Hermetica*, the Qabalah of medieval Jewish tradition has exerted a profound influence on the occult. Like most forms of mysticism, it describes the levels of consciousness and being between the human and the Godhead, but it is not for this reason that it has become the basis of modern magic. The Qabalah employs a complex symbol called the "tree of life" as its central motif. This tree is a pragmatic framework within which to base rituals and meditations, making the Qabalah relevant to the modern occult.

In the Qabalistic tradition— the Hebrew word "QBLH" means an oral or secret tradition—the whole of the manifested universe is said to have originated in *Ain Soph*, the hidden and infinite "god energy," which is without qualities or attributes. The Qabalists believed that as soon as one tried to ascribe qualities to *Ain Soph*, this sense of infinity and limitlessness would be lost.

Above: A third-century mosaic depicting Hermes, bearing his caduceus, carrying the infant Dionysus to safety on his winged feet. Both gods are important in occult tradition, but Hermes was particularly revered by alchemists.

Right: The Qabalistic tree of life, made up of ten hierarchical sephiroth, represents both the manifested universe and human levels of consciousness. It is an important meditational symbol in most branches of occult practice.

…That which is above is like that which is below, to perpetrate the miracles of One thing…Here is the father of every perfection in the world. His strength and power are absolute when changed into earth; thou wilt separate the earth from fire, the subtle from the gross, gently and with care. It ascends from earth to heaven, and descends again to receive the power of the superior and the inferior things. By this means, thou wilt have the glory of the world. And because of this, all obscurity will flee from thee. Within this power, most powerful of all powers. For it will overcome all subtle things, and penetrate every solid thing. Thus was the world created. From this will be, and will emerge, admirable adaptations of which the means are here…

The tree of life describes in effect a type of crystallization process by which the infinite gradually becomes finite; the latter is the world as we see it around us. For the Qabalist, however, there are intermediate stages of being, or mind, energy or consciousness—call it what you will. The *Ain Soph* thus reveals aspects of its divinity to humans, and on the tree of life these are represented symbolically by ten major stages called *sephiroth*. In modern magical usage, whereby magic becomes rather similar to yoga in operation, the *sephiroth* are best regarded as levels of consciousness. Magicians begin with their present level of "earth consciousness" and try to retrace the steps back to the Godhead. The ten levels are designated as follows.

Kether—The crown, or peak of creation
Hokmah—Wisdom (the father)
Binah—Understanding (the mother)
Hesed—Mercy
Geburah—Severity, or strength
Tiphareth—Beauty and harmony
   (the son)
Netzach—Victory
Hod—Splendor
Yesod—The foundation
Malkuth—Kingdom, or earth
   (the daughter)

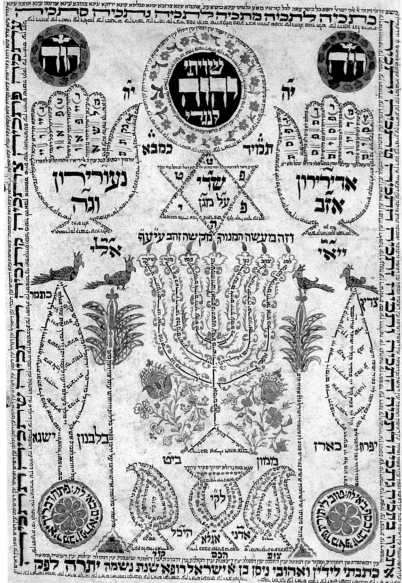

One immediately obvious distinction is that some of the *sephiroth* have "personal" attributes—the father, mother, son and daughter—while others mention only abstract attributes, such as mercy. A closer analysis, particularly of the way in which the tree has been incorporated into magic, shows that this is not a real distinction. Magicians take considerable notice of the gods and goddesses of the different religions of the world and they endeavor to compare and correlate them in terms of the attributes, sacred qualities and aspirations the deities personify. The gods are considered symbols of what the magicians may themselves become, and the mythology is seen as a type of symbolic energy process deep in the spiritual areas of the mind. This is what Jung was

Above: *The purpose of this nineteenth-century micrah is to aid meditational prayer. It is full of Jewish and Qabalistic symbols, including the menorah, the magen david (star of David, also called the seal of Solomon) and a hand whose fingers are believed to ward off evil.*

Left: *A tree of life depicted in a synagogue's elaborate stained-glass window.*

Below: *An etching from Goya's* Caprichos *series illustrates witches en route to a sabbat. The sabbat was held at night, when the moon's influence would arouse animal instincts, which the Qabalists termed Nephesch.*

implying in his theory of the archetypes of the collective unconscious, but for magicians it is a pragmatic reality. They know that the gods are inherent in their minds and they devise rituals and meditations as aids for encountering them.

Returning to the tree, it is apparent that each of the *sephiroth* levels of consciousness plays an important, harmonizing role. The crown, *Kether*, resides at the top of the tree. It is a level that transcends duality, and in this sense resembles the Buddhist state of nirvana, or infinite bliss. The next levels, *Hokmah* and

Below: *An etching from Goya's* Caprichos *series illustrates witches en route to a sabbat. The sabbat was held at night, when the moon's influence would arouse animal instincts, which the Qabalists termed Nephesch.*

Binah, have sexual ascriptions, being the father and mother respectively. Together with *Kether*, these form the Qabalistic "trinity." *Hokmah* is the outward, dynamic and creative force, and *Binah* is the womb of creation from which all is born; as such, she is the mother of us all.

It is interesting to note that the Qabalists regarded their mystery teaching in part as a commentary on the Biblical Book of Genesis, and the remaining seven levels of the tree were said to be the seven days of creation. These seven also have mythological counterparts, and to all intents and purposes the seven days represent the total, mystical universe. The reason for this is that humans were separated from the Godhead by their Fall, and the gulf between the trinity and the rest of the tree can be described as the "abyss." Magicians claim that it is possible to cross the abyss, but at this level of being all notions of ego and self disappear. The finite is transformed into the infinite.

In mythology, the levels represented by *Hesed* and *Geburah* refer to the father of the world as we know it. Often, like Zeus, he is said to reside upon a high mountain, which reaches into the infinite sky: Zeus's home was on the lofty Mount Olympus. *Hesed* represents the father-god in his merciful form, and *Geburah* represents him at war. The Greeks called this latter form Aries, and the Romans, Mars. According to the Qabalah, the universe is composed of a dynamic conflict between life and death—of building up and breaking down. *Hesed* maintains peace and order in the cosmos, while *Geburah* breaks things down once their use is past.

Below them, we come to *Tiphareth*, which is at the center of the tree. As can be seen from its location, it is midway between the human and the Godhead and thus represents the god-man, or messiah. The aim of spiritual philosophies is to allow the human to become the child of the gods, and so *Tiphareth* is the son. In different religions and mythologies, we find that Osiris, Apollo, Dionysus and Christ all have a strikingly similar role as symbols of new life. Usually these figures are also sun gods, since the sun is always reborn from the "death" of night with each dawn. The main aim of the Hermetic Order of the

Golden Dawn was to prepare its practitioners for the mystical experience of *Tiphareth*, and their rituals incorporated both Egyptian and Christian symbols.

Descending farther down the tree, we come to *Netzach*, which represents love, art and the emotions. Opposite, we find *Hod*, which counterbalances *Netzach* by means of rational intellect and reason. Then we come to *Yesod* which, in a sense, represents the lower areas of the mind, when the tree is seen as a symbolic diagram representing the potential of the human mind. In *Yesod*, which equates with the lower unconscious in psychology, we find the basic sexual drives. The Qabalists referred to it as the *Nephesch*, or animal soul, and mythologically it is represented by the Moon. Just as the Moon reflects the Sun (which represents true illumination), lunar worship tends to arouse the animal instincts rather than the spiritual ones. The sexual religion of witchcraft, in particular, with its lunar sabbats, incorporated the worship of the goat (the beast), and the witches rode to sabbats on their brooms (a symbol of the male phallus).

The final *sephirah* is *Malkuth*, which represents our present consciousness. Our task from here is to find our way back into the occult areas of the mind, which are, effectively, the source of all inspiration and knowledge.

In fairness to the classical Qabalists, it has to be admitted that the summary given above presents a modern, occult view of the Qabalah rather than an historical one. Judaism is, of course, monotheistic, and hence it was not appropriate to talk of "the

gods" so much as "the one God." However, it is probably true that the distinction between polytheism and monotheism is overplayed academically, when it tends to be a symbolic division. Wallis Budge commented that even in ancient Egypt all the gods were said to come from one—Ra—although for practical purposes the gods were represented as separate beings in their own right, with distinct characteristics.

Magicians and occultists use the Qabalah and its tree of life as a framework within which to pin the symbols of all Western and Eastern religions. They have thus expanded its use beyond its original Judaic confines. In recent times, too (since the lifetime of Eliphas Lévi over a century ago), a connection has been made between the major-arcana cards of the Tarot and the ten levels of the tree. As such, the *sephiroth* are the levels of consciousness, and the Tarot cards are the "doorways," or "paths," leading to them. The Qabalah has thus become an intricate and profound "modernized" cosmology. It allows humans to harmonize all their mind processes and eventually to rediscover the spiritual illumination that lies within them.

Left: The animal instincts contained in the human lower unconscious are represented both by the Qabalistic sephirah Yesod, *and by the archetypal symbol of the Moon.*

Below: A seventeenth-century Qabalistic amulet designed to ward off the evil eye. The seal of Solomon (so called because Solomon was said to have controlled demons with a hexagram) at its center was believed to have protective abilities. It is contained within a triple magic circle inscribed with words of power.

Right: A page of the
seventeenth-century
alchemical treatise
Claris Artis, *illustrating
a dragon—an important
symbol of transmuta-
tion—swallowing the
elemental fire.*

Right: A page of the
seventeenth-century
alchemical treatise
Claris Artis, *illustrating
a dragon—an important
symbol of transmuta-
tion—swallowing the
elemental fire.*

Right: Hermes *"the thrice
great"* Trismegistus,
*depicted on this page from
the early sixteenth-century*
Tractatus Alchemici. *The*
Hermetica *was a primary
influence on the "science"
of alchemy.*

ALCHEMY, ROSICRUCIANISM AND FREEMASONRY

Although the popular image of alchemists is that of medieval chemists trying obsessively to turn base materials into gold, alchemy is now also recognized as the search for spiritual transformation, thanks largely to the work of Carl Jung. Alchemy is an ancient tradition that dates back two thousand years in both China and India, where it continues to flourish; Western alchemy is a younger, but largely discontinued, practice.

Perhaps the greatest influence on Western alchemy was the *Hermetica*, and the "Hermetic art" was first developed in Egypt, spreading to Europe in the twelfth century. Alchemists believed that the world was created from *prima materia* ("first matter"), and that this was present in everything. By breaking down and then reassembling the ingredients of the *prima materia*, using the process known as *solve et coagula*, they could be transmuted into the most precious substance of all—gold. It was furthermore believed that all things are composed of sulfur (symbolizing the soul and masculinity) and mercury (symbolizing the spirit and femininity)—these dual components were represented by Hermes, the hermaphrodite. Some traditions also included

salt as a third element, symbolizing the body. The ultimate goal of alchemy was perfect transmutation (the "great work"), and in pursuit of this, alchemists searched for the key, the elusive "philosopher's stone" (*lapis*). The

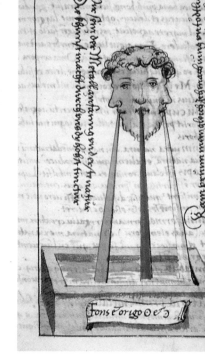

lapis was a hypothetical substance which, it was believed, could cause transmutation into gold (regarded as the perfect metal) as well as conferring complete knowledge and immortality as the "elixir of life."

Jung became interested in alchemy after a dream in which he appeared as a seventeenth-century alchemist. After intensive study of both the Western and Eastern traditions, he became convinced that "the alchemist projected…the process of individuation into the phenomena of chemical change." He reasoned that alchemy was primarily concerned with the attempt to transmute the "base metal" of the human body into spiritual perfection and thus achieve the transformation of the soul, rather than of physical matter. This process involved the alchemists' mystical "death" and "rebirth," their

bodies and souls being symbolized by the substances with which they worked. The hermaphrodite represented the perfect union, both of masculinity and femininity, and of physicality and spirituality, and it was this union that the alchemists were seeking in their quest for true knowledge.

This mystical purpose removes alchemy from the realms of mere pseudoscience, but it has further significance in the occult through the practices of alchemists, who sought spiritual guidance by means of meditation, dreams and visions. Furthermore, it was an esoteric art, whose complicated mysteries and symbols could only be understood by the initiated. And although the advances of science in recent centuries have largely discredited its methods and assumptions, as a mystical belief system its principles have continued to echo down the centuries, in the twentieth century influencing such bodies as the Hermetic Order of the Golden Dawn, as well as New Age thought.

A further school of esoteric belief that has influenced modern occultists is Rosicrucianism, which emerged in Europe in the seventeenth century as a result of the publication of two anonymous German manifestos of the Rosicrucian Order (or the Order of the Rosy Cross) in 1614 and 1615: *Fama fraternitatis des löblichen Ordens des Rosenkreutzes* ("The Fame of the Praiseworthy Fraternity of the Order of the Rosy Cross") and the *Confessio Fraternis* ("Confession of the Fraternity"); these were

Left: The Rosicrucians borrowed many elements of their belief from the Qabalah, including the rose and cross, which the Qabalists had themselves derived from the works of the alchemists of ancient Egypt. The symbol depicted here was adopted by the French Rosicrucian revivalists of the 1890s. Unlike the traditional rosy cross, this version has a magical pentagram at its center.

Left: Isaac Newton, the discoverer of the universal law of gravitation, as depicted by the mystic William Blake. A brilliant mathematician and physicist, Newton devoted the last thirty years of his life to the study of alchemy.

followed in 1616 by *The Chemical Wedding of Christian Rosenkreutz*. As well as inviting people of learning to join the society, these manifestos detailed the probably fictitious life of the much-traveled founder of the order (in 1459), Christian Rosenkreutz (1378–1494), who was said to have brought alchemical, Qabalistic and occult knowledge from Egypt. Although the historical existence of Rosenkreutz and his original order is dubious—authorship of the pamphlets has been attributed to a Lutheran pastor, Johann Valentin Andreae (1686–1754), while Rosenkreutz's experiences have been equated with those of Paracelsus—subsequent Rosicrucian societies were formed whose members included Dr. John Dee and Sir Francis Bacon. Rosicrucianism even influenced German Pietism.

The Rosicrucian tradition is said to be based upon the teachings of Pharoah Thutmose III, whose followers founded the order in 1489 BC, and those of his descendant, Akhnaton (Amenhotep IV). It incorporates elements of Christian Gnosticism and the Jewish Qabalah, as well as of occult and alchemical magic said to date back to the days of ancient Egypt. The cross-and-rose symbol of the order is believed to have been adopted by Akhnaton and rep-

resents death and rebirth, love and secrecy. As in alchemy, the aim of Rosicrucianism is the attainment of perfect knowledge. Initiates progress though twelve degrees of mastery and may be required to undergo a number of reincarnations before they achieve complete cosmic consciousness and union with the supreme being. In modern times, the emphasis has been on spiritual healing and the influence of the planets, thus making it attractive to adherents of New Age thought.

Rosicrucianism continues to influence occult belief, and a number of societies claim their origins in the order, including the Californian Ancient and Mystical Order *Rosae Crucis* (A.M.O.R.C.), founded in 1915 by Harvey Spencer Lewis (1883–1939) and the Rosicrucian Fellowship, which was founded by Max Heindel (1865–1919) in 1909. Other noted modern occultists who are believed to have been Rosicrucians include Rudolf Steiner, Gerald Gardner, Samuel Liddell MacGregor Mathers and Dr. William Wynn Westcott.

Rosicrucianism also influenced Freemasonry, whose eighteenth degree is that of the Knight of the Pelican and Eagle Sovereign Prince Rose Croix of Heredom, but members of the "Craft," as it is called, claim that the

Right: *The greatest of the sixteen U.S. presidents who were Freemasons was George Washington, pictured here in full Masonic regalia at a lodge meeting. Washington became a Mason in 1752, and his refusal to centralize U.S. Freemasonry under his control means that each state has its own Grand Lodge and Grand Chapter.*

EASTERN MYSTICISM AND ITS INFLUENCE ON THE OCCULT

In recent decades there has been an increasing interest throughout the West in the teachings and practices of Eastern mysticism, and a number of schools now present these traditions in various forms in the West, ranging from traditional Sikhs and Buddhists through the brightly robed members of the Hare Krishna Movement to self-proclaimed "messiahs" from India.

The influence of Eastern philosophy in the West is increasing in prominence but is not an entirely new phenomenon: it began at about the same time as the development of Spiritualism in the nineteenth century, when Western scholars first began to recognize that Eastern philosophy offered something more than the crude superstition it was once dismissed as. During this period material revealing the substance of the teachings and practices of Eastern religions was made available to the Western general public for the first time.

This popularization of Eastern beliefs can be linked to two events: the founding of the Theosophical Society in 1875 and the Columbian Exposition in Chicago in 1893. Because of its interest in oriental philosophy and the emphasis placed by its founders on India and Tibet as sources of occult knowledge, the former promulgated many oriental ideas (for example, reincarnation) and encouraged investigation into Eastern scriptures, which had been almost exclusively the domain of the scholar and academic. The Columbian Exposition included a "world parliament" of religions, in which exponents of a wide range of beliefs and approaches were given an opportunity for expression and dialogue. It was through the personality of Vivekananda (1863–1902), a swami and disciple of Ramakrishna (an Indian mystic who died in 1836), that the first adaptation of the "East for the West" philosophy was really made, and eventually the Vedanta Society of America was founded, quickly establishing itself throughout the country. This marked the beginning of a missionary movement from the East to the West, which in later years would have marked effects.

As an alternative to the traditional philosophies of the West, Eastern mysticism has proved very popular, and the success of the initial "missionary" movements inspired

Left: The British Lord Allerton wearing full Masonic garb studded with the esoteric symbols of the "Craft," most notably the compasses and set-square.

Masonic lineage dates back to the builders of Solomon's Temple, especially to Hiram Abiff. Evolving from the craft guilds of medieval English stonemasons, the formal organization of Freemasonry as we know it today began with the foundation of England's Grand Lodge in 1717, whence it spread to become an international fraternity. Although Freemasonry propounds the well-known Christian tenets of brotherly love, faith and charity, it is open to all men—women are specifically excluded—who believe in a supreme being, the "Great Architect of the Universe." Notable Freemasons have included Sir Christopher Wren, Mozart, Napoleon, some European royalty and sixteen U.S. presidents. In common with Rosicrucianism, the highly ritualized and secretive practices of Freemasonry are based on degrees of initiation, involving the individual's "death" and "rebirth," in which increasing amounts of esoteric knowledge are imparted.

The symbols and rituals employed by alchemists, Rosicrucians and Freemasons, as well as their ultimate purpose, are, to an extent, interlinked, and many have been absorbed into the vocabulary of the "mainstream" of the occult. Certainly most modern occultists sympathize with their common quest for spiritual knowledge and perfection.

Right: Intricate wooden carvings of the Sun and Moon at a palace at Bhaktapur in Nepal. These symbols represent sacred concepts the world over, lending credence to the belief of the followers of Bahai in the universality of all religions.

others, of varying degrees of authenticity and importance, to undertake similar work in the West. During the 1960s and 1970s especially, such activity almost reached fever pitch, with a wide range of groups engaging in proselytizing activity. On the superficial level, a popular interest in meditation and vegetarianism, in incense and beads, in chanting "Om," and in reading oriental scriptures, was encouraged. However, it also had a much more lasting and fundamental effect on those disciples who penetrated these shallows to reach the depths beneath. During the 1990s, Eastern mysticism enjoyed a revival.

Among the prominent groups and individuals who claimed to follow the Eastern traditions at the time of their greatest popularity, the following are influential:

The Vedanta Society—the original group founded by Vivekananda, which today continues to hold lectures and classes, and which has monasteries and convents throughout the United States. The philosophy it espouses is based on the *Vedas*, the most sacred writings of Hinduism.

The Ananda Marg—founded in 1955 by Shrii Shrii Anandamurti to spread the teachings of the ancient techniques of tantra, Astanga yoga and meditation. The movement has groups, communes and centers in many cities throughout the world. It also operates schools and engages in various forms of social work.

The Bahai faith—followers of the teachings of Bahaullah (1817–92), who declared in 1863 that he was the chosen manifestation of the supreme being for the age. The religion affirms the universality and validity of all religions and strives to unify humankind with one religion, one political, and one social, order. The Bahai movement has a large membership and has spread rapidly.

The International Society for Krishna Consciousness—the Hare Krishna movement, dedicated to awakening the ecstatic state of "Krishna consciousness," whose disciples devote much of their time to chanting their mantra, "Hare Krishna," and taking missionary work to the streets. The society was founded in 1965 by His Divine Grace A.C. Bhaktivedanta Swami Prabhupada (1896–1977), who claimed to be part of a long line of succession going back five hundred years to Lord Chaitanya, an incarnation of Krishna.

Jiddu Krishnamurti (1895–1986)—an Indian philosopher and mystic who, after leaving the Theosophical Society (which had prepared him to become the vehicle for a manifestation of Christ), established himself as a teacher in his own right. He traveled widely, lecturing on his own highly individualist philosophy. He rejected all attempts to proclaim him as a teacher, in the sense that he believed that truth is something for individuals to discover for themselves; he was opposed to all institutions and defined systems of belief.

Meher Baba (1894–1969)—an Indian man who claimed to be the incarnation of the supreme being (incorporating both Krishna and Christ), who had returned to redeem humanity. Despite his claims to immortality, he died. Most of his disciples throughout the world were, however, undeterred by this apparent disaster, and groups teaching his philosophy continue to operate decades later.

The Students' International Meditation Society—the group headed by Maharishi Mahesh Yogi (1911–), which teaches transcendental meditation, and which spread rapidly throughout the world. The techniques taught by the society have been favorably commented upon by those who have undertaken scientific assessments of their effects on individuals' efficiency and health. The system is based on an initiation at which a trained teacher, whose authority derives ultimately from the Maharishi, gives the student a word as a tool for meditation. A variety of scientists have written on the effects of the tech-

Left: A Buddha figure meditating serenely. During the twentieth century Buddhism became an increasingly attractive faith for many Westerners.

nique, and it has been approved for teaching in some schools and colleges in the United States. In 1992 the Natural Law Party was founded in Britain, bringing Maharishi's philosophy to the world of British politics.

The Divine Light Mission— centering on the person of Guru Maharaj Ji (1958–), who claims to be the supreme being's representative, and whose movement is based upon the Vedantic tradition. A split between Maharaj Ji and his family resulted in his suing for control of the mission in 1975. Although its influence has weakened, the mission still attracts followers.

There is now a greater range of Eastern teachers and traditions in the West. These may be classified in general terms in several categories. The Indian tradition emphasizes meditation and the use of the *Bhagavad Gita*, the *Vedas* and other, similar scriptures. This tradition is often centered on individual teachers, who claim either to be divine or divinely inspired. They encourage the close master/disciple relationship with their students that characterizes Indian schools.

Left: Jiddu Krishnamurti pictured as a young man. After breaking away in 1929 from the Theosophical Society, which had placed him at the head of its Order of the Star of the East in the belief that Maitreya (the future final Buddha) would incarnate into his body, Krishnamurti became a noted spiritual teacher in his own right.

Right: *Bhagwan Shree Rajneesh (1931-90), the founder in 1974 of the Rajneesh Foundation based at Poona in India. After setting up an ashram in Oregon in 1981, he incited controversy over his blatantly material lifestyle (he had over one hundred Rolls Royces). Rajneesh was arrested and fined for fraud in 1985 and then returned to India.*

Yoga includes a wide variety of traditions, from Hatha (the physical) to Raja (the intellectual)—and everything in between, such as Bhakti (devotion), Jnana (knowledge) and Karma (unselfishness). The major yoga teachers recognize that such divisions are largely artificial and that any system of development must be based on an integrated view of humans. Sri Aurobindo (1872–1950), one of India's best-known yogis, certainly affirmed this view, and in his quest for spiritual perfection he developed integral yoga—a combination of various types of yoga—whose aim was the individual's holistic perfection. Hatha yoga in particular has become increasingly popular in the West as an alternative to the frenzied activity that characterizes Western systems of physical culture.

In the West Buddhism was once largely the domain of educated intellectuals who found in it a religious system free of the traditional Western concept of the supernatural, or God. Because of its basic beliefs, the Buddhist religion has tended not to proselytize or engage in any of the more exotic activities common to other Eastern-influenced groups. It became increasingly popular among a wider Western public during the 1990s.

Tibet has always been a place of mystery and fascination for the West from the beginning of their contact. Interest was reinforced by the claims of the Theosophical Society that it was the home of the "masters." Tibetan Buddhism has had an incredible appeal, perhaps because it was once so inaccessible, and so little was known about it. Teachers offering the Tibetan traditions have ranged from such blatantly commercial "lamas" as Lobsang Rampa to a number of legitimate Buddhist monks who have established centers in the West. The exiled Dalai Lama is the best-known representative of Tibetan Buddhism.

Zen Buddhism has emerged from Japan as a system of some considerable interest to many people in the West, especially those who, tiring of the heavy emphasis most philosophical schools place on the intellect, find a refreshing change in the simple approach of Zen. Various Zen communities, centers and teachers have been established in the West to perpetuate this tradition.

The revival of interest in Eastern mysticism in the second half of the twentieth century is mirrored by its resurrection a century earlier. In many ways, the social and religious conditions of the times are very similar. In the 1880s the debate between fundamentalist Christianity and science was taking place, and those people who were unable to accept the total authority of either science or Christianity felt they had to choose an alternative faith. Some turned to Mormonism and Christian Science, while others felt that Theosophy offered an attractive synthesis of scientific knowledge and comparative religion. In England, the Esoteric Section of the Theosophical Society studied the Hermetic sciences, and writers like G.R.S. Mead, its leader, made a special study of Gnostic literature. Meanwhile, the Hermetic Order of the Golden Dawn developed as a rival group, and people who wished to be instructed in such mysteries had to make their choice between one or the other.

The Golden Dawn incorporated some Eastern elements into its magical practices, like *I Ching* divination and the Tattvas, the Hindu symbols for the elements. More importantly, the occult "sciences" also assumed the Eastern concepts of humans, the sources of their cosmic energy and their methods for spiritual advancement.

In the same way that Hindus and Buddhists accept that human consciousness is but a drop in the ocean of Brahma or nirvana, contemporary occultists and magicians accept the view that humans bear the task of universalizing their consciousness. In his book *Magick in Theory and Practice*, Aleister Crowley wrote: "every man and woman is a star"; and, like the tantrics of India, Crowley believed that the harmonized human was one in whom both sexual polarities were apparent and balanced. For this reason, Crowley incorporated a homosexual degree into the occult rituals of the *Ordo Templi Orientis*. Victor Neuburg, the poet and disciple of Crowley, noted that he laid special emphasis on the "divine Androgyne"—the being who transcends duality and limitation.

Unlike Christianity, which stresses compassion and faith, and unlike Islam, which emphasizes human inadequacy before Allah, modern magic has followed Buddhism's precept that the root of all suffering is ignorance.

Consequently, magic stresses that humans have to know themselves, and must also make themselves familiar with the more profound levels of consciousness open to them through meditation and similar methods.

Magic adopts the microcosm/macrocosm concept also found in yoga, which postulates the raising of Kundalini energy through the central nervous column until it reaches the crown (universal consciousness). Kundalini (which means "snake" in Sanskrit) visualizes this consciousness-enhancing energy as a snake that lies in the chakra (a wheel-shaped energy channel) at the base of the spine. Through meditation, Kundalini energy is raised through the body's seven major chakras until illumination is reached at the crown. The Jewish Qabalah, upon which much modern magic is built, may have inherited some of its Eastern concepts as a result of trade-route inroads into the Holy Land centuries before Christ. Whether or not this is so, as a discipline it proposes a similar mystical

Left: The Taoist tai-chi, or yin-yang circle, represents the cosmic harmony that is achieved when the polarities of yin (the dark, passive, feminine force) and yang (the light, active, masculine force) are in perfect balance. The small circle contained within each half represents the seed of the other, demonstrating their interdependence.

Left: Over 1,000 members of Krishnamurti's Order of the Star of the East gathered in California, where Krishnamurti was based, to hear their guru speak in 1928. A year later he disbanded the order.

Right: A practitioner of yoga demonstrates the "full lotus" position, the padmasana *("perfect posture"). This position facilitates the flow of Kundalini energy through the seven chakras from the base of the spine to the head.*

framework: Adam Kadmon is the archetypal human, and in his body are contained all levels of consciousness. Similarly, the task of mystics or magicians is to raise their consciousness to the point of *Kether,* the chakra transcending all duality (and equating with nirvana).

What the yogis call the *sushumna,* the nervous column's central axis—which contains the polar energies *ida* (male) and *pingala* (female)—has a magical equivalent in what is known as the "middle pillar." In an occult sense, this represents all the harmonized or "neutral" levels of consciousness that are found in alignment in the middle of the tree of life. These levels are: *Malkuth* (ground or "earth" level); *Yesod* (sexuality); *Tiphareth* (harmony, love and compassion); *Daath* (knowledge); and *Kether* (cosmic consciousness). Magic uses either ritual or meditation as its main methods for attaining these levels.

Magic similarly employs the essentially Eastern concepts of posture and the mantra. In yoga, the postures adopted by the *chelas,* or disciples, to purify their bodies and to develop muscular control, are known as the *asanas.* Whereas Hatha yoga demonstrates a wider range of *asanas* than are found in Western cultures, magic still makes use of them. The main difference is that magic is based upon a ritual

imitation of Western gods and mythology, particularly those of ancient Egypt. Consequently, in its rituals magic emulates the posture of the gods as depicted in Egyptian sculpture, who are usually seated on a throne. By contrast, the ideal yogic *asana* is the "full lotus" position, in which the yogi sits on the ground, rather than on a seat. The buttocks, rather than the feet, are thus the point of contact with the ground.

Nevertheless, just as the yogi recites mantras like "Om Mani Padme Hum," magic similarly uses the sacred power of sound. The mantras of magic are the so-called "god names" of the Qabalah. Mantras like "Elohim," "Shaddai" and "Adonai" are all terms relating to God, but in magic they are used to focus the consciousness on a spiritual ideal.

Finally, magic and occultism tend to prefer the Eastern concept of reincarnation over the specifically Western doctrine of resurrection. Reincarnation suggests that humans live in order to learn certain spiritual lessons. They gradually evolve to the point at which their subsequent physical incarnation is unnecessary. Magic teaches that humans are, in a sense, in charge of their own mental and spiritual development. It is up to them to purify their lives, and they are ultimately responsible for all their acts, good or bad (which, in Eastern mysticism, is related to the principle of retributive justice known as karma). Rather than relying on an act of grace from God, magicians feel obliged actively to pursue greater levels of spiritual understanding. Like the yogi, they believe that the path leads *inward*; they do not look to external gods or saviors for support.

Some have claimed that reincarnations carry an overtone of wishful thinking, and it is interesting that Aleister Crowley claimed to be a reincarnation of both the occultist Eliphas Lévi and the Elizabethan trance medium Edward Kelley, both of whom influenced him greatly. Modern magic is for the most part, however, pragmatic, and reincarnation is regarded more as a working hypothesis than a fact. As in Buddhism, the emphasis is on testing all precepts by personal experience (as in meditation), rather than blindly accepting them as literal dogma.

Reincarnation

Reincarnation, or the belief that the human soul or consciousness continues to be reborn over a series of lifetimes, is one of the most widespread religious beliefs.

Its most prominent representation is in Hinduism and Buddhism. In the *Bhagavad Gita*, there is a dialogue between Krishna, the noble and wise spiritual mentor, and his disciple, Arjuna. Krishna explains that it is only the spiritually illuminated who know of their former incarnations: "Both I and thou have passed through many births. Mine are known to me, but thou knowest not of thine…I incarnate from age to age for the preservation of the just, the destruction of the wicked and the

establishment of righteousness." Krishna also goes on to say that, according to our deeds in one life, so we find ourselves incarnating into a family appropriate to our spiritual attainment: "the man whose devotion has been broken off by death goeth to the regions of the righteous, where he dwells for an immensity of years and is then born again on earth in a pure and fortunate family; or even in a family of those who are spiritually illuminated."

Tibetan Buddhists believe that the highest lamas continue to be reborn as spiritual leaders of their community. When a Dalai Lama, for example, has died, it becomes necessary to search throughout the world to find a valid successor. In his book, *Meditation, the Inward Art*, Bradford Smith describes how this was done:

> When the previous Dalai Lama died, wise men had gone forth to seek the new holy one, and had found a little boy who recognized things that had belonged to his predecessor and could pick them out unerringly from among similar objects… [This is an example] of the universal religious impulse and of the way man seeks to represent the cycle of death and rebirth that runs through all of nature. In Tibetan Buddhism, with its firm faith in the rebirth of the soul, not

Left: The fourteenth Dalai Lama, Tenzin Gyatso, who was enthroned at the age of five in 1940. It is believed that the Dalai Lama is reincarnated after his death. After a lengthy search, aided by various oracles and tests, a child born at the time of the Dalai Lama's death is identified as his new incarnation.

Left: A mosaic depicts philosophers cogitating in the original Academy, founded by Plato in the gardens of Academe in Greece. Plato was the pupil of Socrates, and both these Greek philosophers believed in reincarnation.

Above: *The French philosopher and mathematician Blaise Pascal (1623-62), who was a child prodigy. Brilliant works accomplished in childhood—like those of Pascal and composer Amadeus Mozart— are sometimes cited as evidence of reincarnation.*

only of Dalai Lamas but of all, and of a progress based upon behavior during past lives, this impulse is dramatically present.

It is widely accepted that the ancient Egyptian followers of Amen-Ra, who believed in reincarnation, derived this belief from observing nature. The Sun sank, or "died," each evening in the west, and was "reborn" in the east with each dawn. The Sun was also a vital symbol of life; Egyptians who threw in their lot with the sun god could be assured of continuing and everlasting well-being. They believed they too would follow the cycles of death and rebirth.

Perhaps as a result of the Egyptian influence on ancient Greece, a number of prominent Greek philosophers continued the idea of reincarnation. Pythagoras (582–507 BC) believed that he had once been a man named Aethalides and later, Euphorbus, who was slain at the siege of Troy. Hermes, the messenger of the gods, had granted Pythagoras the special faculty of being able to remember his previous lives. Socrates and Plato also believed that the soul passed through many lifetimes.

Reincarnation continues to be a popular concept in the West today, and many people feel instinctively drawn to it as a more realistic after-death belief than that of the Judeo-Christian Last Judgement. A London Sunday newspaper, read mostly by English working people, once asked its readers whether they believed in heaven and hell, reincarnation, or whether they simply did not know what happened after death. The editor was surprised to find that a considerably greater number of readers believed in reincarnation than in heaven and hell.

Reincarnation is, after all, a rather appealing belief. It offers all of us the hope of continuing our lives beyond the apparent finality of death, and it is a tangible concept. Heavens and hells are somewhat remote by comparison and are less easy to visualize than another life in the world we already know.

In 1956, in both Britain and the United States, popular interest in reincarnation gained special impetus from the publication of *The Search for Bridey Murphy.* A Colorado businessman named Morey Bernstein had hypnotized a young woman, Virginia Tighe, into a past existence. Under hypnosis, Mrs. Tighe became an Irish girl named Bridey Murphy. She remembered that she was the daughter of an Irish barrister and that she had lived between the years 1798 and 1864. She was able to recall minute details of her incarnation in Cork, and it appeared that there was a strong case for linking the two personalities. It was subsequently discovered, however, that Virginia Tighe had grown up in a house resembling Bridey's; one of her neighbors had the name of Bridie Murphy (only a slightly different spelling), and there was a parallel in the backgrounds of the two people.

More impressive cases have, however, reared their heads from time to time. Some of these come from the files of the British researcher Arnall Bloxham, who, with his wife Dulcie, used retrogressive hypnosis to uncover previous incarnations. The Bloxhams' first case was Ann Ockenden, a girl who entered a state of trance easily. During a two-hour hypnotic session in 1956, she vividly remembered previous existences in prehistoric times. Another of the Bloxhams' sitters entered an incarnation as a British gunner during the Napoleonic

Wars; he described the sea battle and then screamed in agony when he was seriously "wounded" in the leg. Bloxham's tape contained so much detailed historical data that it was given to Lord Mountbatten, an erstwhile naval commander, who played it to a number of experts on naval history.

Some of the most stringently tested cases were those investigated by Dr. Ian Stevenson, chair of the Department of Neurology and Psychiatry at the University of West Virginia's medical school. His 1961 essay on selected reincarnation cases won the William James Prize, and his documented case histories earned him worldwide respect in his field. His preference, from the analytical point of view, was for reincarnation cases involving small children, who could not have known of other social contexts. Among his most-cited evidence are the cases of Shanti Devi and Eduardo Esplugus-Cabrera.

Shanti Devi, who was born in Delhi in 1926, began, from the age of three, to recall and detail incidents from a previous life led at Muttra, eighty miles away. She told her parents that she had been called Lugdi, and that she had died giving birth to a son. Her husband's name had been Kedar Nath Chaubey. After Shanti continued to press her claims, when she was nine, her parents wrote to a relative of the dead woman and were surprised when a letter returned confirming all that Shanti had claimed. Shanti subsequently went to Muttra and was able to recognize relatives of Kedar Nath Chaubey in a large crowd. She correctly led a carriage through the streets of the town to "her old house," which she recognized even though it had been painted a different color. Shanti was able correctly to answer questions relating to the arrangement of rooms and objects in the house. She also correctly claimed that a sum of money had been buried beneath the floor of "her father-in-law's" house. Shanti Devi remains one of Stevenson's best cases. In all, Shanti made twenty-four substantiated statements about her earlier life, and there were no instances of error.

Cuban Eduardo Esplugus-Cabrera was only four when he told his parents of a previous life in Havana. He gave the names of a number of "relatives" and described his "mother" in detail: she had a "clear complexion, black hair, and made hats." Eduardo said that in his previous life he had been known as Pancho. Stevenson says the parents were sure that Eduardo had not visited the location of his earlier existence. The boy was unfamiliar with the route to the house when taken there, but identified the specific house immediately. He did not recognize the inhabitants of the dwelling, but inquiries were made concerning the previous occupants. A family whose names had been given by Eduardo had indeed lived in that house and had moved out shortly after the death of Pancho. All data given to Stevenson by Eduardo proved to be correct, except for "his father's" Christian name.

Stevenson began his researches as a skeptic and was keen to test a number of hypotheses of explanation rather than to assume the reality of reincarnation. He considered possibilities including fraud, "racial memory" and extrasensory perception as alternatives, but nevertheless came to believe that reincarnation was the most likely explanation.

Such cases as those mentioned above could never be said to prove the universality of reincarnation, but they suggest that it may occur in some cases. Together with the out-of-body documentation of researchers like Drs. Robert Crookall and Celia Green, such cases suggest that the faculty of consciousness (and memory) may not be dependent on the physical organism and may, in fact, survive bodily death.

Spiritualism

Every known society has held that, under certain circumstances, it is possible to communicate with those who have died. Opinions have varied as to whether this is good or bad, harmful or beneficial—either to the dead or to those communicating with them. In some societies, formalized institutions have been established to enable regular communication to take place, and mediums, shamans and other psychics have important places in many cultures.

Spiritualism involves four basic tenets, the first of which is a belief in the continuity of the personality after death. A person is more or less the same

Below: A Currier and Ives portrait of the Fox sisters, Margaretta, Catherine and Leah. The series of rappings, allegedly caused by the ghost of a murdered man, at their home in Hydesville, New York, in 1848 precipitated the first Spiritualist seance. Margaretta and Catherine excited huge interest in Spiritualism and went on to become celebrated mediums.

after he or she has given up the physical body: the person can communicate in words and remember events and people after death. The concept that contact with the dead is possible is the next Spiritualist tenet. The dead exist in some dimension not totally separate from our own. They can be contacted there or, alternatively, can come into our dimension to contact us.

A third belief is that some people (usually known as mediums) have specific psychic gifts facilitating communication with the dead by a variety of means, including automatic writing, going into a trance and direct speech. Further, there is a valid purpose in taking advantage of the possibility of contact with the dead. This is usually justified on the grounds that the dead know more (are more enlightened) or, conversely, that they need help to adjust to their new state.

Spiritualism's philosophy is a particular view of life and death, a system of belief that includes the possibility of, and the validity of, contact with dead. Various techniques are employed to make contact with the dead. The results of this contact are usually verbal and frequently of a poor standard; occasionally physical manifestations occur.

Modern Spiritualism differs from Spiritualism in earlier societies in its emphasis on evidence—that is, on its claims that scientific research can, and will, validate its premises and support the thesis that the results of Spiritualist activities derive from communication with the dead. Two principal questions are explored in this research. Can it be demonstrated that the results are achieved by means only explicable in supernatural terms? For example, not by conscious or unconscious fraud on the part of those involved; nor by natural phenomena of various kinds; nor by the workings of the mind, especially in its little-known aspects (such as telepathy). There is considerable scientific evidence to support the thesis that at least some "Spiritualist" phenomena occur outside the realm of the natural phenomena presently understood by modern scienctists. Such faculties as telepathy and psychokinesis are examples in current debate.

Below: A fashionable seance held in Berlin in the early decades of the twentieth century. Interest in making contact with the dead increased after the carnage of World War I, during which the lives of so many young men were lost.

Assuming that it can be demonstrated that the results are supernatural, can it be proved that they result from communication with the dead, rather than simply demonstrating the psychic powers of the living? This is the most difficult area for Spiritualists, since it is difficult to find evidence to support the hypothesis of communication with the dead that cannot also be explained in simpler terms as deriving from the "nondead."

Spiritualism, in its modern manifestation, began in the USA in the second half of the nineteenth century and rapidly expanded throughout Europe. The impact of wars—whose large-scale loss of life resulted in a preoccupation with death and the fate of the dead—increased its influence, and eventually churches specifically proclaiming a Spiritualist philosophy developed. Some of these were Christian in orientation, others non- or even anti-Christian. Since the modern emphasis is on life rather than death, it may be that Spiritualism is destined to fade away, especially as the manifestations that once astonished and amazed people are now no longer its exclusive domain, but are accepted, to a large extent, as phenomena for scientific study. However, popular interest in Spiritualism remains strong.

Spiritualism usually centers on some form of communication with the spirits of the dead. This is attempted through one of the following means:

✦ *A seance*—a meeting specifically intended for that purpose, usually held in semidarkness, with a number of people sitting in a circle invoking the spirits;
✦ *A ouija board*—a board with the letters of the alphabet and various basic words written on it, over which a glass is moved, theoretically by the spirits;
✦ *A planchette*—a pencil-holder on wheels, which, if held lightly in the hand, is said to be moved by the spirits, who will use it to write;
✦ *Automatic writing*—a pencil held lightly in the hand of the medium which is supposed to move at the direction of the spirits;
✦ *Spirit photography*—an unexposed photographic film which, when developed, shows a picture or message;

✦ *Clairvoyance*—when the psychic power of seeing spirits is possessed by the medium;
✦ *Clairaudience*—when the medium hears things that are not audible to ordinary people;
✦ *Clairsentience*—"feelings" or intuitions.

At a seance, a variety of phenomena occur: generally the medium goes into a trance during which he or she is possessed by the spirit of a departed person, or (usually) by a spirit guide—a teacher, or advanced spirit, who assists and protects the medium who has channeled it. The spirit may speak using the vocal cords of the medium, whose voice changes accordingly. Sometimes materializations (the

Above: A nineteenth-century French seance results in the dramatic levitation of a table. Levitation is, however, a rare occurrence during seances, particularly to heights as great as that illustrated here.

Above: A medium pictured with the tools of her trade, including a speaking trumpet. Many mediums were condemned as fakes by the skeptical, and indeed many of them were unmasked as such, thus giving a bad name to the genuine psychics.

physical appearance in the seance room of a deceased person), apports (the manifestation of material objects with no natural explanation—*e.g.* stones falling onto the table), rappings (the spirits knocking on the table to communicate in code) and lights may manifest themselves in the room. In rare cases, ectoplasm (said to be primal, semispiritual matter) pours from the medium's mouth, or extends from beneath his or her clothing. Occasionally trumpets (a speaking trumpet through which the spirit is supposed to communicate) will be used. Psychokinesis (the movement of articles without a natural explanation) sometimes

occurs, with objects floating around the seance room. Levitation (the lifting of the body of the medium, or a participant in the seance, into the air) is rare. Traditionally seances are held in darkness, since the presence of light is said to weaken the power whereby the spirits manifest themselves.

Spiritualist groups also practise healing, usually claiming to work as the agents of spirit guides with a particular interest in medical work. Both the laying on of hands and various forms of massage are used.

Although Spiritualism has been scientifically investigated to some extent, its religious overtones and tendency to require conditions that make scientific assessment difficult, if not impossible, have precluded detailed investigation. However, extensive studies have been made of many famous mediums, especially during the early years of Spiritualism in England. Mediums are generally classified according to the type of phenomena with which they most often work: mental mediums give information about what they see or hear, or are channels through which the spirits communicate by means of impressions; physical mediums are those who are actually possessed by the spirits, and who precipitate various physical phenomena.

The most notable mediums in the history of Spiritualism include: Mrs. Leonora Piper (1857–1950), Mrs. Gladys Leonard (1882–1968), Miss Geraldine Cummins (d. 1968), Mrs. Eileen Garrett (1893–1970), Mr. D. D. Home (1833–86), Mrs. Eusapia Palladino (1854–1918), and Mr. Rudi Schneider (1908–57).

The philosophy and theology of Spiritualism have been derived from the teachings of the spirits communicated through mediums, and accordingly the various teachings given through different mediums tend to differ, not only in emphasis, but also in information. Therefore, various schools of Spiritualism exist, centering on the teachings of different mediums. For example, most French Spiritualists, and those in South America (who usually call themselves "spiritists"), follow the teachings of Allan Kardec (1804–69), which include reincarnation. The majority of English Spiritualists follow the philosophy of W. Stainton Moses (1839–92), as expressed in his book *Spirit Teachings*, or endorse the very popular writings of J. Arthur Findlay. In general terms, all these philosophies diverge in detail but share certain common characteristics, as follows.

✦ The soul is a duplicate of the body, and resides in its natural state in a world which is similar to, although better than, the physical world, with houses, trees, rivers, etc.

✦ The soul is occupied by the spirit, the life principle.

✦ There are a variety of "worlds" that coexist in a hierarchical series, and differ according to "vibration," and the aim of life is to progress from the lower to the higher worlds. It is often taught that these worlds exist in concentric spheres around the earth.

✦ After death, the soul is drawn to that world to which it is best suited by its vibrations: *i.e.*, an evil man will be drawn to an unpleasant world.

✦ Either souls reincarnate until they attain perfection (as the "spiritists", following Kardec, say), or there is a continued progression in other worlds (as the English Spiritualists believe).

✦ God is not as central in Spiritualist belief as in Christian theology.

This philosophy and cosmology draws heavily upon the writings of the Swedish scientist and theologian, Emanuel Swedenborg (1688–1772), and has some relationship to certain teachings of the neo-Platonists.

While some Spiritualist groups are expressly Christian, others are not. The Spiritualists' National Union (of Britain) summarizes its philosophy into a creed that is the basis for many Spiritualist groups throughout the world, with some variations, as follows:

✦ the fatherhood of God;
✦ the brotherhood of man;
✦ the communion of spirits and the ministry of angels;
✦ the continuous existence of the soul;
✦ personal responsibility for individual action;
✦ compensation and retribution hereafter for all good and evil deeds done on earth;
✦ eternal progress open to every human soul.

Most individual Spiritualist groups, as distinct from formally organized churches, have further vague and undefined philosophies deriving from the teachings received through the medium leading the group.

With the increasing revival of interest in the occult, and the modern scientific interest in psychic phenomena, there has been a decline in interest in Spiritualism, although the concept remains popular in some circles. A widespread awareness of psychic phenomena means that the seance room no longer offers the degree of excitement and wonder to the general populace that it once did. One aspect of Spiritualism, however, has been the subject of renewed interest among New Age believers — the channeling of spiritual entities in order to receive information and guidance. Although some believe that these entities are actually speaking from the channeler's own unconscious mind, others are convinced that the channeler is truly accessing a higher being. Renowned channelers include Jane Roberts, channeler of "Seth"; J. Z. Knight, the channel for the 35,000-year-old "Ramatha, the Enlightened One"; Ruth Montgomery; Alice Bailey, the channel for the Tibetan master "D.K."; and Jach Pursel, channeler of "Lazaris."

Below: *Madame Blavatsky and Henry Steele Olcott, the joint founders in 1875 of the Theosophical Society.*

Above: Jiddu Krishnamurti pictured with Annie Besant in 1926. Besant had been a disciple of Madame Blavatsky and became the head of the European Section of the Theosophical Society in 1895. In 1908 she and her colleague Charles Webster Leadbeater proclaimed that the future incarnation of the Buddha Maitreya would occur in the body of Krishnamurti.

THEOSOPHY

In popular usage, the word "theosophy" usually refers to the philosophy popularized by the Theosophical Society. In fact, it is of a much more ancient origin: the word derives from the Greek words *theos* (god) and *sophia* (wisdom) and was used by some of the ancient Greek philosophers, and later in the West. It meant a special knowledge of the divine, similar to that which the Gnostics claimed. Gradually the idea emerged that a tradition of secret knowledge had been transmitted through the ages, constituting an esoteric, or inner, philosophy, which was known as "the ancient wisdom," or "theosophy."

This concept was popularized in the late nineteenth century by a Russian aristocrat, Madame Helena Petrovna Blavatsky (1831–91), whose writings aroused considerable interest and controversy. Her monumental and voluminous *Secret Doctrine* constitutes the source of most of the teachings of the Theosophical Society. Together with Henry Steele Olcott, Madame Blavatsky founded the Theosophical Society in New York in 1875. The society was to prove one of the major catalysts of the occult revival that occurred in the last quarter of the nineteenth century, and was largely responsible for popularizing Eastern religions and philosophy throughout the West; its influence was considerable.

The society, although in theory free of doctrinal foundations, soon established a specific teaching, which it then promulgated. The society's doctrines, which were principally derived from Eastern, and especially Indian, philosophy, were said to constitute an "ancient wisdom," drawn from the historic tradition, but also from living authorities—"masters"—who had attained perfection and now guided and taught others. In the early years of the society, frequent contact with the "masters" was claimed, including the alleged manifestation of mysterious letters, which were said to have been written by them.

During the occult revival, the society expanded rapidly and spread throughout the world. Its headquarters were eventually established at Adyar, in India, where they remain today. The society initiated extensive publishing activities, and groups of Theosophists (known as "lodges") were established in most countries. Within the society there developed an inner group, known as the "Eastern School," or the "Esoteric Section," to which only select members were admitted, and in which secret teachings were promulgated.

After the death of Madame Blavatsky, the leadership of the society was taken over by Dr. Annie Besant (1847–1933), and the emphasis on Eastern philosophy became more marked. In the United States there were several breakaway groups.

Although it still has many members today, the society appears to be in a period of decline, probably due to the lack of charismatic leadership of the nature of Blavatsky, Besant and Charles Webster Leadbeater, Besant's colleague.

The society was further disrupted by its involvement in the messianic movement centering on Jiddu Krishnamurti; after he renounced his claims to messiahship, many members left the society in disillusionment. One major defection at this time was that of the German occultist Dr. Rudolf Steiner (1861–1925), who subsequently formed his own organization, which was known as the Anthroposophical Society.

THE GOLDEN DAWN

The modern occult revival owes much of its direction to the influential Hermetic Order of the Golden Dawn (founded in 1888), which first gathered together the workings of a fully developed magical system. A number of important writers belonged to the order, including Samuel Liddell MacGregor Mathers, the translator of the *Zohar*; A. E. Waite, an authority on the Qabalah, the Rosicrucians, and the Holy Grail legends; W. B. Yeats, the poet; and the fantasy novelists Arthur Machen and Algernon Blackwood. So too did Aleister Crowley, famous as "The Great Beast 666." In any occult bookshop today one will see Waite's Tarot deck displayed in a position of prominence, and perhaps also Crowley's spectacular and visionary cards. Most contemporary occult and esoteric groups who practise magic as a type of Western yoga acknowledge their debt to the Golden Dawn.

The rituals of the order were originally based on five Masonic grades discovered in the papers of a deceased English Rosicrucian. Dr. William Wynn Westcott, a London coroner and a Freemason, asked Samuel (later "MacGregor") Mathers to expand the material so that it would form the basis of instruction for a new occult society. This group would nevertheless claim an ancient lineage and would compete, in a sense, with the Esoteric Section of the Theosophical Society, which had become rather fashionable in London during the 1880s.

The rituals themselves were not merely artificial or theatrical, but were intended to symbolize stages of the enlightenment of mystical consciousness upon a certain cosmic pathway called the "tree of life." The tree of life in itself is a key motif in the Qabalah, or Jewish mystery tradition, and represents ten levels of consciousness between the many and the Godhead.

Starting at the lowest levels on the tree, there are four major levels of consciousness,

XXI

THE WORLD.

in simple terminology representing: our perception of the environment (*Malkuth*); the sexual instincts (*Yesod*); the rational intellect (*Hod*); and the capacity for love and emotion (*Netzach*). Mathers and Westcott aligned these, as well as an initial neophyte grade, with the five Rosicrucian rituals, and these later became the Golden Dawn rituals *per se*.

The next level of consciousness upon the tree (and it must be remembered that the aim of "white" magic is to trace the mystical stages back to the Godhead) is called *Tiphareth*, and this represents the mystical level of the "god-human." Reaching this level is a very profound spiritual experience, in which magicians feel the power of the "god energy" living within them and experience "rebirth." Mathers and Westcott then devised a type of "occult society within

Left: The twenty-first major-arcana Tarot card, The World. *In 1910 A. E. Waite, a Golden Dawn member, published his interpretation of the Tarot with cards designed by Pamela Colman Smith. Many later decks would draw upon the Rider-Waite version, as it became known.*

Left: An ancient Babylonian depiction of the tree of life, an image that members of the Order of the Golden Dawn used to help them visualize the hierarchical stages of their enlightenment.

Below: *Osiris, king of the underworld, and his wife/sister, Isis. The Golden Dawn drew heavily upon Egyptian mythology in their rituals, and as a skilled sorceress who had received her magical instruction from Thoth, Isis was especially revered.*

a society," designating this level, as well as the next two stages upon the tree, "the Second Order." Its existence was kept secret from the initiates to the Gold Dawn grades. It was also given the grandiose title of *Rosae Rubae et Aurea Crucis* ("The Red Rose and the Cross of Gold"), thus linking the order with the Rosicrucians. Westcott, Mathers and another member, Woodford, appointed themselves figureheads of this exalted level of consciousness. Above them on the tree remained three further levels of consciousness: the "trinity," consisting of *Kether* (the crown), *Hokmah* (wisdom) and *Binah* (understanding). Mathers, in particular, insisted to members of lower

rank that he had sole access to these lofty realms of inspiration.

The first Golden Dawn temple, that of Isis-Urania, was opened in London in 1888, and by 1896 there were temples of Osiris in Weston-super-Mare, Horus in Bradford, Amen-Ra in Edinburgh, and Ahathoor in Paris. We can see from the names of these temples that, apart from the Rosicrucian symbolism of the mystical grade of *Tiphareth*, the predominating influence was that of ancient Egypt. The Egyptian gods had been well illustrated in mural motifs and papyri and provided an elaborate pantheon of gods symbolizing the occult potential of humans; it was therefore appropriate that they should have been revived in this particular context.

Mathers, who had assumed increasing influence within the order, eventually sealed its doom by his essentially autocratic manner. He was fond of chastising members like Annie Horniman, who criticized him for withdrawing into a state of élitist isolation. Mathers spent much of his time translating important occult texts, like the *Magic of Abramelin*, and he expected his colleagues to finance and maintain his sojourns in the British Museum and the *Bibliothèque de l'Arsenal* in Paris.

Finally, Mather's exclusive claim to occult authority wore thin, and schisms formed within the order: Florence Farr mobilized her "Sphere Group" around an astral Egyptian entity, and Dr. Felkin formed the breakaway *Stella Matutina* around certain "Sons of Fire" who dwelt in the Arabian desert. With the death of Mathers in 1918, the original Order of the Golden Dawn fragmented completely, although Felkin's group continued to exert an influence, which is still felt today in the form of the Fraternity of the Inner Light (founded by Dion Fortune) and its derivatives.

There were certain lectures on occult knowledge that Golden Dawn members had to master, and these brought together a lot of information on magic, the Tarot, alchemy and astrology that is still of vital interest today. The grade of *Malkuth*, for example, included details of alchemy and the elemental spirits of earth, air, water and fire. Also contained therein were the symbolic connections between the gods of different religions and the ten basic levels of consciousness upon the tree of life. (Aleister

Crowley, who left the order in 1904, compiled a detailed list of such "correspondences" in his book *777*, later republished in the volume *The Qabalah of Aleister Crowley*.) At the stage of *Yesod*, the practitioners learnt the division of the soul, or consciousness, into *Neschamah*, the animal instincts. In *Hod*, they learned in detail the connections between the twenty-two major-arcana cards of the Tarot and the levels of consciousness on the tree, and in *Netzach*, the sacred names of the gods.

All the magicians took part in rituals appropriate to their grade, and these were intended to impress upon the performers a sense of awe and mystery. Between 1937 and 1941, Israel Regardie published the full rituals of the *Stella Matutina*, as they derived from the Golden Dawn; R. G. Torrens's more condensed *The Secret Ritual of the Golden Dawn* presents a slight variation on these. Many occult groups in both the United States and Britain still base their grades on the Golden Dawn pattern, and ripples of the order's influence also continue to find their way into the music and literature of contemporary counterculture.

THE TATTVAS

The Tattvas were one of the most notable Eastern elements in the ritual magic of the Hermetic Order of the Golden Dawn, an inclusion all the more remarkable when we consider that this order was solidly based on the occult inspiration of Western mythology.

Nevertheless, the Tattvas were adopted from their original Hindu context as appropriate symbols of the elements. There are five basic symbols in the series: *Tejas*, a red equilateral triangle—fire; *Apas*, a silver crescent—water; *Vayu*, a blue circle—air; *Prithivi*, a yellow square—earth; *Akasa*, an indigo egg—spirit.

A respected authority on the occult, W.E. Butler, alluded to the Tattvas as tides operating in the magnetic sphere of the earth, so that "The Element of *Akasa* is strongest at sunrise, then it merges into the element of *Vayu*. This in turn merges into *Tejas*, and this into *Apas*, and finally *Apas* merges into *Prithivi*."

However, the major function of these symbols in the occult is as doorways into the visionary recesses of the mind. The symbols may be used either in isolation or with one superimposed upon another. In a sense, they act as a

Left: Mélusine's husband broke his promise never to visit her on a Saturday when her partial transformation into a serpent occurred, causing her to flee from him for ever. Like Mélusine, mermaids have the lower body of a water snake or fish, and such fantastic sea creatures may be encountered in the visions of those meditating upon the symbol of Apas.

directive to the unconscious. The symbols become catalysts for releasing certain imagery, so that magicians who meditate on the red symbol, *Tejas*, begin to experience visions associated with the element of fire. If they meditate upon *Apas*, representing water, they can expect visions of water, which may entail fantasy beings of Western mythology, for example, water spirits or mermaids.

The method used by magicians is as follows. Having prepared their series of pictorial representations on white cardboard, they stare at the symbol until its after-image begins to appear. They then retain the latter in their minds as an image and meditate fixedly upon it. The next step is to imagine that the after-image has become a doorway through which one may pass. If the meditators are able to project their consciousness in this way, they then experience visions appropriate to the element they have selected. They are able to withdraw from the vision, rather in the manner of Hesse's magic theatre described in *Steppenwolf*, by returning through the doorway by which they entered.

The technique of using the Tattvas as "astral doorways" is not intended as an escapist diversion, but is instead supposed to show practitioners that certain active energies are operative in their unconscious minds. These are rendered into human form by the structuring processes of the mind itself and appear in visions as gnomes, elves, fairies, nature spirits

Above: The archangel Gabriel battles against the forces of evil. Those who use the Tattvas may experience visions of Gabriel when meditating on the symbol of Apas. This symbol represents water, with which Gabriel is in turn associated.

and so on. In its most profound form, such meditation could lead to visions of angels and archangels, because these too have a symbolic relationship with the elements. For example, Michael is the archangel of fire, Raphael of air, Uriel of earth and Gabriel of water. In the vision, magicians are able to address the spirit beings and can request certain information from them. In practical terms, they are addressing the repository of their unconscious minds and are bringing to the fore valuable, symbolic insights, which may otherwise have been forever lost. In the Golden Dawn, it was also intended that magicians could harmonize their personalities by encountering those spirits that could counterbalance their weaknesses. A person with an "airy," dreamy approach to life would benefit from a meeting with the gob-

lins of the earth, for example, and a person with a somewhat "watery" disposition could perhaps fortify his or her personality with fire.

The following account of a short Tattvic vision, recorded by Mrs. Mathers of the Golden Dawn, provides an example of the form that the experience can take. Her focusing symbol was the crescent of water, combined with the indigo egg of spirit.

…a wide expanse of water with many reflections of bright light and occasionally glimpses of rainbow colors appearing. When divine and other names were pronounced, elementals of the mermaid and merman type [would] appear, but few of the other elemental forms. These water forms were extremely changeable, one moment appearing as solid mermaids and mermen, the next melting into foam.

Raising myself by means of the highest symbols I had been taught, and vibrating the names of water, I rose until the water vanished, and instead I beheld a mighty world or globe, with its dimensions and divisions of gods, angels, elementals and demons…the whole universe of water…I called on HCOMA [Note: HCOMA, pronounced "He-Co-Mah," is a special magical word for water, based on the so-called Enochian language which was used extensively in the Golden Dawn.] and there appeared standing before me a mighty archangel, with four wings, robed in glistening white and crowned. In one hand, the right, he held a species of trident, and in the left a cup filled to the brim with an essence which he poured down below on either side…

THE NEW AGE

In the later decades of the twentieth century, a number of eclectic movements have emerged that can be categorized loosely as part of the New Age movement. Arising from a widespread dissatisfaction with the modern Western way of life, and finding no spiritual sustenance in the established Western religions, such groups have developed their own systems of beliefs and practices, which, it is hoped, will be fit for the millennium and the "New Age." Although their various credos are too disparate to allow a definitive statement of New Age belief, they share certain basic similarities.

The importance of ecology, of respecting the natural environment and interacting with nature is stressed, as is the feminine principle. The attainment of human potential is emphasized, and the mystical elements of such religions and cultures as Buddhism, Hinduism, Sufi Islam, shamanism and Theosophy are applied appropriately to help in the achievement of spiritual perfection. To this end, too, the intuitive voice is considered important, which may be better heard through meditation. New Age practitioners also use a wide range of traditional mystical methods for gaining spiritual insight, including astrology, channeling and crystals, in the quest for spiritual healing.

As well as incorporating many occult beliefs and rituals into their practices, New Age groups share much common ground with the neo-pagan and Wiccanist movements—particularly regarding the importance of the natural world, and the male-female synthesis. Although the tenets of the New Age are not strictly "new," the willingness to embrace relevant beliefs from a wide variety of religious and esoteric traditions in the search for spiritual fulfillment illus-

Left: Crystals, on sale here in a New Age book-and-artefact emporium in Atlanta, Georgia, are highly prized by adherents of the New Age movement as talismans and natural objects that have healing properties.

trates an enlightened tolerance that was notably lacking in the mainstream societies of earlier centuries—although not, of course, in the realm of occult belief, which has always thrived on the crossfertilization of a tremendous diversity of philosophies and rituals.

Below: New Age believers approach the pyramids of Giza — structures of magical power — in 1978, in preparation for a ritual to prevent the imminent end of the world. Many New Age groups hold millennial beliefs.

Divination Systems

Humans have always been curious about what the future holds. Since most cultures believe to a greater or lesser extent that the universe is controlled by non-human entities—spiritual beings, for example, or stellar or planetary influences—many systems of divination have developed over the millennia for predicting events, often by seeking information from these superhuman entities. This chapter examines some of the world's most important methods of divination, all of which are still in use today. Many of them have been accorded renewed significance by the New Age movement. Included in this investigation are astrology and tribal divination, the oracles and prophets of various cultures, the Chinese systems of *I Ching* and *Feng Shui*, dowsing, Tarot, numerology, palmistry and scrying, as well as a short summary of other systems of divination.

ASTROLOGY

From the time of their very first perception of the universe around them, humans have been overawed by the vastness of space and by the wonders of the Sun and Moon, the planets and the stars. Even today, when humanity's scientific skill has penetrated the depths of space, the wonders of the universe remain mysterious and powerful. In their personalizing of the universe, some attributed to the stars and planets relationships with, and influences over, their own lives.

Astrology is the study of the relationships between the heavens and the Earth and between humans and the planets. It is one of the oldest studies known, having played an important role in every highly developed civilization of the past, from those of Egypt and Babylonia to India, China and South America. Astrological study of the heavens led eventually to the emergence of the scientific discipline of astronomy, while the rules, methods and principles of astrology continued to emerge over thousands of years of usage.

Astrology works upon the basis that the planets exert influences on the Earth that affect individuals, as well as groups. Individuals are especially affected by the cosmic situation in existence at the time of their birth, and the qualities inherent in the individual can, to a large degree, be determined by that situation. In the light of scientific knowledge regarding

Opposite: A diviner consults an oracle to discover the meaning of the pattern drawn in the sand and its implications for the future.

Below: A medieval woodcut depicts the Earth at the center of the solar system, surrounded by concentric circles, representing the paths of the planets, and enclosed by signs of the zodiac.

Right: Following the
establishment of
Christianity in Europe,
astrology was condemned.
The subject was
reintroduced in the
medieval period from
the Arab countries in
which it had continued to
flourish. Illustrated here
is an Arab zodiac.

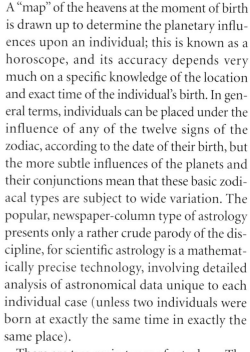

Below: "Zodiacal man,"
illustrating the influence
of each sign of the zodiac
over parts of the body. In
medieval times, diagrams
such as this were used to
diagnose ailments by
means of a process known
as melothesia.

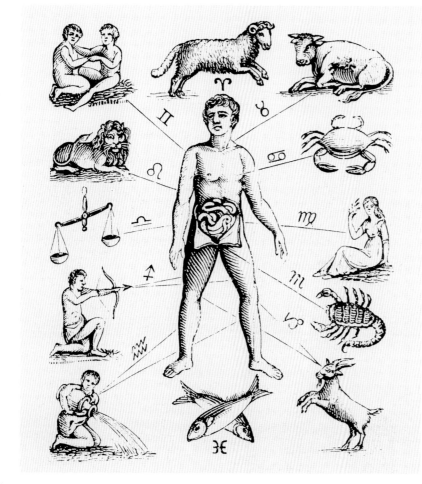

the influences of cosmic radiation upon the Earth, the theories of astrology are perhaps not so fantastic, although it can be argued that the important time as far as the individual is concerned is the moment of conception (at which the influence of the cosmic radiation begins), rather than the moment of birth.

Astrology attributes different influences to different planets and conjunctions of planets.

A "map" of the heavens at the moment of birth is drawn up to determine the planetary influences upon an individual; this is known as a horoscope, and its accuracy depends very much on a specific knowledge of the location and exact time of the individual's birth. In general terms, individuals can be placed under the influence of any of the twelve signs of the zodiac, according to the date of their birth, but the more subtle influences of the planets and their conjunctions mean that these basic zodiacal types are subject to wide variation. The popular, newspaper-column type of astrology presents only a rather crude parody of the discipline, for scientific astrology is a mathematically precise technology, involving detailed analysis of astronomical data unique to each individual case (unless two individuals were born at exactly the same time in exactly the same place).

There are two main types of astrology. The first is mundane astrology, which concerns itself with large-scale phenomena, such as wars, natural disasters and political and social trends. This is based upon the premise that cosmic influences affect large groups of people—and even the physical structure of the Earth. Horoscopes can be drawn up for nations, societies or even races, but these are necessarily far less accurate than those for individuals.

The second type, horary astrology, is based upon the premise that a chart can be drawn up not only for an individual born at a specific moment in a specific place, but indeed for anything to be "born," or inaugurated, at that place at that time. Hence horoscopes can be used to determine the advisability or otherwise of undertaking certain activities at particular times.

Since, by its own claims, astrology is an exact and complex science, it is difficult either to support or condemn its premises in simple terms, and it should not be judged on the pronouncements either of newspaper columns, or of popular astrologers.

The basic premise upon which astrology is founded is that the universe is not a fragmented collection of individual pieces, but a unified, organic whole, in which every part is dependent upon, and in some way connected with, every other part. The universe is seen to be coherent, meaningful and ordered; it has pattern and rhythm and is, to a large extent, predictable. Humans first gained a sense of order and rhythm from their close relationship with the cycles of nature and their observance of the movement of the planets and the stars. Gradually they came to the conclusion that these patterns could be interpreted and understood, and could therefore be anticipated.

It has often been said that the reasoning behind astrology is thus *analogical*, rather than *logical*—it works on the ancient theorem of the occult, "as above, so below." This idea has gained increasing support as a result of modern research into the nature and working of cosmic influences on the Earth and on human behavior. As science investigates the effects of cosmic radiation—not only from obvious phenomena like sunspots, but also the more subtle emanations from outer space—the premises of astrology are receiving more and more support. Even the old belief that the Moon affects sanity has received some measure of support from modern research into the influence of that body on human behavior.

Astrology works on the assumption that the Earth is the center of both the solar system and the universe—and, for all practical purposes, this is a valid assumption in that the universe does revolve around it, as far as humanity is concerned. Astrology pictures the Earth as being at the center of a series of concentric circles: the paths of the planets and the signs of the zodiac. The zodiac is a hypothetical sphere around the Earth, divided into twelve sections—the popularly known signs of the zodiac. Each of the signs is classified as being either positive or negative, and one of the basic elements of traditional occultism (earth, air, fire and water) is attributed to it. The Sun appears to move around this zodiac, passing through the various signs. The sign against which it appears to rise on the day of an individual's birth dictates the sign under which the person is said to be born. Thus a person born on November 4 will be a Scorpio, because the Sun appears to rise in the sign of Scorpio at that time. And the Sun, representing the powerful, energetic and creative principle, is seen as the most important factor in the horoscope.

But the Earth also revolves on its own axis, and so there is a "rising sign" too (that is, the

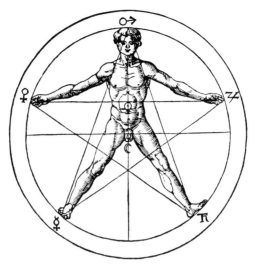

Left: *This medieval illustration depicts cosmic man—a microcosm of the universe. In addition to the planetary symbols, a quadrant bisects him (representing the Earth and the cardinal directions), and the pentagram represents perfection.*

sign against the eastern horizon at the moment of birth), and this is said to be the second most important factor in the horoscope. The actual point of sunrise is called the "ascendant," and this determines a further classification of twelve houses, equal to the twelve constellations. For example, a person born with Scorpio as his or her Sun sign, with the ascendant in Scorpio, would be very different in personality from someone born at a similar time but with a different ascendant; in the former case, all the characteristics of Scorpio would tend to be emphasized and reinforced.

After these basic influences, astrology considers the influence of the Moon (the second most important "planet") and the other

Below: *Women pictured at an astrological meeting held in Berlin early in the twentieth century. Astrology continues to fascinate:— even professed skeptics often sneak a glance at their horoscopes, and some of its assumptions have gained credibility through recent research.*

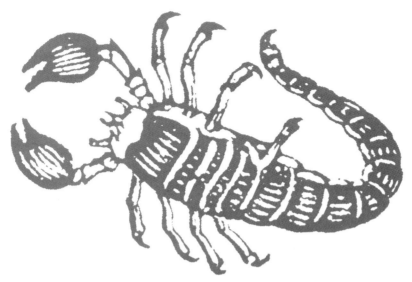

Above: The astrological symbol of Scorpio. According to Greek mythology, Zeus placed the scorpion in the stars after it had stung Orion.

planets. Not only the positions of the planets at the time of birth, but also their relationships to each other, must be taken into account to establish a whole "plan" of the universe at that moment. Different planets in different positions, as well as various combinations of planets, will result in different influences and differing degrees of influence. A fair degree of mathematical skill and accuracy is necessary for such subtle and complex interpretations, and a properly drawn horoscope involves considerable knowledge and ability. The very com-

plexity of such analyses also means that popular accounts of the zodiacal types can never be more than very generalized statements about a whole category of people, all of whom probably display more differences than similarities. All Scorpios, for example, are not necessarily alike, and there are important and subtle influences which only a detailed analysis will reveal.

There is a significant body of modern scientific evidence that supports at least some of the basic assumptions of astrology and that gives a new view of humanity's place within the universe, as well as the influence of the universe on humanity and the world. Investigations into solar and lunar rhythms, the phenomenon of sunspots and the effect of the Moon on the natural cycles on Earth all lend credence to the possibility that the essential claims of astrology (as distinct from the exaggerated pretensions of popular astrology) will be validated scientifically.

TRIBAL DIVINATION

Unlike astrology, which attributes supernatural occurrences to planetary and stellar influences, many tribal cultures, particularly in Africa, believe that the key to otherwise

Right: An African witch doctor and his assistants preside over a healing rite involving the use of chickens. In the rituals of the Zande religion, the behavior of chickens poisoned with benge is regarded as having as oracular significance.

inexplicable events lies in the personal relationships of individuals—either with fellow members of the tribe, or with ancestors and tribal spirits. Much divination is retrospective, in that tribal diviners are consulted to discover the cause of some misfortune; by identifying the cause (such as spirit possession or other evil influences), problems may be rectified. Diviners may be shamans, witch doctors or medicine men, and in African tribes divination is frequently a royal or sacred function.

Tribal divination falls into two general types: mediumistic divination, which is common in shamanistic societies, in which the diviner enters a trance and communicates with the spirit guides; and instrumental, or interpretive, divination, in which materials such as bones, sticks or shells are cast, and the resulting pattern interpreted. A representative selection of tribal oracles can be seen in the divinatory methods used by witch doctors of the African Zande religion: feeding *benge* poison to a chicken and observing the nature of its death (or survival); inserting two sticks into an anthill and drawing conclusions from whichever is eaten; using a "rubbing board," or *iwa*—rubbing two pieces of wood together until the significant moment is reached when they adhere to each other; or by acting as a medium. Whichever method is used, diviners will ask a number of questions of the people consulting them, thus also gaining valuable psychological insights.

A further form of divination is "wisdom divination": that is, applying the wisdom imparted by the supreme being, which is recorded in the form of tribal myths. This form of divination is particularly useful in enabling a decision to be made, for it provides a frame of reference for "correct" behavior. In the Yoruba Ifa oracle, for example, sixteen cowrie shells, palm nuts or similar objects symbolize the sixteen sectors of the world. In consulting Orunmila, the patron deity of divination, the *babalawo* (diviner) has an ultimate permutation of 256 figures to work with, and by casting the shells and reciting the relevant verses attached to the specific sector in which the shell relevant to the individual has fallen, the problem is defined, and is finally answered by the individual's specific choice of verse.

Divination remains an important aspect of tribal culture around the world, and even when there is no specific crisis to be resolved, diviners may be consulted for a range of more mundane reasons, including the most auspicious time to take a journey.

Oracles and Prophecy

Although the consultation of oracles remains popular in many tribal cultures, in the West, where it is frequently considered superstitious, it has been supplanted by other methods of divination. Yet in the ancient Greek and Roman cultures, as in Sumerian, Babylonian and Hittite society, oracles had a sacred position, and no important decisions in the life of either the individual or the state were taken without consulting them.

The ancient Greeks had a specific word for divination—*mantike*. Its purpose was to seek the advice of the gods rather than to discover the future. Although they consulted more primitive oracles—seeing omens in the entrails of slaughtered animals, for example—and sought the help of female, cave-dwelling sibyls, the Greeks developed a sophisticated system of sacred oracles, of which the Delphic oracle is the best known. At the shrine of Apollo at

Left: King Croesus, the last king of Lydia, consulted the Delphic oracle before declaring war on the Persians (in this case with disastrous results). The oracle had, however, correctly predicted the day on which he would cook a turtle and lamb together, and Croesus therefore trusted in its powers of divination.

Delphi, the Pythia, or Pythoness—a priestess—acted as the medium between Apollo and the enquirer; although widely consulted, she often perplexed the enquirer by the obscurity of her responses.

Given that the Romans borrowed many aspects of the Greek pantheon and forms of worship, it is not surprising that the Roman oracles operated in much the same way as the Greek. In addition, the Romans placed particular emphasis on natural occurrences, such as the appearance of birds or lightning over designated *templas* (oracular temples), which they regarded as being portents (*auspicia*) from the gods. *Prodigia* were particularly bad omens, indicating that the *pax deorum* ("peace of the gods") had been broken; they manifested themselves through such unmistakeably dramatic events as earthquakes. As in several other societies, no important state decisions could be taken without prior consultation with the oracles, which were interpreted by *sacerdotes*, or priests, of the college of augurs on the order of the Senate. Also of great importance were the *libri Sibyllini* (Sybilline books)—a collection of prophecies kept in the Temple of Palatine Apollo in Rome—which were consulted by the *quindecemviri sacris faciundis*—another body of priests. Further Roman diviners included the *haruspices* from Etruria, to whom ordinary people went for advice.

Human oracles—people with psychic gifts who enter a trance state in much the same manner as shamans—are still consulted in Tibet, where there are also state oracles located in monasteries. Among the latter, the most important is that of the destructive deity Pe Har, whose oracle is at Nechung Gumpa. It has helped to identify a number of reincarnated Dalai Lamas, and warned the present Dalai Lama of the Chinese invasion of 1959, allowing him to escape; the exiled Dalai Lama now consults an oracle in Dharamsala in India.

In the Bible, oracular messages from God were termed "prophecies," and although they are essentially similar concepts, prophecies are regarded with rather less skepticism than oracles in modern Western society. The prophets were designated messengers of the gods of the established religions, particularly Judaism, Christianity and Islam, of whom the most famous were Moses, Christ and Mohammed respectively. These messengers exclusively revealed the will and purpose of God or Allah. More modern religious prophets include Joseph Smith, Jr. (1805–44), the founder of Mormonism in the nineteenth century.

In occult terms, however, prophecy operates within a less rigidly religious framework. People have been hailed as prophets since the dawn of time, but undoubtedly the most famous secular prophet was Michel de

Notredame (1503–66), or Nostradamus. A French doctor of medicine and an astrologist, he established himself as a prophet in about 1547, receiving his visions primarily by scrying. His two collections of prophecies, written in the form of somewhat elliptical quatrains, and recorded in *Les Propheties de M. Michel Nostradamus* (also known as *Centuries*) in 1555 and 1558, still continue to fascinate today.

The *I Ching*

The *I Ching*, or *Book of Changes*, originated in China at least 1,000 years before the birth of Christ and is one of the oldest books in the world. Confucius and the Taoist sages thought very highly of it, treating it reverently as a sacred book and prizing its powers of divination. Although evidence of similarly ancient Chinese oracles has been discovered, such as the "oracle bones" of the Shang dynasty (*c.* 1523–1027 BC), the importance of the *I Ching* has remained supreme.

With the upsurge of interest in prediction and prophecy as part of the revival of esoteric wisdom, it is not surprising that the *I Ching* has come to be included among popular pastimes.

At the superficial level this is an undoubted injustice to the *I Ching*, since it was intended to provide a serious and penetrating guide to life, and was not meant to be used merely to satisfy idle curiosity or to tell fortunes.

Several commentators, among them the psychoanalyst Carl Jung and a well-known translator of Buddhist and Taoist texts, John Blofeld, have remarked that the *I Ching* seems to work infallibly. They add, however, that the oracle seems to "answer" in terms of the seriousness of the question, and the response—expressed symbolically as one of the meanings given in the *Book of Changes* itself—needs to be interpreted with sensitivity and intuition.

The *I Ching* is structured on the philosophy of the alternating polarities of *yin* and *yang* in the universe. *Yin* represents Earth and is regarded as passive, feminine, yielding, weak and dark. Overall, it is said to be negative. *Yang* represents heaven and is active, masculine, firm, strong and light. Thus it is said to be clearly positive. Other basic concepts of the *I Ching* philosophy are *t'ai chi*, meaning the center of things—a type of absolute and divine stillness—and *Tao*, meaning "the way." The *I Ching*

Below: Chinese diviners prepare to consult the I Ching *as the gods of prophecy look on. Once the yarrow stalks have been thrown to the ground, the patterns that they make will be equated to the hexagrams contained in the* Book of Changes *held by the venerable, seated master.*

Above: Four of the sixty-four hexagrams contained in the I Ching, *which are made up of a combination of* yin *(broken) and* yang *(continuous) lines. From left to right:* Ksi Tsi, *signifying setbacks;* Ta Kuo, *indicating danger;* Lu, *representing travel; and* Li, *signifying correct behavior.*

Right: Marianne Faithfull and Mick Jagger. Marianne Faithfull was convinced that the I Ching *had prophesied the death by drowning of Rolling Stones member Brian Jones in 1969.*

offers us the way for right action. Commentators skilled in its use say that the question asked—and the spirit in which it is asked—brings to light an intuitive response, which in turn responds to the tides of change, of ebb and flow, in the world. Thus the future is not something static, but constantly in flux, affected by the here and now. John Blofeld says that the oracle allows one to perceive the functioning of the *Tao* in oneself, so that a serious and well-intended question about how one should act is answered with a symbolically expressed response that is in tune with the most spiritual side of one's potential. The *I Ching* does not "predict," in the usual sense of the word, so much as it offers the seeker an appropriate course of action for the future based on the cosmic tides of positive and negative influences that shape our destinies.

To consult the *I Ching*, a method of dividing small heaps of sticks, or of throwing coins,

is used. In the first instance, fifty short and long yarrow stalks are divided systematically in heaps until a resulting collection of stalks provides a combination that can be identified as one of the lines in the "hexagram." The hexagram is a combination of six lines, some of which represent *yin* and the others *yang*. The completed hexagram spells the answer to the question asked at the time of the division of stalks. In the latter case, three coins are thrown, and the side of the coin representing its value is taken to be the positive face. The coins are dropped spontaneously from cupped hands, and their fall produces varying combinations of positive and negative forces, from which the hexagram is drawn.

In each method, the procedure must be carried out six times, and the lines must be built up from the bottom to the top (from Earth to heaven, as it were). After the throws have been made, the specific meanings are found in the *I Ching* itself. There are sixty-four hexagrams in all, but the variety of intuitive meanings far exceeds this number.

As a means of divination in the occult, perhaps Aleister Crowley more than any other Western magician made the most use of the *I Ching*. Crowley was noted for his keenness to adapt the Eastern methods of posture (yogic *asanas*) and breathing to modern techniques of the occult, and, according to his book *The Magical Record of the Beast 666*, he also consulted the oracle regularly. However, when one looks through his account of his day-to-day activities, it is clear that much of his intuition was self-oriented rather than emanating from the *I Ching* itself.

Crowley became notorious for his "sex-abbey" at Cefalu in Sicily, and the following extract from his diaries shows how he consulted the *I Ching* before deciding whether or not to buy the property:

Shall we buy real estate in Cefalu?
= Fang, Fire of Sun.
Large abundant! What should be its physical characteristics? Water of Lingam. Leah says: in a high place. I say: water around it, and Phallus, a Pinnacle. This fits the Caldura like a glove; its promontory is washed by the sea for at least two-thirds of it, and it has a magnificently phallic rock.

On another occasion, in 1921, Crowley asked the *I Ching* for a symbolic prediction of his magical work in the world (he had become Lord of the New Aeon in 1904). The answer was: "Sudden rise to fame, though starting slowly," which was probably true, since Crowley's practice of sexual magic, as well as his experimental taking of consciousness-enhancing substances, soon earned him notoriety in the British press.

In the 1960s and 70s the *I Ching*, along with transcendental meditation, yoga and other forms of Eastern tradition and mystical philosophy, were popular with members of the rock-music culture. While she was Mick Jagger's partner, singer and actress Marianne Faithfull frequently used the *I Ching* for divination. At one stage she was particularly worried about the future of Brian Jones, a member of the Rolling Stones. He had become alienated from his friends and was heavily dependent upon drugs. Whenever she threw the coins with him in mind, the *I Ching* would suggest water and evil. "'Where the water is. A pit, a perilous cavity. There will be evil,' it says," she told Jagger. In July 1969, the prediction came true: Jones, a Piscean by birth, drowned in a swimming pool.

New Age thought helped bring about a revival of interest in the *I Ching* in the West in the 1990s. And in Japan, where many businessmen have claimed that the *I Ching* has helped them to achieve commercial success, an *I Ching* software program has even been marketed, thus adapting this ancient divination system to the computer age.

FENG SHUI

Feng Shui is an ancient Chinese form of geomancy that is believed to date back to the Han dynasty (206 BC–AD 220). Translated as "wind" and "water," *Feng Shui* is used to discover the most auspicious sites for, and the forms of, projected buildings (and also graves), by means of analyzing the *ch'i*, or the natural life force, of the surrounding landscape. *Ch'i* is never static, for new geographical features, such as roads, will alter its balance.

Based on the principles of Taoism, as well as on those of traditional Chinese divination systems, since AD 300 *Feng Shui* has been divided into two schools: the first concentrates on the contours of the landscape, while the second employs a cosmic compass and *I Ching* hexagrams, among other tools. *Feng Shui* is important because the consequences of the sites and

Below: *Participants in a* Feng Shui *ritual in Hong Kong dedicate a new building that has been constructed in careful consultation with a* Feng Shui *master.*

forms of buildings are profound: if a structure is erected on a site not in harmony with the surrounding *ch'i*, its inhabitants will be doomed to a life of suffering—or at least of bad luck. The importance of *Feng Shui* even extends to the positioning of furnishings and outdoor plantings; if negative *ch'i* cannot easily be overcome by altering a building's structure, a strategically sited mirror, plant, light, wind chime or garden shrub can be used to balance it.

According to *Feng Shui*, the natural features of the landscape, such as rivers and hills, are influenced by wind and water. There are five basic elements: fire, earth, water, metal and wood. The polarities of *yin* and *yang* are also primary concepts; they make up the *ch'i* central to *Feng Shui*. In its simplest application, the feminine *yin* force (known as the "White Tiger") should be to the left, or rear, of the site, and the masculine *yang* (the "Azure Dragon") to the right, or south. The interaction of the five elements with these two basic natural forces is analyzed, and astrological auspices and the presence of local spirits are further factors to be considered.

Ideally, all structures should face south (which symbolizes fame) for good *Feng Shui*. North is associated with commercial success, west with children's fame and east with a happy family life. Certain sites are regarded as inherently possessing good *Feng Shui*: mountains whose shapes resemble dragons, for example; evenly flowing water (associated with prosperity); or winds that meander around natural features. Roads or rivers that follow a straight line, however, are believed to possess *sha*—a destructive force. Occasionally the *Feng Shui* master will carry out exorcisms of existing buildings, known as *Tun Fu*.

Feng Shui is taken extremely seriously in most Chinese societies, and no corporate building project is embarked upon without prior consultation with a *Feng Shui* master. In many cases, too, roads have been diverted to avoid harming the landscape's dragon spirit. Although similar systems of geomancy have been also used in the West, in the late twentieth century New Age sympathy with the importance of natural forces has resulted in a widespread interest in this centuries-old Chinese tradition.

Dowsing

Often referred to as water-witching or water-divining, dowsing is not necessarily concerned with locating water, but can be used to discover the whereabouts of other natural substances, people, objects or the source of illness. Dowsing as a form of divination was practiced in ancient Egypt and may even be older; it is known all over the world. Because of its high success rate, in the Middle Ages dowsing was associated with witchcraft (Luther proclaimed that it was the work of the devil), but Christian dowsers managed to escape stigma by "baptizing" their dowsing rods and giving them Christian names.

In the popular imagination, the dowser's tool is a forked rod, but it may also be an angled rod, such as a coathanger; a wand or "bobber"— a weighted branch; or a pendulum. Dowsing rods are usually fashioned from willow, rowan, ash or hazel twigs, but metal (particularly aluminum

Right: A dowser holds his forked wooden rod. The rods are traditionally made from wood, but other materials, including metal and plastic, can be equally effective, as can such instruments as pendulums. Some dowsers require no tools at all, but feel indications of the presence of the substance that they are seeking in their own bodies.

and copper), plastic and bone may be used too. In practice, the dowser concentrates hard when "tuning" the rod, then walks across (or stands over the map of) the location believed to hold the substance in question. When the rod detects the presence of the substance, it jerks violently. No one knows exactly how dowsing works, but it is commonly believed that dowsers have an innate psychic propensity. As in *Feng Shui*, the dowser's ability to "connect" with the inherent characteristics of the surroundings or landscape is also important. Other explanations include the sensitivity of the dowser's tools to electromagnetic and electrostatic force fields.

With the nineteenth-century advances in scientific knowledge, dowsing correspondingly declined. It regained its popularity in the twentieth century, largely as the result of the efforts of the French priests Alexis Mermet, Alex Bouly (who renamed it "radiesthesia") and Jean Jurion. Now quite well established and

respected, dowsing has been successfully used in the fields of archeology and geology and in the search for oil, gas and minerals—and even to try to locate missing persons and explosive mines (as in Vietnam). Although medical dowsing is prohibited in the United States, it has been used elsewhere to diagnose illnesses, usually by rotating a pendulum over the patient's body.

THE TAROT

One of the most interesting and popular of all esoteric practices is the use of Tarot cards. Most people know them as the precursors of the standard playing cards, and they are perhaps best known for their use in fortune-telling. They have also appeared as symbols in modern media—from plays to posters.

Tarot cards are popularly believed to have been passed down through history by the Romany people, and there is a certain veneer of superstition surrounding them. However,

Above: A Romany palm-reading consultation. The Romany people practice a number of divinatory methods, and are popularly believed to have introduced Tarot cards to Europe from their supposedly common origin in Egypt. The Tarot is now known to have preceded the arrival of the Romany people in Europe, however.

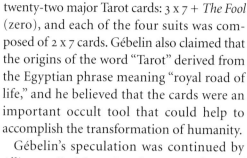

twenty-two major Tarot cards: 3 x 7 + *The Fool* (zero), and each of the four suits was composed of 2 x 7 cards. Gébelin also claimed that the origins of the word "Tarot" derived from the Egyptian phrase meaning "royal road of life," and he believed that the cards were an important occult tool that could help to accomplish the transformation of humanity.

Gébelin's speculation was continued by Alliette, a Parisian wigmaker, or professor of mathematics, according to different accounts. Alliette, who wrote under the pseudonym Etteilla (his own name reversed), declared that the Tarot originated 171 years after the biblical deluge, and was developed by seventeen magicians. From his room in the Hôtel de Crillon, he used to offer pronouncements on the divinatory use of the Tarot, including regarding the fate of his fellow men during the French Revolution.

The next major theorist of the Tarot, and the one who has perhaps influenced modern occultism more than any other, was Eliphas Lévi (1810–75). Lévi was a priest of the Catholic Church, a graphic artist and a political satirist. He was fascinated by the Qabalah, with its ten levels of consciousness, and he made the brilliant discovery that the twenty-two major-arcana trump cards of the Tarot correlated symbolically to the paths leading to these stages of consciousness. Likewise, in the tree of life there are twenty-two links that connect the ten spheres, or the *sephiroth*. Lévi believed that the Tarot was therefore an important representation of the images of mystical consciousness.

Above: It was the eighteenth-century French theologian Antoine Court de Gébelin who first linked the Tarot with the "Book of Thoth," believing that, like the Egyptian pyramids, Tarot cards were a symbolic expression of the profoundly esoteric tradition of ancient Egypt.

Right: The fourth major-arcana Tarot card, The Emperor, *from a French deck. His crown, scepter, throne and eagle-emblazoned shield are clear attributes of authority, while his legs form a cross, signifying the four elements.*

most of the legends concerning the Tarot cards are false. They were certainly not invented by the Romanies of medieval Europe, since they are known to have been present in Italy a century before the Romanies arrived there. Nor did the Tarot originate in ancient Egypt. This particular legend is part of the eighteenth- and nineteenth-century romance of "lost cultures," when people looked back to a "golden age" that possessed a secret, esoteric wisdom, which was then transposed into all sorts of fictitious or symbolic locations, like "initiation chambers" in the Great Pyramid, or the "lost continents" of Atlantis and Lemuria.

Antoine Court de Gébelin (1725–84), a French theologian and student of mythology, was responsible for some of the early, somewhat fanciful tales about the Tarot. In his book *Le Monde Primitifzi* (or *The Primitive World*), Gébelin surmised, without substantial evidence, that the Tarot was part of the Egyptian "Book of Thoth"—the book of divine wisdom—and that the cards symbolized in pictorial form the arcane knowledge of the initiates to the esoteric beliefs of ancient Egypt. Particularly important was the number 7—there are

L'EMPEREUR

Lévi's work was extended by Gerard Encausse or "Papus" (1865–1916), who similarly wrote commentaries on the relationship between the Tarot and the Qabalah and, in particular, on the twenty-two letters of the Hebrew alphabet.

Lévi also exercised a strong influence on the Hermetic Order of the Golden Dawn. A. E. Waite (1857–c. 1940), whose "Rider" pack of Tarot cards is well known, translated a number of Lévi's books, including

THE MAGICIAN

THE LOVERS.

Far left: The Juggler, *or* Magician, *is the first major-arcana card; this version is from the Rider deck. With a halolike symbol of infinity hovering above his head, he holds aloft a wand. Before him on the table are the sword, cup and pentacle of the other three minor-arcana suits.*

Left: This image of The Lovers, *the sixth major-arcana card, is also from the Rider deck. The two human figures are equated with Adam and Eve, an association that postdates the original personification of vice and virtue being threatened by the genius's dart.*

Historie de la Magie, into English and regarded Lévi as the most significant magus of his age. Aleister Crowley even considered himself to be Lévi's reincarnation and drew on Lévi's correlations in formulating his own work on the Tarot, *The Book of Thoth.*

The Golden Dawn magicians used the Tarot cards as pathways into the mind, rather than as a means of divination. Each of the cards can be visualized as a doorway through which magicians can imaginatively pass; they can then have symbolic and mystical visions related to the imagery of the tree of life.

The most commonly agreed correlation of the major-arcana Tarot cards with the Hebrew alphabet (and that followed by A. E. Waite and Paul Foster Case, the American founder of the "Builders of Adytum") is as follows.

Left: Marie-Anne-Adelaide Lenormand (1772–1843), *a noted French clairvoyant who frequently consulted the Tarot on behalf of the Empress Josephine.*

0 *The Fool—Aleph*
1 *The Juggler,* or *Magician—Beth*
2 *The High Priestess,* or *Female Pope—Gimel*
3 *The Empress—Daleth*
4 *The Emperor—Heh*
5 *The Hierophant,* or *Pope—Vau*
6 *The Lovers—Zain*
7 *The Chariot—Cheth*
8 *Strength,* or *Fortitude—Teth*
9 *The Hermit—Yod*
10 *The Wheel of Fortune—Kaph*
11 *Justice—Lamed*
12 *The Hanged Man—Mem*
13 *Death—Nun*

Right: The twelfth card is The Hanged Man. *MacGregor Mathers believed that the card signified sacrifice, and certainly the halo around the head supports this interpretation. The gibbet from which he hangs can be equated with the tree of life.*

14 *Temperance*—*Samekh*
15 *The Devil*—*Ayin*
16 *The Lightning-struck Tower*—*Peh*
17 *The Star*—*Tzaddi*
18 *The Moon*—*Qoph*
19 *The Sun*—*Resh*
20 *(The Last) Judgement*—*Shin*
21 *The Universe*, or *World*—*Tau*

Modern occultists therefore use the major-arcana Tarot cards as their doorways to greater consciousness. The other fifty-six cards, called the "minor arcana," which are divided into four suits—wands and swords (masculine), and cups and pentacles (feminine)—are of less significance. Each of the major arcana corresponds to a certain portion of the psyche, symbolized by the tree of life. The tree is a living, vibrant thing, and each *sephirah* flows into another. The magician too, must flow along the tides of consciousness.

The Tarot images constitute a type of mythology of the mind, rather in the same manner as Jung's archetypes of the unconscious. Magicians meet the gods in their visions, seeing them as embodiments of different facets of their own personalities: the warring aspect, for example, being represented by Mars (*The Chariot*), and the more intuitive, emotional side by Venus (*The Star*). Meditating on the Tarot cards helps occultists to balance their personalities.

Descriptions and interpretations of the major-arcana Tarot cards were incorporated into Golden Dawn teaching. The following brief summaries of these are adapted from *The Tarot*, by S. L. MacGregor Mathers.

0 *The Fool* or the *Foolish Man*. A man with a fool's cap, dressed like a jester, with a stick and bundle over his shoulder. Before him is the butterfly of pleasure luring him on, while a tiger (in some packs, a dog) attacks him from behind. It signifies folly or expiation.

1 *The Juggler*, or *Magician*. Before a table covered with the appliances of his art stands the figure of a juggler, one hand upraised holding a wand (in some packs, a cup), the other pointing downward. He wears a cap of maintenance [a heraldic term] like that of kings, whose wide brim forms a sort of aureole around his head. His body and arms form the shape of the Hebrew letter *Aleph*, to which this

THE HANGED MAN.

card corresponds. The juggler symbolizes will.

2 *The High Priestess*, or *Female Pope*. A woman crowned with a high miter or tiara (her head is encircled by a veil), a stole (or a solar cross) upon her breast and the "Book of Science" open in her hand. She represents science, wisdom or knowledge.

3 *The Empress*. A winged and crowned woman seated upon a throne, holding in one hand a scepter bearing a globe surmounted by a cross, resting the other upon a shield emblazoned with an eagle, on whose breast is a cross. She is the symbol of action, the result of the union of science and will.

4 *The Emperor*. He is depicted crowned and leaning against a throne. His legs form a cross, while beside him, beneath his left hand, is a shield emblazoned with an eagle. In his right hand he bears a scepter similar to that of the Empress. His body and arms form a triangle, of which his head is the apex, so that the whole figure delineates a triangle above a cross. He represents realization.

5 *The Hierophant*, or *Pope*. He is crowned with the papal tiara and is seated between the two pillars of Hermes and Solomon. With his right hand he makes the sign of esotericism, and with his left he leans upon a staff surmounted by a triple cross. Before him kneel two ministers. He is the symbol of mercy and beneficence.

6 The Lovers. This card is usually described as representing humanity positioned between vice and virtue, while a winged genius threatens vice with his dart. It is usually considered to mean proof or trial. [Mathers considered this interpretation, but felt that "it represents the Qabalistical Microprosopus between *Binah* and *Malkuth* (see my *Kabbalah Unveiled*), while the figure above shows the influence descending from *Kether*," and that it symbolizes wise disposition.]

7 The Chariot. This represents a conqueror crowned, bearing a scepter and riding in a cubical chariot surmounted by four columns and a canopy. The chariot is drawn by two horses, one of which looks straight forward, while the other turns his head toward the conquerors. (Two wheels are shown in the complete, single-headed figure.) It represents triumph and the victory of justice and judgement.

8 Justice. A woman crowned and seated on a throne (between two columns), holding in her right hand an upright sword and in her left the scales. She symbolizes equilibrium and justice. [*Note:* the positions of *Justice* and *Strength*, or *Fortitude*, may occasionally be switched.]

9 The Hermit. An old and bearded man, wrapped in a mantle, with his head covered with a cowl, bearing in his right hand the lantern of occult science, while in his left he holds his magic wand partially hidden beneath his cloak. He symbolizes prudence.

10 The Wheel of Fortune. A wheel of seven spokes (the two halves of the double-headed cards make it eight spokes, which is incorrect), revolving between two uprights. On the ascending side is an animal ascending, and on the descending side is a monkey descending; both forms are bound to the wheel. Above it is the form of an angel (or a sphinx in some cards), holding a sword in one hand and a crown in the other. This very complicated symbol signifies fortune, good or bad.

11 Strength or Fortitude. A woman wearing a crown and cap of maintenance, who calmly and effortlessly closes the jaws of a curious lion. She represents strength. [*Note: Strength*, or *Fortitude*, and *Justice* are sometimes switched.]

THE SUN .

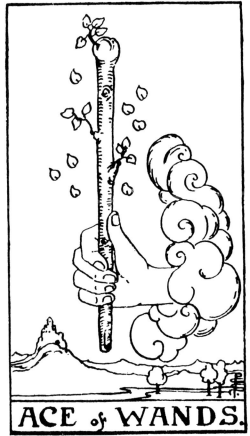

ACE of WANDS.

Far left: The Sun *is the nineteenth major-arcana card. This Sun shines down on a child seated upon a horse (a solar symbol), figures that have been substituted for the Gemini twins of earlier versions. The Sun is a symbol of happiness even when it is reversed.*

Left: The ace card of the minor-arcana suit of wands, a masculine suit that precedes those of swords, cups and pentacles. Each of the four suits represent an element, in this case fire, indicated by the smoking hand that holds a budding branch of the tree of life.

12 *The Hanged Man.* This extraordinary symbol is almost unintelligible in the double-headed cards. Properly, it represents a man who has been hung head downward from a sort of gibbet, to which he is attached by one foot. His hands are bound behind his back in such a manner that his body forms a triangle with the point downward, and his legs a cross above the triangle. Two sacks or weights are occasionally attached to his armpits. He symbolizes sacrifice and is usually depicted with a halo.

13 *Death.* A skeleton armed with a scythe, with which he mows down heads in a meadow like blades of grass. He signifies transformation or change.

14 *Temperance.* An angel with the sign of the sun on her brow, pouring liquid from one vessel into another. She represents combination.

15 *The Devil.* A horned and winged demon with the claws of an eagle, standing on an altar to which two smaller devils are bound. In his left hand he bears a scepter. He is the image of fate or fatality, good or evil.

Right: Aleister Crowley at the time of his first Himalayan expedition. Crowley studied Eliphas Lévi's interpretations of the Tarot before writing The Book of Thoth, *his own work on the subject.*

16 *The Lightning-struck Tower.* A tower whose upper part is like a crown, struck by a lightning flash. Two men fall headlong from it, one of whom is in such an attitude as to form the Hebrew letter *Ayin*. Sparks and debris are falling. It means ruin or disruption.

17 *The Star.* A nude female figure pours water upon the earth from two vases. In the heavens above her shines the blazing star of the Magi (surrounded by seven others); trees and plants grow beneath her magical influence, and on one the butterfly of Psyche alights. She is the star of hope.

18 *The Moon.* The Moon shining in the heavens, drops of dew falling, a wolf and a dog howling at the Moon and, halted at the foot of two towers, a path that loses itself in the horizon (and is sprinkled with drops of blood). A crayfish, emblematic of the sign of Cancer, ruled over by the Moon, crawls through water in the foreground toward the land. The card symbolizes twilight, deception and error.

19 *The Sun.* The sun sending down its rays upon two children, who suggest the sign of Gemini. Behind them is a low wall. The card signifies earthly happiness.

20 *(The Last) Judgement.* An angel in the heavens blowing a trumpet, to which is attached a standard with a cross. The dead rise from their tombs. It signifies renewal or result.

21 *The Universe,* **or** *World.* Within a flowery wreath is a female figure, nude except for a light scarf. She represents nature and the presence of the divine in nature. In each hand she bears a wand. At the four angles of the card are the four cherubic animals of the Apocalypse: above, the eagle and the man; below, the lion and the bull. The card represents completion or reward.

Many different meanings can be applied to the individual Tarot cards, depending on which system of interpretation is used—and MacGregor Mathers' version, although fairly standard, is just one of these. It should also be noted that when each card is reversed its characteristics become a negative mirror image of any positive attributes, and vice versa. For example, although MacGregor Mathers states that *The Lightning-struck Tower* signifies ruin or disruption, in its positive aspect the card can also represent the breaking down of emotional barriers.

ΠUMEROLOGY

From the earliest times, humans have been fascinated by the symbolism of numbers. We find common elements in this symbolism: for example, the numbers 7 and 12 occur in many cultures as combinations of sacred significance.

Modern numerology draws much of its inspiration from the sixth-century philosopher Pythagoras, who believed that numbers represent the essence and qualities of things. Hence, for numerologists, an analysis of the numbers comprising a person's name will reveal what sort of person he or she is inherently.

Pythagoras's views on numbers were expanded by the medieval Qabalist Cornelius Agrippa (1486–1535) in his book *Occult Philosophy*, which was first published in 1533. According to Agrippa, the numbers 1 to 10 have the following qualities.

Above: An Arab scribe at work. Arab mathematicians introduced the figure 0 to Europe, as well as the numerals that we use today (as opposed to Roman numerals). The Qabalists incorporated some Arabic elements into their mystical philosophical system, and the work of the Qabalist Cornelius Agrippa informs many of the principles of numerology.

Right: The scales of justice, the symbol of the zodiacal sign of Libra, are equated to the number 5 in numerology.

1—The origin of all things, God, the central intelligence in the universe, the sun and the alchemical philosopher's stone.

2—Marriage and communion. Alternatively, evil and the number of division.

3—Trinity, fulfillment and sacred wisdom.

4—Solidity, permanence and foundation (associated with the earth). There are four elements, four seasons and four cardinal points.

5—Justice. In medieval Europe, this was interpreted to be Christian justice, there being five wounds in Christ's body. Humans also observe the world through their five senses.

6—Creation. In Judeo-Christian belief, the world was fashioned in six days, God resting on the seventh. According to Agrippa, the numbers also represents labor and service. Six is considered the perfect number.

7—Life. Seven is made up of six (perfection) and one (unity and God). In the medieval conception, life is made up of the body (spirit, flesh, bone and humors—bodily fluids) and soul (passions, desire and reason), making a total of seven elements of life.

8—Fullness. The number eight is remarkably even, for it can be divided twice and still retains the balance of all things. It is also associated with infinity (whose symbol is a horizontal 8).

9—The number of the spheres, with cosmic significance.

10—Completeness—one cannot go beyond 10 without including other numbers. As a Qabalist, Agrippa believed that the world came to be through a divine process of ten stages.

Numerology featured prominently in Qabalism, which developed three systems to discover the hidden meanings of words by assigning numerical values to their letters. In all three systems, the total sum of the assigned numbers was analyzed by reference to other words (especially from the Scriptures) that shared the same totals, to draw conclusions about the significance of the word. *Gematria* also considered the size and style of letters; *notarikon* concentrated on the first (and occasionally middle and last) letters, which were used to form new words; and *temurah* was used to create anagrams, or to organize letters into mathematical structures for eventual substitution with the letters of other words.

According to modern numerologists, the two most revealing aspects of people's lives and characters are their birthdates and commonly used names. The latter is said to be the name that most closely defines the identity (or "essence") of a person. The birthdate is not written as a succession of numbers, but is plotted onto a diagram (0 is not included), which shows the positions as follows:

Mind level	3	6	9
Emotional level	2	5	8
Physical level	1	4	7

Numerologists believe that this represents a threefold division of humanity and that the aim of all mystical teachings is perfection. Consequently, the perfect human would have all these numbers in his or her make-up. One of the authors of this book was born on 1.10.1947, which would be diagramatically represented as:

Mind level			9
Emotional level			
Physical level	111	4	7

This analysis shows a lack of functioning on the emotional level, and this would therefore be an area clearly in need of improvement! Thus, the birthdate numbers show us to what extent we are unbalanced and what qualities of character are needed for a harmonized development of the personality.

Another method concentrating on the birthdate is the concept of the "ruling number." The numbers in the above diagram total 23, which can be reduced to 2 + 3 = 5. The fact that 5 is the number of justice, and also that the author is a Libran (Libra: the scales = balance), offers some sort of compensation for the previous analysis.

The most popular method used for reducing a name to a number is to take the name used by the person under analysis (this would not normally include the middle name) and apply a numerical value to each letter. A is 1, B is 2, and so on, until we arrive at I, which is 9. Since there is no zero, and 10 = 1, J becomes 1, and K, 2, and so on through the alphabet. The full sequence is as follows.

1	2	3	4	5	6	7	8	9
A	B	C	D	E	F	G	H	I
J	K	L	M	N	O	P	Q	R
S	T	U	V	W	X	Y	Z	

It is usually claimed that the birthdate—denoting the beginning of life—is more important than the name, partly because the name is given by the parents, while the birthdate is an integral part of the person (and is therefore a more reliable guide). However, it is also recognized that a person grows up, develops and responds as *one who has a name*. In this sense the name comes to symbolize the personality and, in a very limited sense, "predicts" it. Some names sound hard and aggressive, others soft and poetic, so it is little wonder that numerologists stress the vibrationary qualities of the name.

A person may find the numerical value of his or her name by totaling the sum of its letters. If it comes to a total exceeding 10, it is "reduced," as with the ruling number above. This number may then be slotted into the birth diagram as a further clue to the personality.

As with astrology, numerology offers an analysis of what a person is, rather than of what he or she may become. During people's lifetimes, as they exercise their free will, they make certain decisions as they develop. Numerology merely offers a framework for what people may become if they follow a natural tendency; it does not make any claim to prophecy.

PALMISTRY

In its simplest form, palmistry is the fortune-telling technique of reading hands, popularized at fairground sideshows. This is, of course, but a poor imitation of the discipline that today more than ever lays claim to scientific foundations.

Left: The popular image of the palm-reader: an exotically dressed woman who operates at fairgrounds after her own palm is crossed with silver.

Palmistry (also known as cheirognomy or cheiromancy) is concerned with the analysis of the hands—not simply the lines on the palms, but their combinations and conjunctions, together with other minute details of the hands and fingers. In palmistry, the features of the hand are linked with aspects of personality and character, as well as with other features of the individual—both physical and psychological. Scientific palmists do not postulate simple correlations between this feature of the hand and that psychological characteristic; instead they look for significant aspects, their combinations and relationships. They look for an overall pattern, which will be unique in each individual case.

The palm of a human being develops its characteristic lines and patterns from the time of birth (and even from before that time). These develop and change over the years and may, in their changes, indicate further mutations in the individual's life and personality. But palmistry is not a fatalistic technology: the lines on the palms reflect aspects of personality rather than causing them. Therefore,

palmistry is an analytical discipline more than a predictive one—although the skilled palmist who observes tendencies and interrelationships on the hand can postulate likely trends in the individual's future.

Palmistry has developed from a fortune-teller's art to a realm of legitimate scientific investigation. Its origins are extremely ancient, and references to this method of divination in the ancient writings of India and China date back some 3,000 years. Certainly it was referred to by Aristotle who, it is said, attributed its origins to ancient Egypt. It was not, however, until the sixteenth and seventeenth centuries that palmistry, along with other forms of divination by analysis of the body (including phrenology—or reading the shape of the head), became systematized.

It was during this period that the macrocosm/microcosm theory was expanded (that is, "as above, so below," meaning that humans were linked with the cosmos and an analysis of human nature revealed the wider universe). Hand-reading textbooks became popular; most of these were far from scientific and often worked on the basis of laws of correspondence.

In the nineteenth century, the first attempts were initiated to make palmistry (or "chirology," as it was then often known) respectable to a Western audience. One of the most important works of this time was *Laws of Scientific Hand Reading*, by William G. Benham, an American. It was at this time too that the famous palmist "Cheiro" (the pseudonym of Count Louis Harmon) brought the study to the height of its popularity.

Gradually the interest in scientific palmistry, as distinct from the more popular fortune-telling version, has expanded. A number of scientists, especially psychologists, have taken an interest in the correlation between the characteristics of the personality and the lines on the hand. Many psychologists and palmists believe that, in statistical correlations such as these, some support is given to the ancient premises of hand-reading, especially regarding the relationship between mental disorders and hand characteristics. Certainly, as ever more serious scientific consideration is given to the study of the significance of the lines on the hand, more information will become available on this ancient technique of character divination.

In their analysis of hands, traditional palmists look for a number of features, as follows.

✦ The size and shape of the hands, including the size of the palms, the size and shape of the fingers, and their thickness and width.

Left: The works of Aristotle (384–322 BC) contain the earliest Western references to the practice of palmistry.

Opposite, above:
A Chinese palm-reader uses a magnifying glass to aid a close examination of his client's hand. Palmistry has a long tradition in China, dating back thousands of years.

Opposite, below:
A Tyrolean mother consults a palm-reader while her fascinated children observe the proceedings from behind a window. Perhaps the palm-reader will tell her if there are more to come.

Left: This depiction of a palm is unusual, as it contains Christian images, rather than zodiacal and esoteric symbols—indeed, palmistry was banned by the medieval Catholic Church. Significantly, Christ's cross has bisected and thus shortened the life line.

✦ The flexibility or stiffness of the hand and the fingers.

✦ The characteristics of the fingers—this includes the traditional correlation between the fingers and the different aspects of personality.

✦ The fingerprints are examined by some, but not all, palmists.

✦ The mounts—the "hills" on the hand; different mounts relate to different aspects of personality.

✦ The lines—it was traditionally popularly assumed that these were the only features of concern to the palmist; however, they are only a part of the whole pattern of the hand and must be seen in a total context. Different lines are related to different aspects of the individual, the most important lines being those of the head, heart and life.

Some palmists prefer to read directly from the hand, others like to take prints and analyze these in depth. Other palmists state that the hands are merely a point of contact with the person, and say that they employ some form of psychic perception for the actual character analysis, while others reject all "nonscientific" methods of palmistry.

SCRYING

Scrying (also known as crystal-gazing, or crystallomancy) is an ancient and universal form of divination, involving gazing into a speculum—a transparent stone or reflective surface—in order to see the future in the form of a vision. The fortune-teller of popular Western lore gazes into a polished crystal ball, but quartzes, or precious stones such as beryls, can also be used as specula, as can polished thumbnails (usually in Arab cultures), metal, glass, mirrors (as in *Snow White*), blood or ink. Whatever the object, however, the importance of meditation to induce a trancelike state is paramount. Once this state has been achieved, it is commonly reported that the speculum clouds over and then clears to reveal the vision.

Scrying (derived from the word "descry," meaning to discern) was practiced in ancient Egypt, from whence it spread to the Arab world and thence to Europe. In Elizabethan times, Dr. John Dee's assistant, Edward Kelley, was

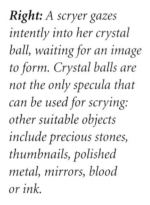

Right: A scryer gazes intently into her crystal ball, waiting for an image to form. Crystal balls are not the only specula that can be used for scrying: other suitable objects include precious stones, thumbnails, polished metal, mirrors, blood or ink.

Left: *A wide variety of divinatory systems are used all over the world. Here a street-based fortune-teller, surrounded by the tools of his trade, awaits potential clients.*

an adept scryer, who communicated with the angels (whom he saw in his black obsidian mirror or crystal egg) in the Enochian language that was later used by members of the Hermetic Order of the Golden Dawn. Nostradamus, too, used scrying to induce his visions. Although in the Middle Ages it was believed that the scryer saw demons trapped by powerful magic inside the speculum, today it is recognized that the art of scrying lies in the clairvoyant skills inherent in the scryer, which can be honed through practice.

OTHER FORMS OF DIVINATION

Countless other forms of divination are employed all over the world. There follows a short summary of some of the best known, presented in alphabetical order.

✦ **Alectromancy**—writing the letters of the alphabet around a circle, placing a grain of wheat on each, then noting the order in which a cock eats the wheat.
✦ **Astragalomancy**—scattering bones on the ground and predicting the positions in which they will fall.
✦ **Belomancy**—writing down advice on tags, which are then attached to arrows. The advice attached to whichever arrow flies the farthest is accepted.
✦ **Geomancy**—observing the patterns made by scattering objects, such as stones, on the ground; or observing points of the Earth.
✦ **Gyromancy**—walking around a circle until one falls; the position of the fall is significant.
✦ **Haruspicy**—drawing conclusions from the physical state of the entrails of slaughtered birds and animals. Also known as *extispicy*.
✦ **Hydromancy**—noting the flow of water by, for example, dipping a ring attached to a string into water; or observing the patterns of tea leaves that have settled in cups.
✦ **Necromancy**—summoning the spirits of the dead (as practiced by the Witch of Endor). Also known as *spiritualism*.
✦ **Oneiromancy**—interpreting dreams.
✦ **Pyromancy**—observing the way a particular fire burns.
✦ **Runes**—interpreting random letters of this early alphabet of the Gothic tribes of northern Europe.
✦ **Stichomancy**—opening a book (such as the Bible) at random and isolating a sentence by chance (for example, by sticking a pin into the page). Its words may be applied to solving a problem. Also known as *sortes*, or *bibliomancy*.

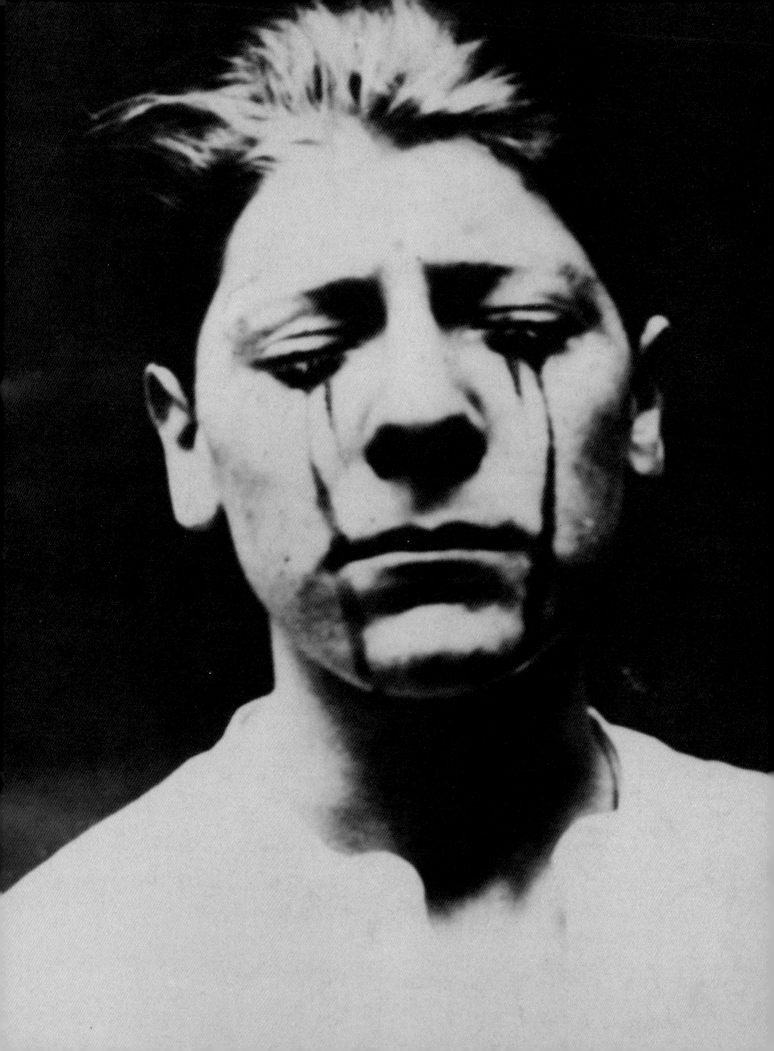

Inner Experience

Inherent in the human mind is the capacity for a rich variety of inner experience. We all generate vivid visions in the form of dreams, from which we can learn more about ourselves, while meditation and biofeedback can also lead us to enlightenment. This chapter examines these experiences and various methods for attaining transcendental states of consciousness, including hypnotism, autosuggestion and relaxation, as well as the more sophisticated phenomena of trance consciousness and out-of-body consciousness. Possession, exorcism and faith-healing are also discussed in the context of the power of the human mind, as are extrasensory perception and psychokinesis. In the words of Fulke Greville (1633), "the mind in her vast comprehension contains more worlds than all the world can find"; this analysis lifts the veils of just a few of those worlds.

Meditation and Biofeedback

Relatively recently in the West there has been an increased level of interest in yoga, Zen Buddhism and transcendental-meditation, popularized by Maharaji Mahesh. It seems that the direction of popular interest has moved away from activity in the outer world back toward the inner world of meditation and contemplation.

Basically, meditation involves the practice of enhancing the quality of inner peace, through what may be termed "alert relaxation." Meditating people are not drowsy, but their train of thought changes, so that instead of observing all the details of external reality, they are more involved with the source of thought itself and with the underlying "oneness" of the manifestation of thought.

Meditation is a key practice in the Zen sects and in Raja yoga. In the West it also plays a significant part in magical practice and in Catholicism, especially in the Cistercian and Carthusian traditions. William Johnston, a Western theologian with a specialized interest in Eastern mysticism, pointed out that just as Zen uses paradoxical *koans*, or tales that force the meditator to transcend rational thinking, and just as yogis use the mandala in meditation, Christianity has certain parallel practices. According to Johnston, meditation resembles Christian "contemplation," and he noted that once a Zen practitioner demonstrated to a group of Christians that the cross could be used as a type of *koan* symbol.

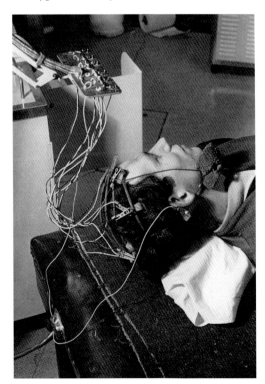

Opposite: *The tears of blood issuing from the eyes of this individual are an example of the extraordinary phenomena that can occur during a trancelike state. The best-documented cases of spontaneous bleeding are those that manifest themselves in Stigmatics, fervent Christians who, during meditation, develop wounds that parallel those of Christ's crucifixion.*

Left: *When wired up to an E.E.G. machine, as illustrated here, a subject's brain-wave patterns may be monitored and recorded, thus giving valuable information about the changes that occur in the brain's activity during meditation.*

Above: *Seated in a comfortable chair, this subject is connected to an E.E.G. biofeedback device, which will measure her brain-wave patterns and then report them to her by means of light or sound. Biofeedback techniques enable subjects to monitor and control their mental activity and thus achieve enhanced states of consciousness.*

It seems clear, then, that meditation itself is a mental process that is not exclusively bound to any particular religious or mystical school. Edward Maupin described it as "deep passivity, combined with awareness." In yoga and other Eastern meditative disciplines, the practitioner sits cross-legged, often in the "full lotus" position, so that the right foot rests on the left thigh, and the left foot rests on the right thigh. In yoga the meditator is allowed to close his eyes, but Zen, which is more oriented to the "here and now," requires that the eyes are open. The gaze is cast downward, directed about a meter in front of the knees.

It was once difficult to assess what types of mental activity were occurring in yogis and

mystics as they meditated. However, analytical science has recently enabled the specific tabulation of their brain-wave activity under laboratory conditions. The meditators can be wired to an electroencephalograph (E.E.G.) machine, and all their brain-wave functions can be meticulously recorded, giving at least one kind of description of this mental state.

The existence of brain waves was first established by a German scientist, Hans Berger, shortly after World War I. Berger attached two electrodes to the scalp of a young, psychologically disturbed patient and, with the help of an indicator, noted that there was an electronic response. Berger believed that there were two main types of brain-wave patterns: alpha, connected with passivity; and beta, associated with concentration and problem-solving. It has since been found that there are four main types of brain-wave activity.

Alpha, the first type, has a frequency of around 8–12 cycles per second and enables the subject to focus on inner states of awareness, including mystical consciousness. Most people who close their eyes produce some alpha waves; they are harder to produce with the eyes open. The presence of high-level alpha activity indicates a state of deep concentration.

The second type, beta, occurs in alert, waking consciousness and measures around 13 cycles per second. Where alpha relates to the inner world of thought, beta is more a part of the external world of action. Theta is linked to the mental state of drowsiness and to the condition immediately preceding sleep. It measures around 4–7 cycles per second. Delta rhythms are produced in deep sleep, and measure 0–4 cycles per second.

Experiments were conducted in Japan and the United States to identify which of these brain-wave patterns occurred during meditation. Drs. Akira Kasamatsu and Tomio Hirai of Tokyo University employed the services of forty-eight Zen Buddhist monks, recording their brain-wave patterns on E.E.G.s during meditation. Some of the "masters" produced alpha waves after only 50 seconds, and the electrodes did not appear to interfere with the process of meditation. It was noted that if a clicking noise was made, this sound blocked the production of alpha waves for 3–5 seconds by interfering with the concentration. (This was not the case in a separate study of Raja yogis, who were totally oblivious of any movement or noise in their environment.) Kasamatsu and Hirai noted that their Zen subjects sometimes passed straight from the alpha state into theta. By contrast, in the Raja-yoga study of Anand, China and Singh (1961), the meditators produced persistent alpha waves, which were heightened during *samadhi* (deep concentration).

In 1958 Dr. Joe Kamiya of the University of Chicago conducted research on the brain-wave activity registered during the sleeping state and, in particular, the spasmodic traces of alpha patterns. He wired up a subject to an E.E.G. machine to record his brain-wave patterns and asked the subject to report his own state of mind. At first the subject guessed correctly at only the normal rate of 50 percent, but by the fourth day he had guessed his mental activity correctly (that is, coinciding with the E.E.G. readings) 400 times in a row. This was an amazing discovery, because it showed that individuals could, with practice, learn to identify their own mental states. Kamiya later discovered that it was also possible for a person to learn to sustain a given state, such as alpha; the modern technique of biofeedback was about to be born. The next step was to invent a machine that would transform the presence of alpha waves, as measured by the E.E.G., into an audible sound that could be heard by the meditator, thus showing his progress. The biofeedback device was thus developed as an aid to maintaining a positive, contemplative state of mind.

Further devices have since been invented to allow people to recognize all the postulated types of their brain-wave activity, and in some cases the signal is a light rather than an audible tone. Biofeedback became especially popular in the United States, where it was enthusiastically hailed in some circles as a "short cut to mystical enlightenment."

Several commentators, including William Johnston, have been keen to point out that while contemplative states contain alpha, alpha in itself does not equate with mystical consciousness *per se.* In fact, theta waves may be just as important: many artists and writers gain inspiration from the theta dream state, which is generally associated with creativity. Marvin Karlins and Lewis Andrews also pointed out

that each of the mental states has its place, and that the pursuit of alpha for its own sake is not necessarily a good idea. Some subjects have found the transition from beta to alpha "a source of anxiety and apprehension," not the state of well-being and passivity that is usually claimed, and they go on to say that "some alpha experiences are strictly a function of the subject's expectations."

Nevertheless, biofeedback put mystical states of consciousness onto the scientific map. We can now better understand meditation and be more sure of its positive effects. Through E.E.G. recordings, we can tell how deep a state of contemplation is and, through biofeedback, ordinary people, who may not have had the opportunity to join a Zen monastery, can now improve their meditative—if not spiritual—development by means of a machine.

Below: This machine, demonstrated by an apparently skeptical subject in 1938, was invented by H.C. Lavery to "do the work of a psychoanalyst." It was not until the 1950s, however, that biofeedback was taken seriously as a valid scientific technique, largely as a result of the research carried out by Dr. Joe Kamiya.

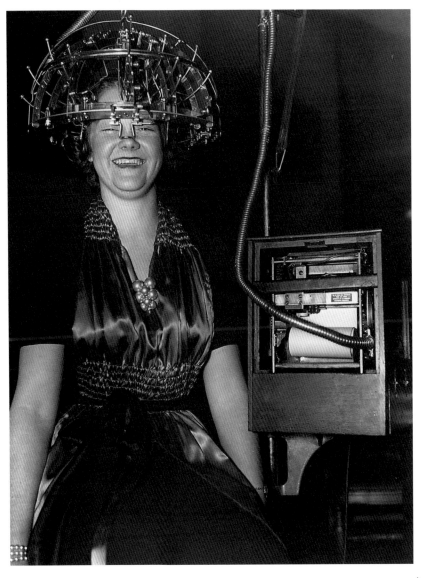

Above: This sleeping subject's brain-wave patterns are carefully observed by scientists from Harvard University and the Boston Museum of Science.

Opposite: As is illustrated in these photographs from Bergamo, Italy, and Bethesda, Maryland, researchers disagree over the degree of comfort their sleeping subjects require.

DREAMS

Throughout history, humans have regarded the dream state as something awesome and mysterious, in which strange, supernatural omens can be revealed or perhaps new courses of action and behavior demonstrated. In the Bible we find the account of Joseph, who dreamed that one day his whole family would bow to him. His dream did not show the members of his family in the literal sense, but used the language of symbols: "Behold, I have dreamed a dream more; and behold the sun and the moon, and the eleven stars made obeisance before me…" In this instance, Joseph's dream followed the mythological symbolism of representing

his father as the Sun, his mother as the Moon and his brothers as companion stars.

A quite different culture, that of the Native American Iroquois, also pays special attention to the symbolism of dreams. An early Jesuit missionary among the Iroquois, Father Fremin, wrote that they had substituted the dream for a divinity; in other words, they had made dreams their "god." In 1642 a Huron man (the Hurons are an Iroquois tribe) dreamed that a non-Huron Iroquois had captured him and burned him alive. When he awoke, a council of chiefs was held to discuss the portents of the dream. The chiefs decided that the events of the dream must not come to pass, so several members of the tribe procured firebrands and tried to trap the dreamer and burn him to death. Realizing the extreme danger that he was in, the dreamer grabbed a small dog and paraded around with it over his shoulders, begging that it be sacrificed instead of him. Finally the dog was clubbed to death and roasted in flames as an offering to the demon of war, "begging him [the demon of war] to accept this semblance instead of the reality of the dream…"

Dreams have exercised a special fascination from ancient times to the present. The Egyptian pharaohs believed that dreams were messages from the gods, and Hippocrates, the "father of medicine," wrote a lengthy treatise on dreams. The classical Chinese Taoists were interested in speculating on whether dreams were more real than everyday life, and many societies, including that of the Fiji islanders, believed that dreams represented the wanderings of the soul. In modern times August Kekulé von Stadowitz, an organic chemist, was pondering on the structure of the benzene molecule when he had a dream that revealed its formation. The dream included the symbolism of a snake eating its tail—a symbol of alchemical mythology. One of the most famous predictive dreams is Abraham Lincoln's dream of his own assassination, while another dreamer, J.W. Dunne, formulated the philosophy of "serial time" on the basis of his dreams. He had developed the particular faculty of predictive dreaming, and on one occasion he dreamed that the *Flying Scotsman* steam train would crash near the Forth Bridge in Scotland several months before it did so, in April 1914. Dunne speculated that the universe consisted of parallel bands, or spectra, of events and that events occurred at one level before another. In this way, he thought, the dreamer or clairvoyant may have access to a plane of reality before the events they "see" are manifested in the everyday world; dreams thus reveal a different dimension of causality.

Dreams play a special role in esoteric and occult thought. Apart from their elusive and mysterious quality, dreams are also regarded by modern-day occultists as being significant for two major reasons. First, Jung's analysis of dreams has provided us with several important concepts—like the collective unconscious and the theory of the archetypes—which are the basis of much modern magical thinking. Secondly, the dream may be used as part of a technique for "astral traveling."

While it is true that Freud first showed that dreams relate to the *dreamer*, rather than being portents from external deities, Jung discovered that the religious side of dreaming could be explained by potent, mystical energies buried deep in the psyche itself. Originally, Freud had thought that dreams were most relevant to a person's *conscious* thoughts. He soon discovered, however, that when patients were encouraged to discuss their dreams, they would uncover *unconscious* elements as well. These often revealed neuroses, and thus, if the patients could recognize the symptoms, they could benefit therapeutically from the analysis of their dreams.

Freud tended to analyze dreams from the viewpoint of their having certain motifs whose meaning was constant. The following is a typically Freudian dream analysis, and was made by a particularly fervent follower of Freud, Angel Garma, a Spanish psychoanalyst.

Dream: "A lion was pursuing me and I wanted to escape. I was shut up in a room, and I could not find the door to get out. I felt terribly anxious…" **Garma's explanation:** *"Dreams such as this are frequent in women who have not yet started a normal heterosexual life. An unmarried woman often has the above dream. The lion, like wild animals, monsters, or abnormal, or bad, people, represents a sexually excited man pursuing her. She cannot escape because of her own desires."*

Right: Sigmund Freud (1856–1939), the founder of psychoanalysis and author of The Interpretation of Dreams *(1900), was a pioneer in the field of dream analysis. He and his former pupil, Carl Jung (1875–1961), would disagree over their respective dream theories, Jung later going on to propound his arguments for archetypes and the collective unconscious.*

Another, more contrived, Freudian analysis follows.

Dream: "My father tells me that if I do not pass my B.A. examination I shall not be able to marry George...." **Explanation:** *"A woman dreamed this shortly before her marriage. She doubted her instinctive capacity, which appears as anxiety about her B.A. exam. The father is her superego, or psychoanalyst, telling her that she cannot marry unless her genital response is normal."*

Where Freud and his school have tended to uncover sexual motifs in dreams, Jung was anxious to discover why certain symbols rather than others occurred in dreams. For example, a key in a lock, the wielding of a heavy stick, or a battering ram may all occur in dreams as sexual motifs. Jung wrote: "The real task is to understand why the key has been preferred to the stick, or the stick to the ram. And sometimes this might even lead one to discover that it is not the sexual act at all that is represented, but some quite different psychological point."

Jung furthermore made the vital discovery that not all the contents of a dream relate to *personal* memories or neuroses; this is extremely relevant to magical theory. "There are many symbols," he wrote, "that are not individual but collective in their nature and origin…" These were images that Jung called the "archetypes of the collective unconscious," and in effect they represent a body of mythological images that recur throughout the psychic history of humankind, in all human creative functions: for example, in art, music, legends and poetry. Jung believed that because humans had experienced certain "constants" in their environment, like the Sun, Moon, stars, ocean and changes of season, they began to formulate these as basic images in their psyches. However, they were not impressed upon humans in an abstract way, but as deities of nature, so that all these forces of nature became gods. As a result of thousands of analyses of dreams from this level of the mind, Jung claimed that what was revealed was the myth or symbol—the *archetype*—rather than the process or event itself. The mind, he believed, tended to formulate these experiences in an anthropomorphic way.

The Sun is an especially significant archetype and has long been an object of veneration because of its eternal nature, and because it is the source of life and light. Sun gods are found in many religions—Apollo Helios in Greece; Ohrmazd in ancient Persia; Osiris in ancient Egypt; and Christ. They invariably represent life, rebirth, light and purity. Jung said that they are relevant to our psyches because they represent symbols of inner harmony and integration. He believed that one of the main functions of the psychoanalysis of dreams was to come to terms with what the subconscious was trying to say in the dream. In other words, one has to recognize both the personal and archetypal content of the dream and try to learn the lessons of the symbolism.

Many practitioners of modern magic accept the Jungian view that the gods of mythology, which may be revealed in dreams, visions, trances, or rituals, represent inner processes that are normally subconscious. Using the tree of life, which equates these gods to symbols of the mind, magicians gradually come to understand and integrate the more transcendental processes of their minds.

The second major function of dreams in esoteric thought is their use as a method of astral projection (or out-of-body experience). Dr. Celia Green noted in her book *Lucid Dreams* that we can now separate as a special category those dreams in which dreamers know they are dreaming. They find themselves conscious within the dream and are sometimes able to direct their dreams—and their actions within them. When this occurs, dreamers may experience the very remarkable process of finding themselves "outside their bodies." It is as if they have entered a new time-space location, which is populated not by the objects of the real world, but rather by their thoughts, their imaginings and perhaps the symbols of their unconscious minds.

Magicians recognize in this phenomenon an extraordinary new dimension of life and being. They find new access to their creative energies and sources of inspiration; they find themselves in weird and surreal mythological landscapes; they discover that they can move without the limitations of their physical bodies to any location they will themselves to go to.

Because of this strange application of the dream state, psychical researcher Sylvan

Muldoon decided to formulate an exercise of dreaming in which one willed oneself to dream in a certain way. The dreamer had to try to retain his or her consciousness in the dream state and could then *will* certain images to appear in a certain sequence by "directing" his or her dream. Out-of-body experiences are related to dreams of flying and floating, and Muldoon suggested that if people willed themselves to dream these sequences, they could find themselves traveling astrally into new dimensions of the mind.

Dreams are thus valuable not only for an analysis of sexual and other neuroses, but they may also be used as a technique for acquiring magical consciousness. The dream, on the one hand, is a sequence of visual events that demands understanding. But it is also the realm of ideas and processes of thought—a realm that allows magicians to impose their will upon these ideas and to use the dream to increase the range of their perceptions.

Opposite and above:
Rather than taking them at face value, psychologists agree that the surreal and irrational images that appear in our dreams should be regarded as symbolic messages from the unconscious mind, to be interpreted analogically and not literally.

Below: As well as its use as a suggestive technique, hypnosis may also unlock areas of the mind that cannot be accessed consciously — sometimes with extraordinary results. In this photograph the Reverend Carroll Jay of Virginia hypnotizes a subject who speaks no German, but who can speak this language fluently under hypnosis. Many subjects speak of their past lives during regressive-hypnosis sessions.

Hypnotism, Autosuggestion, and Relaxation

Hypnotism, as a device for inducing a sleep-like trance, is an age-old technique. In general, it depends on the abilities of hypnotists to relax their patients and allow them to enter a mental state in which they become more suggestible to commands. In most cases, a skilled practitioner can induce a hypnotic state in around ten minutes, and the effects can be startling.

As an object of amusement, hypnotic and posthypnotic suggestion have often been used as a stage act. People may, for example, be given an instruction while under hypnosis that they should cough ten minutes after awakening. They return to their seat as members of the audience and, quite without knowing why, begin to splutter and choke as commanded.

There is, however, a more serious side to hypnotism, and this is as a medical therapy. Dr. Harvey Doney, working at the Toronto Rehabilitation Center, used hypnotism to suggest to cardiac patients that clean, fresh air was coursing into their lungs and filling their bodies with oxygen and energy. Electrocardiograms showed that, after a six-month period of the therapy, these patients were as healthy as the members of another group, who had had to practice regular physical exercise.

Hypnotism has been used successfully as an anaesthetic in surgical operations and by dentists. It has also been found that difficult childbirths can be rendered virtually painless by hypnosis. Dr. George Newbold, a British gynecologist, stated: "After witnessing many labors during which the patient is restless and dis-

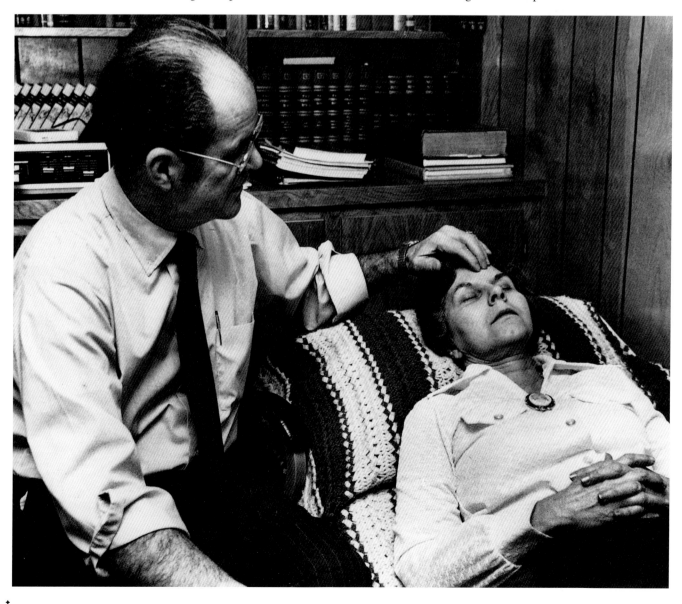

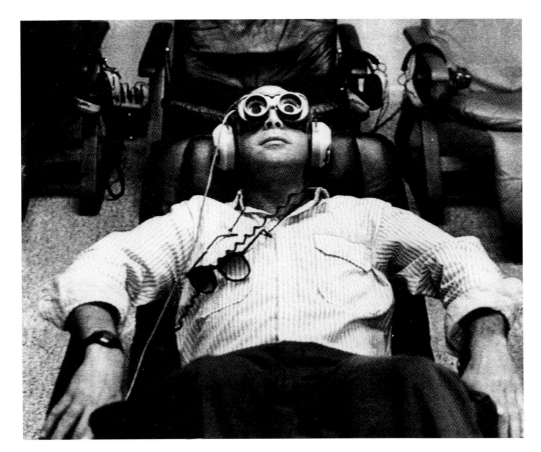

Left: Various methods can be employed to achieve a relaxed state of mind, including visualization. At "Mindworld" in Miami, Florida, a subject relaxes by listening to calming music and wearing special goggles. Many occultists advocate such "active" techniques of relaxation for achieving enlightenment over the traditional, passive, forms of hypnosis.

tressed from pain and discomfort, the sight of one conducted under hypnosis may well seem to the onlooker to be something in the nature of a revelation."

As a technique of the esoteric world, hypnotism has not attracted as much attention as might be expected, mainly because it places the "patient" in a state of passive helplessness. Currently, disciplines like yoga and meditation, which stress that people have to achieve higher states of awareness by themselves, have proven more relevant. However, the technique of autosuggestion, which is, in effect, a form of self-hypnosis, does play a significant part in the occult, both as a relaxation exercise and for visualization purposes.

One of the best methods is a relaxation technique used in recent Mind Dynamics training and similar fields. It is also found in a related form in practical Gurdjieff training. We include it here because meditators have to tell themselves that certain things are becoming real to them, and that their consciousness is moving, as it were, into "new areas." The method is as follows. Meditators first inform themselves that they are becoming drenched in beautiful, red colors; as they relax each part of their bod-

ies in turn—from their heads down to their toes—they are becoming filled with "redness." Then they imagine that, as they become more restful, their bodies are now filled with an exquisite, orange color. They gradually work their way downward, passing through all the colors of the rainbow. Thus they become increasingly relaxed.

According to the Mind Dynamics organization, this produces an alpha state of mind, which allows much greater mystical awareness. The organization has established a visualization exercise, in which the meditator "builds" a "workshop" in yellow colors in an imagined, peaceful environment called "the passive scene in nature." In this workshop are placed time-control devices, special medicines and equipment, and an inexhaustible library, all of which are "imagined into reality." They become useful mental aids for reaching into the subconscious and for finding solutions to problems that perhaps could not be solved in the conscious, awakened state.

Magic makes use of similar techniques of relaxation. Once in a relaxed state, magicians have to imagine themselves into a context that they wish to enter. If they want to "balance"

Right: As well as being used as a medical therapy, suggestive hypnosis may also have a place in surgery. In cases of patients who are particularly responsive to hypnotic suggestion, even anaesthetic drugs are rendered unnecessary. During the operation pictured here, which was carried out in Milan in 1961, the patient, Pierina, made medical history by successfully eschewing anaesthetics in favor of hypnosis.

their personalities with intellect, they may will themselves to see the form of Michael, the archangel of fire (intelligence), and converse with him. They build up a visual impression of Michael, calling him forth in a type of mental invocation. Here, magicians are asking a particular facet of their minds to appear in a visual form. They are bringing into their consciousness certain faculties and energies that were hitherto unconscious.

Again, by means of autosuggestion when in a relaxed state, magicians may wish to explore their minds by traveling along the symbolic Tarot paths. They have to tell themselves that the imagery of, say, *The Star*, or *The Chariot*, is becoming increasingly real to them in all its detail. They visualize the environment in its symbolic form portrayed on the Tarot card. They then find that their consciousness has uncovered new, mystical areas of their minds that they might never have suspected were there.

Thus, magic makes use of hypnotic suggestion only as an adjunct to visualization. It places the meditator, rather than another person, in control. It operates with certain visual aids in mind, like the Tarot cards, or images

from mythology, and it is used primarily to achieve transcendental states of awareness.

Tʀᴀⁿᴄᴇ Cᴏⁿsᴄᵎᴏᴜsⁿᴇss

The main viewpoint underlying trance methods in magic is that we all have a number of bodies of perception, not merely the one we use in our daily lives. If we are able to put our physical body to "sleep" by some means, we then have other, optional realms of perception open to us. Going into a trance is a means of rendering the physical body inert, so that the consciousness is free to go on a mystical journey. It is thus an area strongly related both to out-of-body experiences and shamanism.

Trance consciousness has been traditionally important in indigenous societies, such as in South America and Indonesia, but it also plays a major role in modern magic. It was the main method employed by two remarkable trance occultists, Austin Spare and Victor Angel, both of whom relied on trance inspiration for their painting.

The occult technique for entering the trance state is an extension of a gradual relaxation exercise, in which the body is "put to sleep" in stages. However, it is equally important that the full spectrum of consciousness is retained, even though the physical organism is gradually made inoperative. Occultists who use the tree of life symbol in their meditations regard the tree, in one sense, as growing within them. It becomes a representation of the divine energies that dwell in all of us. For this reason, it is also connected with energy centers known in yoga as *chakras*. Occultists try to activate their *chakras* to allow them greater visionary activity, while their bodies sink deep into a state of trancelike relaxation at the same time.

The activation comes first. Occultists imagine a white light descending from above their heads and they vibrate to the mantra "Eee-Hee-Yeh," a sacred name taken from the Qabalah. The light now descends to the throat and is imagined to radiate forth in the form of mauve light. This time the mantra is "Ye-Ho-Waa-El-Oh-Him." Descending further, it reaches the region of the heart and solar plexus. It has now been transformed into a golden-yellow light, and the mantra is "Ye-Ho-Waa, Al-Oaa, Vaaa Daath." Now it moves from the heart down to the region of the genitals … and the light changes from yellow into a rich, deep purple; "Sha-Dai El-Haiii." Finally the light reaches the feet, and the colors of earth—russet, citrine, black and olive—are visualized. The final mantra is "Aaa-Doh-Naii, Haaa, Aaa-retz." These mantras are the names of God in the Qabalah and are used because

of their uplifting, vibrationary qualities. Thus the first stage of activation is completed.

Occultists now imagine white light streaming down their left sides, beneath their feet and up their right sides to the top of their heads. They then visualize a similar band of light energy traveling from their heads down along their noses to their chests and legs, once again beneath the feet, and up past the back of the legs to the head. In their minds, they have thus enclosed their bodies, which may be lying horizontally or be seated in meditation. Their breathing is deep and regular. They imagine that the boundaries of light define a type of translucent container, which is actually their own "consciousness."

The second, crucial stage is to transfer the consciousness out of their bodies. The meditators now have to imagine that their "containers" are filling up, perhaps with liquid, and that the remaining space inside the container, the "air," represents the extent of their consciousness. As the liquid fills the body, so that part slowly relaxes and goes to sleep. At first the legs are filled, and one is aware of the body only above the knees. Then the level rises, and consciousness extends only to that part of the body above the chest. Soon the only conscious part remaining is the head, for the rest has fallen into trance and is, to all extents and purposes, "inert." It is at this last stage, when the consciousness, or "mind," is leaving the body, that the act of astral projection occurs. As

Left: By touching the forehead of this American Indian Movement activist, Lakota Sioux medicine man Leonard Crow Dog induces a state of calm concentration. Such relaxation techniques have parallels with trance consciousness, whether for religious or magical meditation.

already mentioned, occultists believe that if the external, physical body becomes inactive, the next, "inner body" is awakened. All the perceptive processes are now transferred to an area of the mind that would normally be unconscious. But it is like transferring one's perception to a living dream: one is no longer bound by the body and can travel according to one's will. Sometimes fantasy elements from the unconscious also appear, and these will seem as real as "normal" reality.

Meanwhile the body remains in a state of trance. Some projectionists claim that a silver cord can be seen connecting the physical and "astral" bodies, although according to Dr. Celia Green, a prominent researcher into out-of-body experiences, this is not always the case.

Magicians who use the Qabalistic mantras usually find that chanting in itself becomes a type of directive to the unconscious mind to unleash certain visionary experiences. It becomes possible at this stage to imagine oneself into locations that are totally subject to the will of the practitioner, and it is this faculty of creative imagination that is the essence of magic. If occultists are using the Tarot cards as stepping stones, they will try to imagine themselves confronting the maiden of the last Tarot card, *The Universe* or *World*. They can then travel along the paths represented by the other cards in turn, until they get deeper and deeper into the spiritual areas of their minds.

In the meantime, the physical body remains in a state of trance. Should the occultists wish to return, they may gradually ease themselves back into their bodies and "awaken." The controlled act of projection has led a number of writers to theorize that this trance technique in some respects resembles the act of dying.

Right: Many methods may be used to attain trancelike states. Adherents of the Brazilian Macumba faith, like this woman, dance to a hypnotic drumbeat or chant to achieve a state of ecstatic consciousness. Occultists, too, employ mantras (as well as visualization techniques) to help them escape the "domination" of their conscious minds.

Left: In mythology, the rainbow is a symbol of the bridge between heaven and earth, and it is thus often equated with the silver cord that connects the physical and astral "bodies." The colors of the rainbow can also be used as meditational aids to relaxation: members of the Mind Dynamics organization, for example, visualize their bodies being successively saturated with each color of the rainbow's spectrum until they have attained an enlightened state of consciousness, or complete (white) light.

Out-of-Body Consciousness

In past decades, the phenomenon originally known among occultists as "astral projection" has assumed a position of prominence in parapsychological circles. It has been the subject of special investigation by researchers like Professor Charles Tart of U.C.L.A., and Dr. Celia Green, who headed the Institute of Psychophysical Studies at Oxford, England.

An out-of-body experience (O.B.E.) is one in which someone feels that he or she is observing his or her surroundings from a position away from the body. One of Celia Green's subjects suddenly felt himself floating high in the sky while riding a motorbike at speed through the countryside; normally, however, the body is more passive.

An out-of-body experience usually takes place when a person is drowsy, relaxed, sick or inert. E.E.G. readings have revealed that these experiences share some characteristics with dreams, but there is one important distinguishing feature: they seem to be subject to *will*, unlike most dreams (which incorporate random images), and they are characterized by a perceptive quality that is as clear as normal waking consciousness.

According to Ernest de Martino, an Italian ethnographer, out-of-body experiences in "primitive" societies have been documented in myths and legends as the "wanderings of the soul," and the worldwide belief in an afterlife may be a folk memory of this phenomenon.

In Western society, it has only been in the twentieth century that astral traveling has been documented in detail, although several references to it are found in classical literature.

The three most noted modern pioneers of the out-of-body experience were Sylvan Muldoon, Oliver Fox (the pseudonym of Hugh Callaway) and Robert A. Monroe, although others, including researchers Ralph Shirley, former editor of the *Occult Review*, and "Yram" (Marcel Fohan) also made significant contributions.

Sylvan Muldoon came from a family interested in spiritualist matters, and it was while attending a spiritualist meeting in Clinton, Iowa, at the age of twelve, that he had his first out-of-body venture. He felt he had fallen into what he called a "silent, dark and feelingless condition," and then suddenly found that he could project a part of himself outside his body: "I managed to turn around…There were two of me!"

Muldoon also described a feature that is regarded by many as characteristic of out-of-body experiences: the silvery, elastic cord that is said to join the astral body to the physical body. As Muldoon "walked around in the air," this cord maintained a connection between his astral consciousness and his inert, slumbering body. He had merely transferred his perception outside his normal frame of reference. Muldoon believed that the astral body was, in a sense, more "real" than the physical body and, in fact, constituted the "life" element. On death, the astral body would sever the cord-link with the

Above: Guardian angels watch over infants as they sleep. Many who have reported near-death experiences recall that they encountered in their out-of-body state benevolent supernatural beings, like angels, who told them to return to their physical bodies because it was not yet the proper time for them to die.

physical body and would not return. Soviet parapsychologists similarly formulated the idea of the "bioplasmic body"—a type of energy prototype of the physical which, like the D.N.A. code, regulates and maintains the physical organism. This view also found support from the American researcher Dr. Stanley Krippner.

Muldoon, however, not only described his subsequent experiences in his important work *The Projection of the Astral Body* (1929), but went on to outline the means of achieving this state of consciousness. He evolved techniques of dream control whereby people would try to will themselves to dream a sequence of events that would involve the separation of the astral and physical bodies. One of these techniques was to imagine oneself ascending in an elevator and alighting on the top floor. Others were to swim, fly or ride in a balloon.

Muldoon highlighted another important aspect of the out-of-body experience: usually the perceived surroundings correspond exactly to reality. Sometimes one may feel one has traveled to a friend's or relative's house and is observing current situations that can be subsequently verified for accuracy. The second major category of experience, however, entails

fantasy elements from the subconscious mind. These were present in the accounts of both Oliver Fox and Robert A. Monroe.

Oliver Fox's accounts of his experiences outside his body first appeared in the *Occult Review* in 1920. Like Muldoon, Fox placed a strong emphasis on dream control. He believed that the out-of-body experience occurred with the "dream of knowledge," which happened when one *realized* that one was dreaming and could then act within that framework. (This type of dream was referred to by Celia Green as the "lucid dream.") The dreamer could now enter the realm that had hitherto been unconscious. He often found himself observing people who were shrouded in an aura of rich and dazzling colors. Similar descriptions of auras are given in Bishop Leadbeater's book on clairvoyance and the astral planes.

Initially, Fox considered that the "dream of knowledge" was the only means available for attaining the out-of-body state. Later, he realized that the relaxation of the body could produce a similar effect. During relaxation, one would feel oneself autohypnotically overcome by a sense of numbness; then it was almost like escaping through a trapdoor in the brain. Fox called this the "pineal door" method. On one occasion, Fox felt that he was falling down a long shaft, and the tunnel is a common motif in out-of-body experiences. Fox was overcome by a sense of darkness and silence and then noticed that he seemed to be naked and bleeding, as if from wounds; it occurred to him that he was dying. Then, as if he had suddenly entered the realm of Greek mythology, he heard a voice demanding: "Say thou art Theseus. I am Oliver Fox."

Strange, mythological encounters and visions such as Fox's are commonly reported in the out-of-body state and in near-death experiences and lend some credence to the view of *The Tibetan Book of the Dead* that on death one's consciousness leaves the body and has visions of heavens and hells which are, in reality, states of harmony and disorder in the mind.

Through the work of such researchers as the American physician Raymond Moody, whose book *Life After Life* was published in 1975, and Kenneth Ring, a founding member of the International Association of Near-Death Studies at the University of Connecticut, a further phe-

nomenon related to out-of-body (
has also been identified: that
experience (N.D.E.). In comm
of-body state, some indi
approaching death, or inde
dead, experience the ser
their physical bodies,
detachment. Other as
feeling of peace; trav
a bright light; meet
"angels" (or even
tell them to re
despite their r
tics believe
attributabl
nomena
describ
tual c
R
Jo

it.
ork
ewed
n, and
iological
es Tart at
experiences
ring sessions
ta during sleep.
served the same
ribed and said that
trapped in a vise.
strange sensation that
ody in an elastic way
fines; he was able to feel
usual reach. But another
ed itself: his fingers were not
nodox sense, but were passing
al objects. A number of subjects
claimed that during out-of-body
they have floated upward through
ceilings and observed with remark-
ty the night sky and surroundings, as
from a considerable height.

Monroe subsequently discovered that he could travel to see his friends in the out-of-body state. On one occasion, he observed a friend loading an unfamiliar mechanical device into the back of his car and, when discussing the incident with him later, discovered that it was a generator. Like Fox, Monroe also entered strange, inner-plane locations, which he designated "Locale II" and "Locale III"; "Locale I" represented more ordinary, everyday imagery. On the former occasions,

lved in time-warp phe-
enery and, on one occa-
ic location similar to the
t card (The Last) Judgement.
criptions parallel those found
works of writers who have used
ss-enhancing substances.
characteristics of the out-of-body
e are therefore as follows.
onscious component (the mind, or
) appears to leave the body, and the lat-
emains apparently inert, as if in a state of
p sleep or trance.

Sometimes, but not always, the person seems to have a second body, connected to the first by means of a silver cord.

✦ It becomes possible in the astral state to travel through physical barriers and to travel considerable distances "at the speed of thought." The *will* is an important feature, since it determines the form the experience will take or the location one will visit.

✦ Astral traveling can involve purely physical locations, fantastical locations of the mind, including heaven and hell, or episodes apparently taken from mythology. In such instances, they become as real to the observer as is reality in waking consciousness.

Left: Astral travelers and dreamers may meet figures from mythology during their out-of-body experiences or dreams. One explanation for this phenomenon may be that they are encountering facets of their own imaginations that are symbolized by mythological archetypes. Another viewpoint postulates that such visions are the result of the disintegration of the conscious mind, revealing the disordered and fantastical world of the unconscious.

Possession and Exorcism

Throughout history and across a wide range of cultures and societies, various states of consciousness, specifically those associated with ecstasy—including poetic and artistic inspiration, religious fervor, drunkenness, sexual frenzy, trance and other states outside the usual range of ordinary, everyday experience—have often been classified as resulting from the influence upon individuals of forces, powers or beings outside their own personalities. The cause of such influence has been given a variety of explanations—such as devils, gods, spirits, the dead, elementals, nature spirits, angels and ghosts—but inevitably the idea has developed that humans can be taken over by an external force, which operates through individuals without their conscious cooperation and usually against their will. This concept is reflected in popular exclamations like "he is not himself today," or "something has got into him," implying that the individual can, sometimes literally, not be "him- or herself."

Possession is not a new concept: throughout history, virtually all societies have recognized that it is possible for people to be "taken over" by an influence or entity outside themselves. Two types of possession have been universally recognized. Voluntary possession occurs when individuals allow themselves to be possessed by an entity—as do Spiritualist mediums—to enable the entity to manifest itself when it could not ordinarily do so. This includes possession by the spirits of the dead, spirits of nature and the gods—especially for the purposes of prophecy—as well as the type of possession that is found among Christian Pentecostalists. Involuntary possession occurs when individuals do not freely allow themselves to be possessed, but are taken over involuntarily by an external force that is generally evil, and destructive to them.

In popular terminology, the word "possession" covers a wide range of phenomena, but in more precise usage it should only be applied to one category of a group of three. Individuals can be influenced by external forces in a variety of ways. The first category can be termed "influenced." Individuals may be aware of an influence, of varying degrees of power, that affects their thoughts or behavior and does not originate from within them. In some methods of divination, individuals allow themselves to be influenced by external forces. At its simplest level, influence includes the sorts of "feelings" that many individuals get in certain localities, and about certain people.

In the second category, obsession, individuals are aware of an influence that is affecting their thoughts and behavior to a more marked

Below: This painting by Fungai (c. 1460–1516) graphically depicts St. Catherine of Siena (1347–80) successfully exorcising a devil from a possessed woman. Officials of the Catholic Church perform exorcisms in accordance with the centuries-old Rituale Romanum; *within other Christian churches the power of exorcism is believed to have been granted by the Holy Spirit to the charismatic minister.*

degree than is caused simply by "influence," and are unable to liberate themselves from it. It has, so to speak, become attached to them, but remains "outside" them. Possession itself describes a state in which individuals' personalities are displaced by other entities that gain control, to varying degrees, of their bodies. Individuals need not necessarily be aware that anything is happening, or have any memories of it after the possession is over, since they were not "there" at the time. Individuals come under the influence of external entities in a variety of ways, sometimes quite accidentally (for example, by entering a house in which a restless entity exists) and sometimes due to their own action (for example, by playing with occult rituals); in each case, the actual degree of influence varies.

Whether or not individuals can actually be possessed by external entities remains a matter of speculation; nevertheless, there have been innumerable cases in which it appears that the subjects were, and in which exorcism proved successful as a therapy.

The psychologically unbalanced, particularly those suffering from specific types of disorder (e.g. paranoia or schizophrenia), may believe that they are being persecuted by someone, or something, external to themselves, or even that they are being attacked from within by various forces. Individuals suffering from compulsive thoughts or desires may interpret these as originating from outside themselves, believing that they are being "planted" in their minds by enemies or evil spirits. It certainly appears to the individuals so affected that they are being "made" to do things against their will by someone, or something, else.

A wide range of influences can cause the experience of believing oneself to be obsessed or possessed. Sexual frustration or imbalance is influential in causing the welling-up of psychic energy, which is unsuccessfully seeking an outlet and is therefore introverting, causing a variety of conflicts within the individual. This is especially evident in cases in which devoutly religious and highly puritanical individuals suffer from what they interpret as obsession or possession, characterized by "impure" thoughts and desires. It must be recognized that the majority of cases in which possession, obsession or even influence are alleged can be

Left: Ectoplasm issues from the mouth of a medium whom Conan Doyle once consulted. Although widely derided as a product of trickery, many believe that ectoplasm is the physical materialization of the spirits that mediums have voluntarily allowed to possess their bodies.

explained in much simpler psychological terms, and the terms relating to possession should be reserved only for those cases in which all alternative explanations fail. These would be characterized by: symptoms that do not respond to the usual methods of treatment, either medical or psychological; cases in which the individual is otherwise healthy and well-balanced and exhibits no indications of being mentally disturbed (apart from the actual symptoms of the possession or obsession); cases in which there is an indication that unorthodox (from a psychological point of view) treatment—in the traditions of exorcism—will cause a response and an improvement.

Whether or not they are accepted as cases of possession or obsession in the traditional sense, there are cases in which these conditions are fulfilled, and which respond to exorcism but not to traditional medical or psychiatric techniques.

There are many case studies in the field, although some of them can be explained in terms other than those involving possession or obsession. Some examples may help to clarify the three concepts.

A classic case of possession is as follows: a young boy, after a period of showing signs of disturbance and restlessness, nightmares, loss of appetite, uncontrolled aggression and loss of concentration, suddenly begins lapsing into

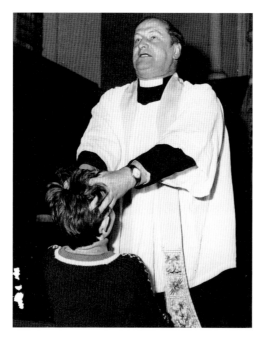

states of violent anger, during which his body is thrown into an uncontrolled frenzy, and he screams and shouts. In the course of these "fits," he converses with onlookers, almost as though he is "someone else"; when he returns to his normal state, he is unable to remember anything that happened, but suffers nevertheless as a consequence of the contortions of his body. His physical condition endangers his health. Extensive medical and psychiatric diagnoses reveal that the symptoms do not result from any physical cause (e.g. epilepsy or brain damage) and that the boy, in his normal state, is quite healthy psychologically. However, he continues to manifest a secondary personality of a violent, destructive nature. Eventually, a rite of exorcism is performed and, after several repetitions, the symptoms completely disappear. This is a case in which conventional medical and psychiatric treatment had no effect, and in which possession can be advanced as a reasonable explanation.

The following example illustrates obsession: a woman begins to find that thoughts are intruding into her consciousness, encouraging her to go to live with an aunt whom she dislikes. The thoughts eventually manifest themselves as voices, which are audible to the woman but not to anyone else. She is consciously aware that they are not her own thoughts, but is unable to prevent them or put them out of her mind; it seems to her that someone is actually talking to her. She begins to "see" the aunt in her mind, and the image becomes annoying because of its frequent occurrence. She undertakes all types of activities—physical and intellectual—to distract herself from the obsession, but cannot do so. A doctor determines that her health is good but is being undermined by this problem. She consults a psychiatrist, who can locate no immediate cause of the problem. She has no guilt feelings about the aunt and presents herself as a well-balanced, healthy woman. Despite both medical and psychiatric treatment, the problem continues. The woman eventually consults an occultist, who tells her that the aunt is involved in witchcraft and has been employing an obsessing entity, created by some form of ritual magic, to try to get her to live with her. The occultist performs a magical exorcism, and all symptoms cease.

Influence can be exemplified as follows: a man consults a Spiritualist medium and thereafter feels that he is being followed by a vague, undefined figure, which is neither hostile nor friendly, but simply annoying. There is no feeling of obsessive influence: the figure simply follows him, and this in itself is disturbing. Believing it to be a problem within himself, rather than an external reality (possibly relating to the fact that he, because of his religious background, feels guilty about attending the Spiritualist seance), he consults a psychologist. After a period of treatment, the figure still remains. The psychologist refers him to a religious minister, who performs an exorcism. The figure disappears and never returns.

These three instances, simplified in the telling from the original cases, give clear-cut examples of types of possession; in detail, actual cases are rarely as straightforward or as easily resolved.

Genuine cases of possession, obsession and influence are exceptional; most alleged instances have alternative explanations. Unfortunately, with the modern revival of an often uninformed interest in the occult, there is a tendency to accept at face value every claim of possession, and to offer exorcism as an immediate and practical solution. It should be remembered that exorcism itself, when performed in cases in which there is no possession or obsession, can cause the individual to be exposed to all manner of undesirable influences.

Any belief systems that allow for possession and obsession, or for the influencing of individuals or places by evil forces, necessarily include provision for the destruction of those evil forces. Exorcism—the casting-out of evil forces or devils—has been a part of human history ever since humans first personified the forces of nature and divided the powers around them into good and evil. Every society that recognizes possession also recognizes, and makes provision for, some form of exorcism, in which a superior power or skill is invoked to combat the evil. Essentially, exorcism refers to people, but it can also refer to the expulsion of evil influences from places (e.g. haunted houses).

Traditionally, exorcism has worked according to several basic principles: make things unpleasant enough for the possessing entity, and it will go away; use reason to trap the entity into doing something rash, and thus force it to go away; or summon a greater power and invoke it to force the entity to leave.

The methods used in different societies vary: some burn leaves; whip the possessed individual; create large amounts of noise in the expectation of frightening the entity away; try to trick it away from the body by placing tempting objects—food or sometimes animals—around the possessed individual; or summon the gods to banish the entity. Christian exorcism, although working on the basis of a different world view, traditionally employs the same procedures: incense, holy water and bells may be used to discomfort the entity; interrogation, challenges and threats are made to persuade the entity to leave; and, finally, God (or the Holy Spirit), is invoked to drive it away.

It is assumed almost everywhere that possession is accompanied by physical symptoms, including extreme loss of energy, nausea, pain and bleeding, and may give rise to supernatural powers on the part of the possessed (e.g. speaking in unknown tongues, or levitation). It is also widely recognized that most people cannot exorcise spirits, but some can do so by virtue of their natural skills (such as those in charismatic ministries), and others by virtue of the authority invested in them (for example, priests). Either way, the exorcist is in very real danger. The methods actually employed

in exorcism vary from one tradition to another and are usually chosen to suit the beliefs of the possessed person.

With the resurgence of interest in all things occult, psychiatry is taking a fresh look at exorcism (as well as possession)—not so much as an explanation, but as a technique that, even if it is founded upon nonscientific premises, tends to work effectively.

In general, exorcisms operate on the basis of a standard formula with three elements: the invocation of powers believed to be greater than those possessing the individual; the invocation of the possessing entity—and an attempt to discover who or what it is—while under the protection of the power previously invoked; and the direction of the exorcist's power to drive out the entity. The exorcist also casts a "protective field" around the possessed individual, in order to prevent the entity from re-entering the physical body.

Exorcism works on the basis of a belief in the existence of various powers in the universe, all possessing varying degrees of strength and engaged in a struggle for existence in this world through the agency of humans, who are thus caught in the middle of a cosmic battle. It is in the individual who is possessed, and is receiving exorcism, that this battle is most clearly manifested: the struggle between darkness and light, between good and evil, between God and the devil and between life and death.

There are a wide variety of techniques and traditions by which exorcism can be carried out. These traditions can be broadly classified as Christian, ritual magic or witchcraft. The Christian techniques essentially derive from the power of Jesus Christ and are based upon

Below: Evidence of possession is believed to manifest itself in the victim in various—generally unpleasant—ways, including abusive language, violent behavior, and involuntary convulsions.

the scriptural account of his disciples giving him the authority to cast out devils. The Christian techniques in turn divide into two branches. In the traditions of the Catholic and Eastern Orthodox churches, the power and authority to exorcise spirits is given to individuals by virtue of their ordination to the priesthood. Exorcism is performed sacramentally, in a ceremonial form, according to a carefully defined formula, with set rules and procedures. In the Protestant tradition, the power to exorcise spirits is taken as having been given to all Christians by Christ, but it is believed to manifest itself especially through individuals who have received that particular gift of the Holy Spirit, and thereby exercise a charismatic ministry. The exorcism tends not to have a prescribed formula, but will vary according to the wishes of the exorcist. It will generally not be ceremonial in form or follow any specifically defined procedure.

In ritual magic, the authority to exorcise spirits derives from knowledge, as magicians do not work by virtue of any authority given to them, but because of the power that they have acquired through self-preparation and learning. The exorcism will usually be ritual in character, making use of ceremonial forms and symbols, often involving the invocation of powers and leading ultimately to a confrontation between the possessing entity and the will of the magician. In some magical traditions, magicians may invoke the aid of the particular order or school to which they belong.

In witchcraft, the underlying principles for exorcisms are similar to those of ritual magic, although the emphasis is a more explicitly religious one, with exorcists invoking the gods and powers of their religion to drive out the possessing entity, and employing a range of traditional witchcraft rituals.

In their various approaches, many religious traditions, such as Judaism, Islam and Buddhism, also have provisions for exorcism, although they are not central to the concepts of the religions themselves.

Faịth-healịng

The term "faith-healing" is widely used to described a range of healing methods, many of which have nothing to do with either the faith of the healer or the faith of the patient, but they employ methods that are either unorthodox or presuppose some form of supernatural intervention in the healing process. They exclude such natural healing methods as naturopathy, osteopathy and homeopathy, which employ something—chemical or natural—that may be described as "medicine" and presuppose a physical origin and physical cure for illness. There are, however, exceptions, and the healers of the Philippines, for example, could be classified in either category, since they employ physical, but supposedly supernatural, methods in their healing.

Although the phrase "faith-healing" can be somewhat misleading, one can look at a tradition of healing dating from the earliest times to which this term can be applied. In some societies, shamans and magicians are called upon to drive out the evil spirits that are believed to be causing illness. They are traditionally regarded as diviners who can diagnose the nature of the sickness (usually a curse applied by another magician, the malevolence of an enemy or the invasion of an evil spirit) and then successfully cure it. These healers use a variety of techniques, often characterized by exorcism, and sometimes administer natural remedies (such as herbs) or provide spells or rituals for healing.

Right: Mary Baker Eddy (1821–1910), the founder of Christian Science (or the Church of Christ, Scientist). An invalid, she found temporary relief in the services of faith-healer Phineas Quimby, but later became disillusioned with his practices and turned instead to God's power of healing, which she promulgated through her church.

Faith-healing is characterized by its emphasis on the mind—or, in some approaches, on the soul or the spirit—as distinct from the body. The power that heals through faith-healing is believed to derive from a variety of sources—gods, spirits or natural forces—or simply from the power of suggestion that the healer holds over the patient. Usually, however, it is believed to originate from outside the healer, who is thus merely a vehicle through which it functions.

In the Western world, people who possessed natural gifts of healing were originally part of society, but as a result of the increasing power of the Christian Church, they tended to disappear, principally because their gifts were inevitably interpreted as the powers of the Devil, and they were therefore believed to be witches. The Church, keeping to itself the power of healing through the sacraments, declined to recognize that such gifts existed outside it, except through the agency of Satan. There were, however, individuals within the Church, including many of the great saints, to whom gifts of healing were attributed, or to whose remains or relics people flocked in search of healing. The miraculous cures associated with places like Lourdes provide examples of faith-healing within the context of the Church, but outside the established domain of the clergy.

It was Franz Anton Mesmer (1734–1815) who really began the fashion of faith-healing that has continued to modern times. Mesmer, an Austrian, claimed to cure his patients by placing them in contact with sources of "magnetism," which, he believed, was the vital life force, the absence or depletion of which caused illness. His patients sat around tubs filled with iron filings into which metal rods were stuck, and these rods, held by the patients, were said to convey magnetism into the patients' bodies. Convulsions, trances and comas were common among Mesmer's patients, and many of them afterward reported their illness cured or significantly improved. Mesmer claimed that his cures were based on natural scientific principles, not on anything miraculous or on divine intervention. His disciples continued to employ his techniques, but eventually much of the paraphernalia of Mesmerism, as it became known, disappeared, and it became a purely mental process, carried out without the help of iron rods or tubs of iron filings.

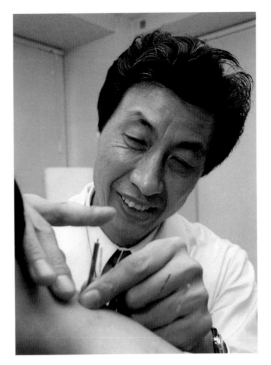

Left and below:
Acupuncture (left) differs from faith-healing, as practiced by Brother Isaiah, "Miracle Man of the Mississippi" (pictured below in 1943), in that it presupposes a physical cause for ailments which can therefore be alleviated by the insertion of needles in strategic points of the body. Brother Isaiah, on the other hand, believed in the traditional Christian power of prayer and the laying-on of hands as effective forms of faith-healing.

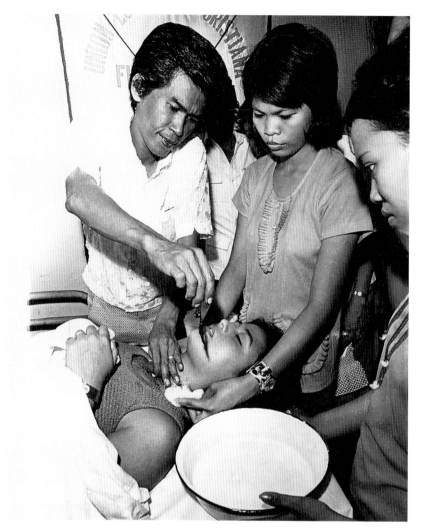

Above: *Psychic surgeons like Alex Orbito, pictured at work in Manila in 1974, claim to be able to carry out invasive surgery using psychic concentration as their only surgical tool. The psychic-surgery tradition is particularly prevalent in the Philippines and South America.*

In America, faith-healing was continued by Phineas Quimby, and it was later developed into Christian Science by his student, Mary Baker Eddy, who eventually came to deny the existence of matter, illness or death, believing them to be "errors" of the "mortal mind."

With the development of Spiritualism, a variety of associated healing techniques emerged, depending largely on mediums through whom various healers were said to manifest themselves. Some gave diagnoses and prescribed treatment, while others actually gave treatment, such as massage and the laying-on of hands.

An increasing interest in healing in the early years of the twentieth century stimulated a variety of approaches, and the Church also began to consider the restoration of the healing ministry which, in primitive times, had been so much a part of its work. Among the various Christian churches, the greatest interest in faith-healing was displayed by the Church of England, but other churches, both

orthodox and unorthodox, began to undertake healing. And the revival of interest in witchcraft also led to the emergence in that movement of healing techniques.

The techniques of faith-healing can be classified as follows.

⋆ *The laying-on of hands*—this is the traditional Christian method and is used by a variety of churches in conjunction with prayer.

⋆ *Sacramental healing*—used in the churches of the Catholic tradition, involving anointment with holy oil and the laying-on of hands, and known as Holy Unction.

⋆ *Prayer*—some groups use no physical actions at all but simply pray, either silently or out loud, for those who are to be healed.

⋆ *Ritual massage*—this technique, which involves running the hands over the body, is not intended to affect the physical body in the same way as, for example, physiotherapy, but is believed to affect invisible forces and to radiate healing power from the healer's hands.

⋆ *Ritual techniques*—as employed in witchcraft groups and by magicians, utilizing various symbols and ceremonies for the healing of the patient.

⋆ *Persuasion*—New Thought and Christian Science groups employ nothing more than the intellectual method of persuading the patient that the illness either does not exist or is not a natural state, and therefore that the mind is capable of overcoming it by the power of positive thinking.

⋆ *Psychic surgery*—used by some groups and healers, especially in the Philippines and South America, when the healer claims actually to open parts of the patient's body and to remove diseased material physically.

A wide range of groups employ various methods of faith-healing today. Church groups, especially Protestant bodies, use prayer and the laying-on of hands. Various associations of healers, such as the Order of St. Luke, have been formed as ecumenical groups in which healers from different churches can work. Christian Science and allied traditions, including New Thought, place a decided emphasis in their teaching and work on the ministry of healing, which they endeavor to accomplish by stressing thought and positive thinking. In Spiritualism, the healing ministry is accomplished largely through mediums whose spirit guides have been physicians or healers. Witchcraft uses spells and rituals for the healing of the sick. Additionally, there are a number of individuals—such as the British psychic Matthew Manning—who have claimed gifts of healing.

Does faith-healing work? There are certainly sufficient instances of individuals who claim to have been cured of a variety of illnesses to suggest that it does. But there are a number of possible alternative explanations. At one extreme, some say that faith-healing does not work at all: either those who claimed to have been healed were never sick, or else their healing was achieved by quite natural processes unrelated to faith-healing. Alternatively, faith-healing does not work in the sense of curing physical illness, but the applied effect of suggestion on the individual leads to the cure. Many of the illnesses cured by faith-healing are psychosomatic rather than "organic" in origin, according to this explanation. A third explanation holds that faith-healing employs natural techniques of utilizing forces presently unknown to orthodox science, but ultimately to be recognized as science advances. Kirlian photography is one phenomenon that suggests this possibility. Finally, some believe that faith-healing is dependent upon supernatural intervention by nonhuman forces and is therefore outside the domain of natural law.

The scientific evidence, based on intensive studies of a wide range of faith-healing techniques, suggests that there are some cases in which faith-healing has achieved the healing of disease. Further, the majority of cures effected by faith-healing are of diseases that are psychosomatic in origin, and not organic. Isolated cases still remain in which organic disease, conventionally diagnosed by medical doctors, appears to be cured by faith-healing, contrary to the expectations of medical science. In the vast majority of cases of alleged faith-healing, there has been no adequate diagnosis before the healing, and claims of cures for all manner of terrible diseases are unsubstantiated because it was never established that the patient suffered from them.

Ultimately, it would be very difficult to prove a cure. The patient would have to be suffering from an organic disease of a serious nature, which would not then cure itself by natural remission. The disease must be accurately diag-nosed by a number of independent physicians and preferably recorded in some way (e.g. by X-rays). This disease must not respond to any medical treatment, and the patient should not receive medical treatment close to the time of the alleged healing. The healing would have to be total, complete and immediate—that is, the disease would simply disappear at the time of faith-healing. The patient would then be re-examined extensively and diagnosed as being free of the disease. Such thoroughly proven cases are virtually unknown. As the purpose of healing is not the conversion of the skeptical, but the relief of the patient's pain, few healers would be interested in engaging in such scientific experiments.

Extrasensory Perception

Extrasensory perception (E.S.P.) is the ability to transmit and receive information by means other than the recognized senses. People sometimes surprise each other by simultaneously referring to obscure thoughts in conversation. Perhaps they act upon intuition about an unforeseeable course of action that later proves to be correct. Others will foresee an event before it occurs (premonition) or may receive "mental impressions" from friends while concentrating. All of these occurrences could be cited as examples of E.S.P., which is normally divided into three areas: clairvoyance, the extrasensory perception of events; telepathy, the direct "transmission" of ideas; and precognition, the perception of future events.

Below: Many research studies have indicated that twins—especially if they are identical—often possess an inherent ability to communicate telepathically with each other. Telepathy, like other forms of E.S.P., is believed to be inherited.

Above: *A laboratory at the Society for Psychical Research (S.P.R.), the organization set up in 1882 to investigate scientifically such paranormal phenomena as telepathy, hypnotism, clairvoyance, and spiritual apparitions. Despite its emphasis on scientific experimentation, some of the cases that the S.P.R. claimed to be genuine were later uncovered as frauds.*

Although such phenomena have always had a mystical tinge about them and have been traditionally regarded as faculties of soothsayers and oracles, the serious, scientific study of E.S.P. occurrences is less than a century old. In the nineteenth century, E.S.P. was considered to be a possible "sixth sense" and was researched by a number of important scientists, including Sir William Crookes, Sir Oliver Lodge and Alfred Wallace. In 1882 the famous Society for Psychical Research (S.P.R.) was founded at England's Cambridge University, with Henry Sidgwick as its first president.

As with all esoteric phenomena, for every possible genuine occurrence of E.S.P. there are countless falsifications. In this respect the S.P.R. got off to a bad start. In July 1882 Sidgwick prematurely announced that he had found conclusive evidence of E.S.P. in a clergyman (the Reverend Creery), his five daughters and their servant. Later, to Sedgwick's embarrassment, it was discovered that they had been using a code with which to trick the researchers. Another such case followed hard on its heels: that of Messrs. Smith and Blackburn. Smith would hold Blackburn's hands, concentrate, and would seem to read his thoughts as Blackburn imagined them. The S.P.R. investigated and recorded the case accordingly in its annals as being genuine. Years later, in 1908, however, Blackburn made the sensational admission that he had cheated during the sessions.

The test conditions for the early investigations were very poor, and the S.P.R. decided to try to improve and regulate its experimental procedures. From this time onward, research into E.S.P. took the form of tests in which subjects had to attempt to record above-chance odds in telepathic guessing sessions.

In England, G.N.M. Tyrrell constructed a device made of five boxes, each containing a light bulb. The circuitry was designed so that a certain bulb would light up when the lid of its box was lifted. The experiment tested possible telepathic communication between the subject and the experimenter, who decided which light would illuminate on each occasion. One of Tyrrell's subjects, a Miss Johnson, gained some high scores using this device. However, a colleague of Tyrrell's, G.W. Fisk, claimed that the experiment could only be valid if the selection of the lights was completely random. He said, quite rightly, that a person would tend not to choose the box that has just lit up. In the case of random numbers, however, a given number will follow itself about half the time. When Tyrrell introduced a "randomizer" into his device, Miss Johnson scored at only the normal rate of chance.

In the 1930s, serious research into E.S.P. was well under way in the United States, under the auspices of Dr. Joseph B. Rhine and his wife, Louisa, at Duke University. Earlier experiments had been carried out by Professor John Coover at Stanford and Professor William McDougall at Harvard, but Rhine's work was to be the most far-reaching. In 1932 he had some good results while using Zener cards with thirty-two subjects in a clairvoyance experiment. The cards had been designed by a colleague, K.E. Zener, and incorporated five distinct symbols: a square, a circle, a cross, three wavy lines and a star. Rhine's subjects scored 207 successes out of 800 tries, while chance results would have expected only 160. The odds against this happening were in excess of a million to one.

Rhine gradually discovered that his subjects performed best under certain conditions. In *Extra-Sensory Perception* (1934) he stressed that, for the best results, subjects should be open-minded, allowed an informal atmosphere rather than a restrictive one, and should be neither extravagantly praised nor discouraged in their results. He also found that subjects tended to improve after the first hundred test runs, and that friends often demonstrated a better "psychic" rapport than strangers.

Rhine's work received considerable attention in the 1930s, but several skeptical psychologists, including W.S. Cox at Princeton and J.H. Heinlein at Johns Hopkins, were unable to duplicate his findings. Some critics argued that it was easy to see through the cards or detect the imprint on the back surface of each card. Rhine insisted, however, that his results had been obtained using thick, opaque cards, and that his subjects had not been allowed to touch the cards in any way.

Another psychologist of the period, J.L. Kennedy, suggested in 1938 that future E.S.P. experiments should attempt to minimize all sensory cues—whether visual, auditory or "subliminal"—between experimenters, and that they should eliminate all types of preferences or nonrandomness. He also considered that at least two people should keep independent records of the scores and results.

In 1940 the Duke researchers published a book entitled *Extra-Sensory Perception After Sixty Years*. Professor Rhine and his colleagues considered a test held in October 1938 and February 1939 to be one of their best E.S.P. trials, because of its "advances in experimental precaution." There were two experimenters, J.L. Woodruff and J.G. Pratt, together with the subject. Pratt acted as "observer"; meanwhile, Woodruff sat at one end of a table, separated from the subject, who was seated at the other end, by an 18-inch-high screen. The screen had a one-way aperture, which allowed the experimenter to observe a pencil pointer held in the subject's hand. The subject had to guess the top card in the experimenter's hand by pointing with the pencil to one of five optional E.S.P. symbols on his side of the screen. Since the experimenter's pack consisted of twenty-five cards, this was the number of trials in each series. The "observer" also carefully recorded the symbol sequences as an extra check. Woodruff and Pratt held over 2,000 runs of twenty-five trials in this manner.

The result showed that thirty-two subjects scored 12,489 successful "hits" out of 60,000, when they could have expected 12,000 by chance. Nevertheless, the odds against the additional 489 hits occurring by chance were in excess of a million to one. One of Rhine's staunchest critics, Professor C.E.M. Hansel, admitted that there were "clear indications that something other than guesswork or experimental error was involved in this experiment, and also that its effects were by no means negligible in the case of at least one subject." However, Hansel believed that the case was not conclusive because there was no proof that the cards were properly shuffled between runs.

In England, Dr. S.G. Soal, a leading parapsychologist, attempted to duplicate the Rhine experiments, at first without success. However, Soal noticed that two of his subjects achieved significantly above-chance scores for both the card ahead and the one behind. One of these subjects, Basil Shackleton, was tested for E.S.P. by Soal and Mrs. K.M. Goldney between 1941 and 1943. Shackleton had to guess the identity of cards with drawings of certain animals on them. He sat in one room, while the experimenter sat in another, calling out when Shackleton should guess. They could not see each other. Meanwhile, the experimenter would show a random number to another person in the room (the "agent"), who would glance at a corresponding card. The test was to see whether Shackleton could telepathically predict which card would come next.

On one occasion, Shackleton managed to obtain scores of the "+1" type, that is, he guessed one card ahead. In 3,789 trials he was successful 1,101 times, when he should have

Left: The late Jerry Garcia, a member of the rock group The Grateful Dead. Known for its mind-expanding music and acceptance of countercultural practices, in 1971 the group and its audience participated in an experiment into "psychic transmission" with the parapsychologist Malcolm Bessent and the Maimodes Dream Laboratory.

Right: At a subsequent press conference, Edgar D. Mitchell, an astronaut in the Apollo 14 mission, discusses the experiment that he supervised in which astronauts communicated telepathically with four Earth-bound "recipients." Mitchell claimed a modest success rate.

scored only 776 by chance. In fact, he managed to achieve high scores on several occasions, and the tests were widely regarded as among the best ever held.

Most of the pioneering E.S.P. research was based on documented card-guessing sessions, and correspondingly most of the criticisms that arose were an attack on the "tightness" of the laboratory testing procedures. In recent decades, however, E.S.P. research spread to wider horizons. The *Apollo 14* astronauts undertook an E.S.P. experiment with colleagues on the Earth in 1971 and produced an above-chance test result. Dr. Eugene Konecci of NASA told an international astronautical conference in Paris in 1963 that the United States was now pursuing E.S.P. research more seriously, since it was apparent that the Soviets were investigating it as a means of communication in outer space.

In *Psychic Discoveries Behind the Iron Curtain*, Sheila Ostrander and Lynn Schroeder described Soviet attempts to "catch the tracks of telepathy as it arrived in the brain." Dr. Lutsia Pavlova of the University of Leningrad and Dr. Genady Sergeyev, a well-known mathematician, harnessed one of their best telepathic subjects, Karl Nikolaiev, to an electroencephalograph (E.E.G.) apparatus. His respiration, heartbeat, eye movements and brain-wave patterns were all recorded. Meanwhile, his friend Yuri Kamensky, a biophysicist, attempted to communicate telepathically with him from Moscow. Kamensky began to concentrate, and, three seconds later, Nikolaiev's brain waves changed drastically on the monitoring devices at Leningrad University. Dr. Pavlova said that, following further E.E.G. documentation of both subjects, it was clear that

when telepathic rapport was achieved, "the brain activation quickly becomes specific and switches to the rear, afferent regions of the brain."

This focusing of force-field waves had also been noted in the E.E.G. registration of another remarkable subject, Nelya Mikhailova, who was able telepathically to order objects to move. Under laboratory conditions she willed the white and the yolk of an egg to separate. Dr. Sergeyev said that, while most people generate three or four times more electrical voltage in the back of their brains than in the front, Mrs. Mikhailova generated fifty times the amount. He had therefore concluded that measuring the voltage in the rear of the brain was a good indicator of E.S.P. potential.

Interesting E.E.G. research was also done in the West by the Maimonodes dream-state researchers in New York. Basically, the testing was for the occurrence of psi (paranormal or psychic) phenomena in the dream state. Researchers Montague Ullman, Stanley Krippner and Alan Vaughan wanted to establish whether, under laboratory conditions, a psychic person could influence by will the images occurring in the dreams of another person, perhaps situated miles away.

Rapid eye movements (R.E.M.) indicate when a person is dreaming, so the Maimonodes team argued that the best period of dream recall would be just after this phase of sleep. Meanwhile, they selected certain images for telepathic transmission, which included detailed and distinctive paintings by Henri Rousseau, Salvador Dalí, Marc Chagall and other artists.

A subject would try to "beam" the picture to a given recipient, who was being monitored under laboratory conditions elsewhere, and who would be wakened after the R.E.M. period of sleep for dream recall. A panel of judges would scrutinize the imagery content of the dream and would decide on objective criteria as to whether there was sufficient parallel to warrant claiming an above-chance "psychic transmission." Their results were generally quite impressive. One example involved the English parapsychologist Malcolm Bessent and the rock group The Grateful Dead. In early 1971 the group gave six concerts in Port Chester, New York. During these sessions, large-scale images were projected onto a screen, and the rock group asked the audience to try mentally to transmit the images to the dreams of Bessent, who was located forty-five miles away at the Maimonodes Dream Laboratory in Brooklyn.

Bessent was to go to sleep at 11:30 PM, during the second concert. The target image was a picture called the *Seven Spinal Chakras* by Scralian, which shows a man meditating in the yoga lotus position. The seven chakras, or spiritual centers of the central nervous column, are depicted as bright orbs of energy in the painting. Forty-five miles away, Bessent dreamed the following:

> *I was very interested in…using natural energy…I was talking to this guy who said he'd invented a way of using solar energy and he showed me this box…to catch the light from the sun, which was all we needed to generate and store the energy…I was thinking about rocket ships…I'm remembering a dream I had about an energy box…and a spinal column.*

The dream is suggestive, and there are certain overlaps, particularly if we remember that the mind operates symbolically. The human frame, in yogic terms, can indeed be equated with a box for storing energy, and the spinal column is the vital causeway along which Kundalini energy is raised.

Experiments in dream telepathy are still being refined, but the work of the Maimonodes team was praised by leading psychologists Sir Cyril Burt and Dr. John Beloff.

What is most notable in contemporary research is the positive attitude among scientists to researching E.S.P., an attitude that barely existed even a few decades ago. And the new direction of research is attempting to take E.S.P. away from the spiritualist "fringe" into an area of systematic knowledge, so that it may complement what is already known about the functioning and potential of the brain.

Psychokinesis

Closely linked to E.S.P. is psychokinesis (P.K.)—influencing physical objects through mind power. The best-known exponent of psychokinesis is the Israeli psychic Uri Geller, who shot to popular fame through his apparent ability to bend spoons and affect the working of watches, through his psi abilities. Other examples of psychokinesis include levitation, apports and the movement of objects for which there is no rational explanation (sometimes attributed to poltergeist activity).

After studying E.S.P., Dr. Joseph Rhine turned his attention to P.K. and recorded startling results with a subject who seemed to be able to influence the fall of dice. Rhine came to the conclusion that E.S.P. and P.K. were closely interlinked, and later attributed P.K. to the success of faith-healing. Many psychics, including Englishman Matthew Manning, have also been noted faith-healers. Following Rhine's pioneering work, P.K., which had previously been dismissed by most as trickery on the part of fraudulent mediums, became the subject of more intensive scientific study. The American physicist Helmut Schmidt, a researcher of micro-P.K. (invisible effects that are validated statistically), devised an apparatus called the "electronic coin flipper" in the 1960s, the forerunner of subsequent random-event generators, which subjects with psi ability try to influence. Macro-P.K. (observable) phenomena, of the type demonstrated by Geller, were also studied. In Geller's case, his success rate was lower in the laboratory than on television.

Although it is not yet fully understood, like E.S.P., P.K. is now recognized as a legitimate area of scientific study. It is still a relatively young subject of interest, but who knows what the researchers of the future will discover?

Below: *Linda Cristal marvels at the spoon that she believed her fellow judge of the 1977 Miss Universe pageant, Uri Geller, bent by means of his psi abilities. Although Geller became a media favorite, he performed less spectacularly under scientifically monitored conditions.*

ESOTERIC CULTURE AND LORE

During the twentieth century, much esoteric culture and lore crossed over into the mainstream of popular belief. It is a remarkable fact that esoteric beliefs that would once have resulted in persecution—or worse—are now readily embraced by millions in the Western world. Even scientists are no longer so inclined to be dismissive, while the imperative to seek scientific "proof" seems to have faded in our millennial, more spiritually aware age. This chapter outlines a number of prevailing esoteric beliefs, including those concerning lost continents; ley lines and power points; mystical sites; supernatural and occult beings—vampires, werewolves, zombies and ghosts in particular; and the best-known types of Fortean phenomena. The exploration concludes with a discussion on how the occult has influenced the arts, focusing on fine art, literature and mystical music.

LOST CONTINENTS

Throughout history, humans have tended to look back toward an elusive age of perfection: a time when human achievements were greater, lives were happier and the world was generally a better place. In religious terms, this has often meant a time when the gods lived upon earth; in secular terms, it has led to theories of prehistoric civilizations whose technology exceeded, or at least equaled, that of the modern world.

Because none of these early civilizations left conclusive, visible remains, the theories concerning them have had to explain their almost total disappearance. Most have done so by locating them on continents that subsequently

sank beneath the oceans, never to be found again. The vastness of the oceans encouraged the idea that such expansive space could not have been "wasted," and that, at some time, there must have been land occupying it.

According to the theory of the lost continents, several points are assumed. Continents existed in the now "empty" oceans of the world: the Pacific, Atlantic and Indian oceans. Civilizations developed on these continents, and a high degree of scientific, cultural and

Opposite: A detail from Hieronymous Bosch's fantastical The Garden of Delights.

Below: The 1967 eruption of the Kilauea Volcano in Hawaii. It is believed that the lost continent of Mu was destroyed by such a natural disaster.

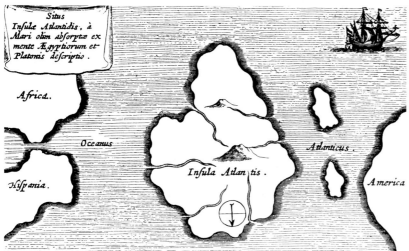

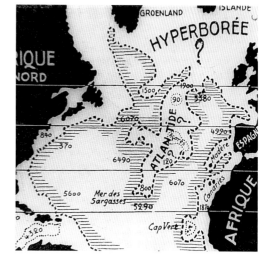

Above: *Two maps depicting the supposed position and topography of the lost continent of Atlantis, which the cartographers believed was located midway between the Americas and Africa.*

Below: *Stories about Atlantis were recorded by Plato (c. 428–347 BC) and have held the popular imagination since. Here, a still from* Atlantis: The Lost Continent *depicts both its advanced civilization and the cause of its destruction.*

technological achievement was attained—perhaps even higher than that known today. Eventually these continents and their civilizations were destroyed—either by natural disasters (such as earthquakes or movements in the crust of the Earth) or by manmade means. Some theories suggest that these civilizations developed nuclear power and were destroyed in a nuclear explosion. Virtually all traces of these civilizations and continents were therefore removed from the face of the Earth. However, some small clues remain. For example, alleged similarities in culture between two peoples on different sides of an ocean are cited as evidence that they derive from the same source; and legends of a "golden age" are cited as "racial memories" of the lost continents.

Speculation about and investigation into the supposed lost continents have ranged from mainstream scientific and archeological research through the whole range of pseudosciences to the occult. Many occult traditions claim that their origins lie in the religious beliefs of the lost continents. In Hawaii, for example, the esoteric tradition of Huna is said to have been derived from extraterrestrial people who settled on the lost continent of Mu. When it was destroyed, their descendants, the *Manahuna* ("people of the secret power"), intermarried with Hawaiians, thus founding a lineage of psychic *kahunas* (priest-sorcerers). But at present there is little historic or scientific evidence to substantiate the speculation that such lost continents actually existed. This is not to deny their existence, but merely to place them in the realm of theory rather than of fact.

There are three principal lost continents of the past. Atlantis, located in the Atlantic Ocean, has attracted the widest belief. Speculation about this continent developed from the reference by the Greek philosopher Plato to Atlantis as an advanced civilization, which was destroyed because of its evil. A number of authors, especially during the nineteenth century, wrote extensively on the subject, and it featured in many religious, occult and anthropological theories. Modern research suggests that historical references to Atlantis may have derived from a civilization based on the Mediterranean coastline that was destroyed by a volcanic eruption.

The second continent, Lemuria, supposedly the original Garden of Eden, was located by some theorists in the Indian Ocean and by others in the Pacific. The British zoologist Philip Sclater and the German biologist E.H. Haeckel called the continent "Lemuria" after the lemur, which is found in Africa, India and Malaysia. Life on Lemuria was generally held not to have reached the advanced civilization of Atlantis. Helena Blavatsky and Rudolf Steiner believed that the Atlanteans were descended from the Lemurians.

The third principal lost continent, Mu, was located in the Pacific Ocean, according to its "discoverer," Colonel James Churchward, and boasted a highly advanced civilization that was destroyed by natural causes.

A slightly different set of theories places such lost civilizations *inside* the Earth, which is said to be hollow, with openings at the ends.

Like the Hawaiian Huna belief, the theory of ancient astronauts, propounded by Erich von Däniken in his book *Chariots of the Gods* (1971), holds that in ancient times extraterrestrial beings visited Earth, possibly mating with humans and teaching them astonishingly advanced technological and esoteric knowledge. Thus are extraordinarily sophisticated early feats of construction and engineering—such as the Egyptian pyramids—explained, as are U.F.O. abductions (regarded as the monitoring of human progress by "ancestral" extraterrestrials). Although the theory is generally derided, ancient depictions of beings who appear to be wearing spacesuits (for example, in the Val Camonica cave paintings in Italy) can be seen in Europe, Africa and South America.

LEY LINES AND POWER POINTS

Occultists have always believed that certain sites and structures are imbued with magical power, but it was not until the twentieth century that this belief was regarded more seriously by researchers investigating the interrelated phenomena of ley lines and power points. The theory of ley lines was first propounded by Englishman Alfred Watkins in his book *The Old Straight Track* (1925). According to Watkins, sacred sites of all ages in Britain are connected by invisible ley lines—the "old straight tracks" of prehistoric times—that were mapped by ancient "Dodman surveyors." His theory excited much initial interest, which was renewed in the later decades of the twentieth century by New Age enthusiasts.

Although skeptics claim that the theory is flawed because sites from all historical periods were included in Watkins's investigation, many adherents believe that leys represent lines of energy contained in the Earth (or, according to Ernst Hartmann, that they indicate a network of underground streams). The points at which ley lines cross are particularly significant and are sites at which Fortean phenomena are often reported. Sympathy with this Earth-energy concept has been underlined by the existence of other geomantic traditions, most notably *Feng Shui*, which is based on the related, universal-energy principle of *ch'i*. Similar types of alignment have been identified linking sacred sites in Peru and Bolivia.

Below: Bell Rock, at Sedona, Arizona, is believed by the Yavapai tribe to be home to their totemic spirits. Visitors to this power point of "harmonic convergence" are variously said to experience visions, transformations and paranormal phenomena.

Right: The Japanese god Fudo, the deity of wisdom and fire and the destroyer of evil. His shrine by a waterfall on the Shiratake mountain near Ohara, Japan, is said to possess supernatural powers. In one story, a woman successfully invoked the god's help in restoring her blind father's sight after standing under the waterfall for a hundred days.

Below: England's Stonehenge is the world's most famous megalith. Although its original purpose remains uncertain, it is the subject of a variety of myths, and its stones are said to have mystical powers of healing. It is an important site for New Age adherents.

As well as claiming to be able to detect ley lines, dowsers are said to note strong reactions at "power points"—sites or objects that are believed to be sacred or inhabited by supernatural spirits. Rivers, lakes and mountains are among the most significant natural power points: such mountains as Olympus (the home of the Greek gods), the San Francisco

Peaks (inhabited by Hopi ancestral spirits) and the Himalayan Mount Kailas (in which the Indian god Shiva is said to live), for example, are believed to be sacred to the gods through their proximity to the heavens. Water may be credited with healing properties (such as the River Ganges), or its source may lead to the underworld. Sedona, Arizona, is located on another kind of power point: the Yavapai tribe believe that their totemic spirits live inside the region's rocks, and the mystical phenomena reported there have caused thousands of people to visit it.

Many of the major power points are said to be marked by manmade structures (including the Egyptian pyramids), and here the theory of ley lines is relevant, for their presence may have influenced the siting of such structures. As at the intersection of ley lines, paranormal activity is frequently recorded at power points—in the scientific view, perhaps as a result of the presence of powerful geomagnetic fields.

As well as being important elements of New Age thought and occult belief, ley lines and power points are increasingly becoming the subject of scientific research. Evidence of unusual activity is sufficient to suggest that the existence of such lines and points cannot simply be dismissed. Deeper study may lead to an understanding of the "Earthmind," as Paul Devereux, the founder of the British Dragon Project Trust that researches such "Earth mysteries," terms it.

MYSTICAL SITES

Whether or not they are built on ley lines, there are many examples around the world of manmade structures that are believed to be endowed with mystical powers.

The ancient megaliths—standing stones—of the Neolithic and Bronze Ages are regarded as important power points. Megaliths are either dolmens (tombs) or menhirs (single stones or groups of stones, of which the best-known group is Stonehenge in Wiltshire, England). It is commonly agreed that megaliths were constructed to serve astronomical, social, political and sacred functions, but speculation continues as to their exact purpose. Many myths are attached to menhirs: some are said to dance at night; others are supposedly people who were turned to stone. Spirits are also believed to gather at menhirs, and, along with the magical powers attributed to them, this is a possible reason why witches and other practitioners of esoteric arts congregate around them. Many are claimed to possess healing powers, particularly those that have been hollowed out (equating them with symbols of the "great goddess"). Tests have established that some menhirs radiate light, and possibly also electromagnetic energy.

Although Carnac, in France, boasts the largest collection of standing stones (estimated at 11,000 originally), and Avebury in Wiltshire, England, is the oldest megalithic site (2600 BC), Stonehenge is undoubtedly the most famous. The subject of many legends (one says that it was built with the help of Merlin), it is believed to have been constructed to serve as a solar temple or stellar observatory. Stonehenge is aligned on the midsummer sunrise and midwinter sunset, yet, despite popular belief, there is no clear evidence that it was associated with the ancient Druids. In the twentieth century, however, it became an important site for Druids, neo-pagans and Wiccans, who celebrated the festival of the summer solstice there, although they have been recently discouraged from this practice in order to protect the megalith.

An equally important site for Druids and similar groups is Glastonbury, in England's West Country. Believed to stand at the intersection of ley lines that connect it with Avebury and Stonehenge, Glastonbury—which may have been sacred to the Druids and is associated with the legends of King Arthur and the Holy Grail—comprises a town (equated with Avalon); an abbey (in whose grounds monks claimed in 1190 to have found the remains of Arthur and Guinevere); and a tor. Glastonbury Tor—522 feet of terraced, volcanic rock—is central to many myths: for example, it is said to have been Arthur's fortress, which led to Annwn (the underworld); or the dwelling place of Gwynn ap Nudd (or the Fairy King), king of Annwn. The apparently inexhaustible Chalice Well at the foot of the tor is believed to contain magical water (which has been proved to be radioactive), and, according to legend, Joseph of Arimathea threw the Holy Grail into the well. Joseph of Arimathea is also associated with the abbey, whose famous Glastonbury Thorn is said to have grown from his staff. The abbey fell to ruin after 1539—as a result of Henry VIII's dissolution of the monasteries—and was excavated in 1907 by Frederick Bligh Bond, who believed that the spirits of long-dead monks had guided him in

Left: The standing stones of Carnac, in Brittany, France, are believed originally to have numbered some 11,000, although only 3,000 now remain. The oldest stone is thought to predate the Egyptian pyramids and, like many such sites, these standing stones are said to possess magical properties.

his task. Reinforced by Katherine Maltwood's discovery in 1929 that the twelve zodiacal signs appear in natural formations in a circle in the Glastonbury region, and the occurrence of unexplained lights over the tor, the area's mystical significance makes it extremely important to twentieth-century occultists, including Dion Fortune (author of *Glastonbury: Avalon of the Heart*), who lived next to the tor.

Although not as old as the megaliths, the Nazca lines of Peru, which are thought to date from between 500 BC and AD 500, are also believed to have been created to serve a mystical purpose. The "lines" are actually enormous drawings of humans, animals and geometric figures, covering a forty-mile-long area. They were made by cutting away the pampa to reveal yellow soil. Because they can only be fully appreciated from the air, author Erich von Däniken excited much popular interest when he postulated that the Nazca lines were intended to guide extraterrestrial astronauts to Earth. Other researchers, including Paul Kosok and Maria Reiche, claimed that they were astronomical maps, but this theory has recently been discredited. The conventional explanation is that the lines represent Nazca gods, or the spirits seen by shamans, and that they were used in sacred rituals.

The "medicine wheels" of the North American Plains region have been the subject of similar speculation. Constructed by early Native Americans, and of uncertain date, they mostly consist of a cairn of rocks surrounded by circles of smaller stones, which are sometimes connected by "spokes." In most cultures, the circle is considered to have mystical powers, and in Native American belief it is regarded as possessing powers of healing—hence the "medicine-wheel" appellation. About fifty such wheels exist in Canada and the United States, of which the most famous is the Bighorn Medicine Wheel at the foot of Medicine Mountain in Wyoming. Although undoubtedly sacred sites, the purpose of medicine wheels remains uncertain; some, such as George Grinnell, believe that they represent the plan of a medicine lodge; others, including John Eddy, that they are aligned according to the summer solstice. Whatever the original reasons for their construction, today medicine wheels are also constructed by other mystical groups for ceremonial purposes, which are generally connected with healing rituals.

SUPERNATURAL AND OCCULT BEINGS

All religions and mythologies describe a vast array of supernatural beings that guide humans, trick them, and offer them enlightenment or occult secrets. Joseph Smith, the founder of Mormonism, described how the angel Moroni appeared in a blazing vision and showed him certain sacred tablets. Madame Blavatsky, the famous Theosophist, used to claim to her followers that she had a constant mystical rapport with certain spiritual "masters," including one Koot Hoomi, who lived in a mysterious region of the Himalayas. Mathers, the cofounder of the Hermetic Order of the Golden Dawn, similarly claimed that he had contacted beings whom he called "secret chiefs," while Aleister Crowley believed that he had received an occult revelation from Aiwass, who was a mysterious Egyptian entity. Of course, if we look farther back into Christianity, Judaism, Islam and other religions, we find accounts of angels appearing to the prophets, and other types of strange entities, such as the Kerubim (Cherubim) of the Book of Revelations.

The world of esoteric wisdom is one in which the entire universe is filled with mysterious personages and beings. Occultists can beseech some of these for help in their quest

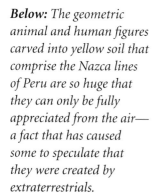

Below: The geometric animal and human figures carved into yellow soil that comprise the Nazca lines of Peru are so huge that they can only be fully appreciated from the air— a fact that has caused some to speculate that they were created by extraterrestrials.

for greater knowledge; others—some of which may be encountered on the astral planes—are horrendous and frightening, and are to be avoided at all costs.

The ancient Gnostics, whose magical universe was rather similar to that of modern magicians, described some of these beings. One of them was Paraplex,

a ruler with a woman's shape whose hair reacheth down to her feet, under whose authority stand five and twenty archdemons which rule over a multitude of other demons. It is those demons which enter into men and seduce them, raging, and cursing, and slandering; it is they which carry off hence and in ravishment, the souls and dispatch them through their dark smoke.

The Gnostics, rather like the medieval, so-called "hell-fire" Christians, conceived of grotesque hells, and in particular of the twelve dungeons of "outer darkness."

These accounts of strange, supernatural beings are not confined to the West. Tibetan Buddhists believe that when people die they are confronted by a vast array of entities, which are really a reflection of the good and evil tendencies inherent in the human mind. One of the so-called "wrathful deities" is an awesome being known as "the great glorious Buddha-Heruka," who is said to appear on the eighth day after a person dies:

Dark brown of color it had three heads, six hands, and four feet firmly postured, the right face being white, the left red, the central dark brown; the body emitting flames of radiance, the nine eyes widely opened in a terrifying gaze; the eyebrows quivering like lightning.

Of course, not all such supernatural encounters are horrific or demonic. Recall John's Apocalyptic vision from Revelations I: 13–15:

And in the midst of the seven candlesticks [I saw] one like unto the son of man, clothed with a garment down to the foot, and girth with a golden girdle. His head and his hairs were white like wool, as white as snow; and his eyes were as a flame of fire.

And his feet were like unto fine brass, as if they burned in a furnace; and his voice as the sound of many waters .

Magicians and occultists believe that they have access to the far reaches of the mind and, like Carl Jung, they consider these beings a reflection of different levels of consciousness. Those who have opened their minds to the spiritual, regenerative side will have visions of God, Christ or Buddha, for example; those who are besieged with doubts, worries, hatred or greed will perhaps be tormented by devils that are essentially of their own making.

Above: *The appearance of the angel Moroni to Joseph Smith (1805–44). During the vision, Moroni revealed the existence of gold tablets inscribed with the "true" Christian gospel. Smith subsequently located these near Manchester, New York, and founded the Mormon Church of Jesus Christ of Latter-day Saints a few years later.*

Above: A Tibetan illustration of the god Shiva, the multilimbed "destroyer" of the Hindu trinity (trimurti).

Right: The legendary terrible, multi-headed hydra, which was slain by the Greco-Roman hero Herakles (Hercules).

The practice of magic, at least in its ritual form, is to invoke and evoke supernatural beings that are representative of the entire manifested universe. In medieval belief, a sure way to recognize witches was by identifying their familiars—usually cats or other pets—which were believed to be demons in disguise. In modern occult practice, however, the evocation of supernatural beings is not so crass. White magicians invoke angels and other spiritual beings because they believe that they will bestow knowledge and grace upon them. Black magicians are seeking to enhance the more hedonistic, animal side of their natures, and they thus evoke elementals and familiar spirits of a lower order than themselves. In a sense they are moving in a counterrevolutionary way, for they are seeking to revitalize their basically animal drives and instincts.

In the Qabalah, the main basis of modern magic, each of the ten levels of consciousness on the tree of life has an archangel associated with it, as well as other angels and planetary ascriptions. The names of these archangelic beings, which are the most exalted individual entities for each level, are as follows.

1 Metatron—*Primum mobile* (beginnings of the cosmos)
2 Raziel—The zodiac
3 Tzaphquiel—Saturn
4 Tzadquiel—Jupiter
5 Kamael—Mars
6 Raphael—The Sun
7 Haniel—Venus
8 Michael—Mercury
9 Gabriel—The Moon
10 Sandalphon—The Earth (four elements)

According to occultist Franz Bardon, there are also spirit beings for every degree of the planetary zodiac. For example, Ecdulon, a spirit of the zodiacal sign of Aries, "can initiate the magician into the magic of love. If desired by the magician, he can change hostility into friendship, and secure for the magician the favor of very important persons." But there are also other supernatural beings in the magical universe. Sometimes they are human, but not always. Ancient myths and legends refer to several fabulous beasts that were often "combination animals." For example, the mantichora was a Persian beast with a lion's body and a human head; it could shoot poisonous barbs from its tail and had a voice like a trumpet. The hydra, against which Hercules pitted his strength, was a dragon with seven or nine heads; each of the heads was immortal and, if any were cut off, new ones would spring up in their place. The beast called the hippocampus was half horse and half fish, and drew Poseidon's chariot, while the harpies were aggressive vultures with female heads and breasts. The chimera, a creature described by Homer, was a combination of a lion, a serpent and a goat.

Such fanciful creatures are regarded by most of us as being figments of the imagination, but for magicians who venture out onto the astral planes it is quite a different matter. Such beings can confront them as if they were real, since magicians are really journeying into the "mythological" areas of the mind.

One of the most positive and far-reaching contributions of the magician Aleister Crowley was to relate the tree-of-life levels of consciousness to the gods of different religions. He also correlated the Tarot paths on the tree with other mythological visions, such as those of imaginary animals. For example, according to Crowley, Path 25 of the tree, represented by the Tarot card *Temperance*, is a location in which one might see a centaur or a hippogriff. A centaur is, of course, the famous half-man-half-horse, and is none other than Sagittarius, who fires his arrow upward toward the

Above: *The Chinese dragon is a hybrid creature which, in the Orient, is believed to have fearsome powers, yet which is mercifully benevolent and protective toward humans.*

Below: *The fire-breathing chimera was described by Homer as having the body of a lion, the tail of a serpent and a goat's head growing from its body. It was the offspring of the monsters Typhon and Echidna.*

Right: For many movie goers, the actor Bela Lugosi, who played the "undead" Transylvanian count in the first Dracula movie in 1931, was the definitive king vampire. Popular belief in vampires dates back centuries and spans many continents.

Below: Dr. Stephen Kaplan, a self-proclaimed "vampirologist," pictured in New York in 1977. Directly above his head, center left, is a medieval woodcut of Dracole Waida ("the impaler"), the historical personage on whom Bram Stoker based his novel, Dracula.

Sun. The hippogriff is a variation of a griffin, and this creature was sacred to the sun god Apollo. The centaur (or hippogriff) occurs here because the card of *Temperance* leads to mystical visions of the Sun and sun gods when used for meditative purposes.

We can see, then, that magic regards all supernatural entities as being, at least in one sense, real. Even if they are only figments of the creative imagination, they are real on that level. And, as magicians expand their consciousness and move farther into the mind, they have to learn to expect almost anything.

VAMPIRES, WEREWOLVES AND ZOMBIES

Three types of supernatural monsters are particularly (if sometimes erroneously) associated with the occult: vampires, werewolves and zombies.

Although the vampire has been a figure of popular mythology in various countries throughout history, it was not until the publication of Bram Stoker's novel *Dracula* in 1897 that the mythology of the vampire became firmly established. Stoker consolidated widely varying traditions about the vampire into the popular figure who has now been portrayed in hundreds of novels and innumerable movies, of whose unusual characteristics most people are aware, and who still manages to inspire some strange fear.

Stoker based his novel on legends of blood-sucking ghosts, who returned from the grave

to cling to life by drawing vitality from the living—who, in turn, would probably die and come back to haunt yet another generation. But Stoker's vampire was not simply a ghost: it was the "undead," one who has died, been buried and risen from the grave in the same physical body to roam around seeking the fresh blood that is necessary to sustain its life.

In Stoker's account, the vampire was a creature of the night, who could be destroyed by the rays of the Sun. The creature was unable to cross moving water, was terrified of crucifixes and possessed incredible occult powers. It is this figure—powerful, striking and sinister—that constitutes the vampire of modern myth. But there is a wide variety of other, lesser-known traditions, from those of central Europe, through the Americas to Australia. And an obsession with drinking blood is not unknown to psychiatrists, suggesting that, at least in some cases, historical "vampires" have actually been the demented and the insane, especially in societies in which blood was accorded a sacred value and was seen as the embodiment of the powers of life.

In simple terms, a vampire is a human who has died, yet who rises from the grave to

become one of the "undead," and who needs regular supplies of fresh human blood in order to remain so. The causes of vampirism are uncertain: some traditions trace it back to possession, some to the principle of heredity, and others to some action of the prevampiric individual; most trace it to contamination by another who was already a vampire. Being bitten by a vampire is almost certain to infect the victim, who then becomes a vampire too. By day, vampires sleep in their graves, rising only when the Sun has set to stalk their victims, and employing strange, hypnotic powers to fascinate and ensnare them.

In Stoker's tradition, vampires can only be destroyed by having stakes thrust through their hearts; following this, the body should be burned, if it hasn't already (as in the horror-movie tradition) crumbled away to dust. In the coffin, the body of a vampire is characterized by the freshness and suppleness of the skin, which is enhanced by the ghastly trickle of blood on the lips.

In addition to the physical vampire, many occultists have talked of "psychic vampires," that is, of people who vampirize the vitality and energy of others, sometimes unintentionally, sometimes consciously. Garlic, crucifixes and holy water—such things are said to be effective against both the psychic and the physical vampire. But ultimately it must be destroyed.

Like the vampire, the voodoo zombie is also "undead"—a corpse that has been reanimated by voodoo magic. Some African tribes believe that zombies were lazy people in life, whose slothfulness condemned them to eternal labor in death. In voodoo, zombies are said to be created by *bokors*—sorcerers—to act as their slaves. There are various ways of creating a zombie: in one, the person selected to be a zombie is killed with a strong poison and buried, before being magically resurrected after a few days in his/her grave by the *bokor*, who then renames it. (Anthropologists have established that the putative zombie is not actually killed, but put into a deep coma before being revived with antidotal substances.) Another method is the capture by the *bokar* of the victim's spirit, the *ti bon ange* ("little good angel"), which remains on earth for about a week after death. The deceased's relations often decapitate the corpse or stab it in the heart, as a preventative

measure against the *bokar*, who sucks the spirit out of the victim's body. Voodoo believers do not fear the zombie *per se*, for it is rarely threatening, but are terrified of being transformed into one. Once created, the zombie, who exists in a robotlike state, is forced to slave for the *bokar* in perpetuity—usually in the fields. *Bokars* forbid zombies to eat salt, which revives their senses and sends them back to their graves—this is usually their only means of escape from their posthumous life of drudgery. Unlike vampires, zombies are sad, powerless figures with no malevolent intentions; werewolves, however, are very different, entirely evil entities.

Tales of werewolves ("were" is derived from the Old English word meaning "man") have existed since ancient times. Ovid, for example, told the story of Lycaon, the king of

Above: Wade Davis, a Harvard University student, pictured with the voodoo paraphernalia he brought back from a botanical field trip to Haiti.

Left: The werewolf—half man, half wolf.

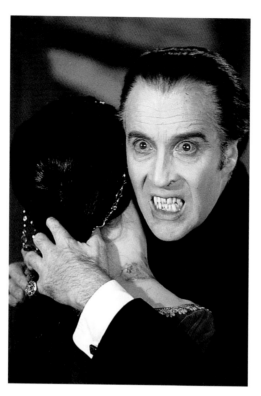

Right: Christopher Lee, another celebrated portrayer of Dracula on the silver screen, whose blood-red-tinted contact lenses are reported to have caused him great discomfort. The characteristics of the celluloid Dracula were dictated by Hollywood, and are not accurate to the less attractive descriptions of vampire legend.

Arcadia, who was turned into a wolf by Jupiter, while St. Patrick is said to have transformed Vereticus, a king of Wales, into a wolf. In popular belief, there are many causes for lycanthropy, including being conceived under a full moon; being possessed by a demon; wearing a belt made of a wolf's pelt; being cursed; or being bitten by a werewolf. Witches, too, were said to be able temporarily to transform themselves into wolves, regarded in the sixteenth and seventeenth centuries as incarnations of the devil, thus connecting lycanthropy with the occult.

In early European times, when sightings of "werewolves" were common, wolves were a persistent threat to the population. In countries where wolves don't exist, similar were-animals are also said to roam, such as were-jaguars in South America, were-tigers in India, and were-lions in Africa. Lycanthropy is also a psychiatric condition in which patients believe themselves to be wolves, and this may also have led to the popular belief in werewolves.

Werewolves are commonly believed to be human during the day, but to transform themselves into wolves at night (particularly when there is a full moon), when they prey on humans, especially children and young girls. Encounters with werewolves are usually fatal, although a yew or ash twig might hold them off for a while. Like vampires, werewolves can only be destroyed by arcane methods: for example, with a silver bullet or with a weapon blessed in a chapel of St. Hubert, the patron saint of huntsmen.

GHOSTS AND HAUNTINGS

Human history has proven consistent in the fear of the unknown—especially when the unknown has to do with death. Every society has speculated on the fate of those who have died, and most have believed it possible for some, if not all, of the dead to return, usually in a nonphysical form, to haunt the living. Generally believing that the dead are dangerous, most societies have taken some precautions to prevent this happening: funeral rituals to drive the spirit away, gifts to appease it, tombs in which to trap it—all constitute part of the process of protection against the wandering dead. It has generally been assumed that the dead, if restless and returned from the grave, would be attracted either to their relatives or people with whom they had had some close association during life—or to places that had a special meaning for them. The deceased's relatives therefore would have to be especially careful, but so would anyone moving into a house in which someone had died. Some societies even forbade the mention of a dead person's name (which is still echoed today in modern society's injunctions against "speaking ill of the dead"), and individuals sometimes shifted their location in order to avoid the return of the dead.

In general terms, the phenomena popularly known as ghosts can be divided into several categories. The mildest form is influences, which are the vague sort of "feelings" that adhere to places (or occasionally to objects), often unpleasantly, but which manifest themselves in no more tangible form. Poltergeists are the noisy ghosts popularized in movies. These manifest themselves by rather destructive outbursts of energy, which cause physical results of various types, usually involving the destruction of household objects, or loud noises. Research (for example, that of Harry Price or Carl Jung) tends to suggest that these are not ghosts in the traditional sense, but the externalization of psychic energy, often associated with adolescents.

Apparitions are the traditional ghosts of popular fiction, the shadowy figures that

in another. Such apparitions usually indicate: people who are on the point of death, who manifest themselves to someone closely involved with them; people who are conveying some message of urgency (for example, the mother who appears to warn her child of impending danger); or people who are asleep at the time and who project their astral bodies accidentally or intentionally.

Although popular movies and novels have characterized the ghost as a white, ethereal figure that drifts around terrifying spectators, ghosts are not necessarily visible, frightening or ethereal. Indeed, many have been mistaken for solid, physical individuals. And ghosts can furthermore be perceived in a variety of ways, often visible only to psychics, while nonpsychics merely "feel" their presence. Perceptions of ghosts can be experienced by several means. The ghost may appear physically in one form or another, and thus be seen visually. There may be noises, voices, music or other sounds that suggest the presence of supernatural phenomena. Ghosts can be experienced through other sensory perceptions, including the perception of a change of temperature (often said

Left: A classic recreation of the ghost, head in hand, that is said to haunt England's Lullingstone Castle. The spirits of the murdered are often said to return to the scene of their death as a reproachful or vengeful reminder.

Below: *A delicate Victorian woman is pictured swooning at the sight of a ghostly marriage in this "trick" photograph. One theory holds that events imprint themselves on the substance of the environment; because they are thus trapped in the fabric of time, their images are eternally re-enacted and may be visible to those who have psychic abilities.*

appear and disappear, often in semidarkness, and are usually associated with historical locations. The fourth type of such phenomena is haunting, in which the characteristics of apparitions and poltergeists are combined to result in psychic phenomena of an alarmingly high degree, with various manifestations.

Modern parapsychological research has investigated some "ghosts" in depth, and a number of scientifically based theories have been advanced as to the nature and functioning of these shadowy figures.

The term "ghost" usually conjures up an image—peaceful or tortured—of the spirit of someone who has died, although some apparitions have been of the living, and others have been of animals or objects, for example, ghost ships, phantom animals or mysteriously appearing and disappearing objects.

Apparitions of people who have died are either associated with the person to whom they appear (for example, the appearance of a relative to pass on a message from "beyond the grave"); or with the place in which they appear (for example, the almost classic theme of murder victims haunting the houses in which they were murdered).

Phantasms of the living are apparitions of people who are still alive, but who appear in one place while their physical body remains

Right: In 1977, this devout New Mexican woman was overcome to see what she believed to be the face of Christ manifest itself in the tortilla that she was frying. According to the Catholic Church, such apparitions are mystical manifestations authorized by God. Another, non-religious, explanation may be that the unconscious need of the believer to see the object of his or her devotion is projected into a physical object. Such externalizations of psychic energy may also explain the phenomenon of poltergeists.

to fall in the presence of ghosts), movement (when breezes are said to occur in otherwise still rooms) and touch (invisible fingers running through the hair, or across the face).

If individuals possess some psychic faculty, they may perceive the ghost either by means of vision (clairvoyance), sound (clairaudience) or feeling (clairsentience). Ghosts can also be perceived indirectly, by means of physical phenomena. In the case of poltergeists, the ghost may manifest itself by moving or levitating objects (by psychokinesis or telekinesis); other indirect "sightings" include the mysterious appearance of writing or apports, and ghosts perceived through any of the means employed

in Spiritualism. Finally, there can be a simple intuition, or "feeling" that someone or something is making its presence felt.

Whether or not individuals who believe themselves to be in the presence of "ghosts" actually perceive someone or something, there remain questions regarding what, and how, they perceive. Generally, theories regarding ghosts have employed one or more of the following basic premises.

✦ The discarnate personalities of individuals can remain in contact with the physical world after death (the Spiritualist hypothesis).

✦ Some type of energy mass can exist in association with places, objects or people, which gives rise to various phenomena. The energy mass is not human, although it may have been stimulated by human action. For example, murderers' anger and hatred may remain once their crimes have been committed and may manifest themselves by means of various phenomena. (This is one of the more frequently cited scientific explanations).

✦ Events leave indelible prints on the total substance of the environment and may manifest themselves in various ways (a variation of the energy-mass theory).

✦ There is always a rational explanation for any such manifestations (the ultimate rationalist explanation).

✦ Such manifestations have no existence in reality, but are caused by psychic influences on the individuals who claim to perceive them.

Right: Mrs. Parker, of Denver, Colorado, claimed in 1973 that her house was haunted by a malevolent ghost that physically attacked her. Clearly, her alleged experience went beyond the more common, indirect "feeling" of a ghostly appearance.

FORTEAN PHENOMENA

"Fortean phenomena," or Forteana, is the collective term applied to paranormal occurrences that have no natural explanation. This mode of description is named after the American journalist Charles Fort (1874–1932), who dedicated himself to collecting information about such unexplained events, publishing four collections of his findings. Fortean phenomena include mystical religious experiences, such as stigmata or weeping religious statues; spontaneous human combustion (S.H.C.); "rains" of unlikely objects, such as fish or snakes (which Fort postulated emanated from the "Super-Saragossa Sea," a superterrestrial region that collects earthly matter and then redeposits it on Earth); ghosts; mysterious creatures like the Yeti and Loch Ness monster; and unidentified flying objects (U.F.O.s) and other extraterrestrial manifestations.

Sightings of U.F.O.s are believed to be centuries old, but popular interest in the subject is a phenomenon of the twentieth century, dating back to 1947, when pilot Kenneth Arnold reported seeing nine unidentifiable objects, which he estimated to be traveling at a speed of 1,600 miles per hour. That year too marked the "Roswell incident," when three alleged U.F.O.s crashed in New Mexico, killing their alien passengers. Since then thousands of similar sightings have occurred, prompting official investigation, notably by the U.S. Air Force under the supervision of J. Allen Hynek of the Astronomy Department of Northwestern University.

Hynek's research concluded that there were a number of common categories of sightings, including disk-shaped objects, Earth lights, and three types of close encounters. Close encounters of the third kind, in which people come into contact with extraterrestrials (E.T.s) have excited much speculation, particularly regarding those people who claim to have been abducted by aliens (whose physical characteristics may vary). Common features of such alleged abductions include being beamed into a spaceship, physically examined, and then returned to the site of abduction. Many abductees have little memory of their ordeal, and this is termed "missing time." Occasionally they may be visited subsequently by mysterious "men in black," who forcefully dissuade them from pursuing their claims. Skeptics explain away sightings of U.F.O.s as misinterpretations of natural weather phenomena or secret, experimental aircraft, while those who have close encounters are believed to be suffering from wish-fulfilling delusions for contact with beings of higher consciousness.

Sightings of U.F.O.s are often linked with reports of Earth lights—bright balls of light that move about randomly—which sometimes seem to display intelligence in their movements, as at Marfa in Texas, and which may be associated with sacred sites such as Glastonbury Tor. Indeed, Earth-light sightings are centuries old and have been incorporated into many tribal myths: Australian Aborigines, for example, call them *min-min* lights and believe them to be either evil entities or spirits of the dead, while certain Native American tribes consider them to be gateways to the heavens, or sources of knowledge. Apart from prosaically explaining their appearance as beams of light from car headlights or other manmade sources, the various scientific theories regarding Earth lights include the belief that they are luminous manifestations generated by electromagnetic energy, or ionized gas.

Also connected to theories of extraterrestrial beings is the recent phenomenon of crop circles—patterns that appear in the center of fields of mature crops of grain that are occasionally heralded by the presence of Earth lights. Crop circles were first seen in the 1980s,

Below: Despite hoaxes, delusions and misperceived natural phenomena, many U.F.O. sightings remain undisproved. These are sometimes substantiated by physical evidence (like photographs and radar data) that has been subjected to rigorous scientific testing procedures.

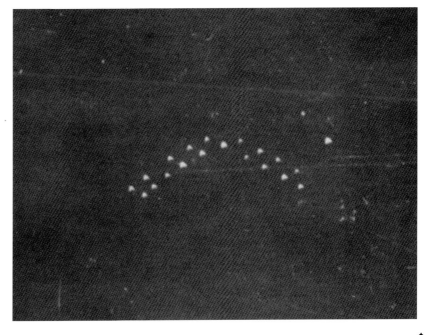

Right: The tourist who took this scenic photograph in British Columbia was unaware of the putative U.F.O. that appears top right until the negative was developed. Although the photograph was authenticated by leading expert Dr. Richard Haines, skeptics believe that such images as these are either fakes or subject to perfectly logical, natural explanation.

Right: Most alleged extraterrestrial encounters involve human contact with U.F.O.s and their alien passengers. Former "Heaven's Gate" cult leaders Marshall Herff Applewhite and Bonnie Lu Nettles were more unusual, however, in that they firmly believed that they were themselves "unearthly" beings who only temporarily inhabited their human bodies, or "vehicles." In 1997 cult members committed mass suicide in the millennium-triggered expectation of joining extraterrestrials in a U.F.O. in the tail of the Hale-Bopp comet.

and since then hundreds have appeared. They are not necessarily circular in shape, but can also represent other geometrical forms—or even, in one case, Sumerian hieroglyphics. Some crop circles have been unmasked as hoaxes, but the fact that many have no tracks leading to them, and that the affected grain is crushed but not broken, has puzzled scientists. Current theories regarding their formation include the action of "stationary whirlwinds," temperature imbalances and excess irrigation. Some people, however, remain firmly convinced that crop circles are either pictorial extraterrestrial communications or evidence of the presence of visiting U.F.O.s.

Finally, another focus of the popular interest in Fortean phenomena is the Bermuda Triangle, an area of the Atlantic Ocean bounded by Bermuda, Puerto Rico and Florida, into which many airplanes and ships have inexplicably disappeared without warning. Perhaps the most famous incident occurred in 1945, when six U.S. Navy airplanes were lost, but this was by no means the first—or the last—such disappearance. Also known as the Hoodoo Sea, the Limbo of the Lost and the Devil's Triangle, local fishermen have always believed that the Bermuda Triangle is populated by malevolent, monstrous demons,

while Christopher Columbus noted that his compass behaved abnormally in the region, and that a mysterious light hovered above sea. Along with most such phenomena, the Bermuda Triangle's power has been explained in rational terms as the result of natural, if exceptional, causes. Others attribute it variously to U.F.O. activity, time warps or the influence exerted by the remains of Atlantis.

OCCULT ART

With the exception of painters of fantasy like Hieronymous Bosch (*c.* 1450–1516), Lucas Cranach (1472–1553), Pieter Bruegel (d. 1569) and the visionary mystic artist-writer William Blake (1757–1827), before the 1880s art was, in a broad sense, representational. The fashionable use of consciousness-enhancing substances, and an interest in dreams and the occult among the Symbolists in Europe, saw the emergence of visionary painters like Gustave Moreau (1826–98), Richard Dadd (1817–87) and Jean Delville (1867–1961), but the work that is termed "occult art" is very much a phenomenon of the twentieth century.

Of all the major movements of modern art, the most trenchantly occult has been Surrealism, certain of whose members were themselves trance, or Satanic, occultists. Surrealism developed in Paris between the world wars, during a period that saw the near-total breakdown of society, and a type of mass alienation from all perspectives of "normality." In place of rational thinking, which then appeared to them to have failed, the Surrealists proposed a new dimension of fantasy. In the *First Surrealist Manifesto*, issued by André Breton (1896–1966) in 1924, he explained why he believed in the omnipotence of the dream. He considered that dreams were not only a reflection of life, but were ultimately a valid visual representation of reality, since their

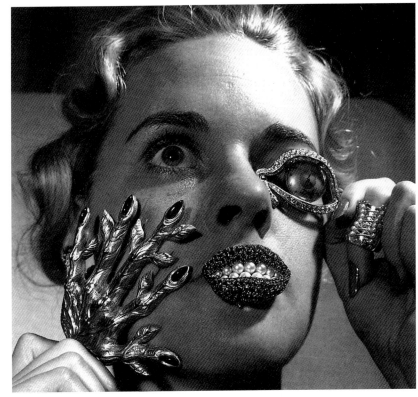

structure was unimpeded by rational processes of thought. They thus offered a new freedom. They also constituted a commentary on humans' inner beings, which were increasingly felt to be more real than their outer beings, or their "social degradation."

The work of the Surrealists was not generally structured; some preferred to emphasize abstract techniques of painting, while others painted using the meticulous detail of the living dream.

Wolfgang Paalen (1905–59), an Austrian painter who lived for a time in Mexico, invented a technique known as "fumage." He would hold canvases freshly coated with oil paint above a candle, so that the smoke would trace eerie, random patterns on the wet paint. He then overlaid these images with surreal, supranormal detail, as in his work *Conflict of the Principles of Darkness*. Paalen was very absorbed by the Tarot and also fused animistic, Mayan influences into his paintings. Max Ernst (1891–1976) developed a similarly suggestive technique, known as "frottage." He would rub a pencil lightly on sheets of paper placed on his floorboards, thus allowing the uneven surface to come through on the paper as a texture. When Ernst looked carefully at his frottages, he found a mystical process coming into play:

Above: *Salvador Dalí, the most famous of the Surrealist artists, was noted for painting and creating three-dimensional objects, including furniture, stage sets and jewelry. The jewelry modeled here by Madelle Hegeler in 1959 reflects the witty, yet nightmarish and hallucinatory, qualities that characterize Dalí's oeuvre.*

Left: *The flamboyant Salvador Dalí, sporting his carefully waxed trademark mustache, is welcomed to New York in 1955 with Oscar, the bantam rooster—a stage-managed event typical of the man whom his contemporaries nicknamed "Avida Dollars."*

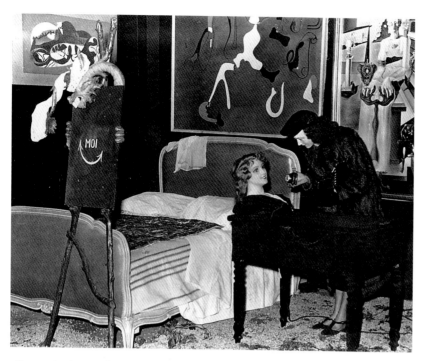

Above: *An image from the Surrealist exhibition that was held in Paris, France, in 1938. The primary aim of Surrealism was to challenge reason by juxtaposing or fusing everyday objects with the irrational and fantastical, thus freeing the mind to explore uncharted areas.*

"When gazing at these drawings," he wrote, "I was surprised at the sudden intensification of my visionary faculties, and at the hallucinatory succession of contradictory images being superimposed on each other."

Within the more representational category of the Surrealists, we find the self-confessed "black" magician Félix Labisse (1905–82), whose painted figures were often a macabre combination of animal, vegetable and human forms. But, like all occultists, he knew of the power of transformation. On a subconscious level, he believed, anything the magician could imagine could actually happen. As an artist, he felt obliged to convey this opinion in his paintings. Similarly, although both employed imagery of a familiar kind, Salvador Dalí (1904–89) and René Magritte (1898–1967) created a strange, nightmarish quality in their works by counterbalancing objects taken out of their normal context. Magritte overcame reality by representing images in combinations that defy reality: a mermaid with the head of a fish and the legs of a woman lies hopelessly stranded upon a beach; a succulent green apple fills a room; plants that are also birds grow upon a rocky mountain top.

The Surrealists offered a new means for observing the universe, which allowed almost anything to occur. This in itself constituted a potentially occult basis on which ensuing art could build. Outside the mainstream of modern art, however, there have been some interesting offshoots. In at least three important instances, the relationship of art to trance mysticism or the occult was developed even further.

The first major English Surrealist was Austin Spare (1888–1956)—in fact, his work precedes the European school by about a decade. His early illustrations, for books like Ethel Wheeler's *Behind the Veil* (1906) and a book on aphorisms entitled *The Starlit Mire* (1911), were fairly orthodox, but meanwhile Spare was training as an occultist as well as an artist. It is thought that around 1910 he joined Aleister Crowley's occult order, the *Argentinum Astrum*, after which he sought a new, mystical direction in his art.

He came to see humans as alienated from the cause of all being, which he called "Kia," and he considered that the role of humans was to learn how to open themselves to its creative energies and life processes. Contained in his remarkable work *The Book of Pleasure (Self Love): The Philosophy of Ecstasy* (1913) were some important new concepts. By now, Spare had developed a theory of sigils, which were symbols said to express the human will in a concentrated form. These sigils would express a command that Spare would make to his subconscious while in a state of trance or ecstasy. He hoped that he would thus enhance his access to his subconscious and all its imagery, and that he would be able to open himself totally to its potential. Like most occultists, Spare believed in reincarnation and thought that all his earlier personalities were lurking deep in his mind. In the trance state, which, interestingly, he called the "death posture," he would try to summon these half-human, half-animal forms and would attempt to identify with them as earlier facets of his own existence. Spare felt that if he retrogressed far enough, he would rediscover all his personalities and finally reach the primal cause of all.

The work of Spare is a forceful reminder that occultists who totally surrender themselves tend to become obsessed by the imagery of their subconscious. Many of Spare's paintings contain swirling, atavistic imagery, and there is also an inherent animal sexuality in much of his work. It represents a merging of trance occultism and art.

Australia offers two further examples of the blending of art and the occult. The first of these is represented by the work of the self-confessed witch Rosaleen Norton, whose paintings continued the tradition of Norman Lindsay (1879–1969), with a marked swing toward black-magic imagery. Norton was familiar with the writings of the Surrealist/occultist Kurt Seligmann and the magical theories of Dion Fortune (who called herself the "black Isis"), Aleister Crowley and Eliphas Lévi. In her work, she detailed many of the so-called *Qlippoth*, the images of the "black," or negative, tree of life. Like Spare, she appears to have sometimes used a tantric, or sexual, technique to attain visionary ecstasy, for she says in the commentary to her monograph that "Kundalini, who sometimes assumes the shape of a serpent, is my most powerful familiar." For her, the power of the orgasm was an inroad to occult consciousness.

The other noteworthy Australian occult artist was Victor Angel, who began his career as a commercial artist. Angel had no noteworthy talents and was responsible for some thoroughly mediocre landscapes. However, at the age of twenty-seven he felt that he was becoming possessed by a spiritual force, which urged him to adopt a new approach to his painting. Like Spare, Angel summoned the presence by means of a sigil, or symbol, which he would hold in his mind. In a clairvoyant state, he then became able to perceive remarkable mythological imagery hovering above his blank paper. Spare, who worked in gouache, claimed no credit for such works, for he said that he merely filled in the detail that was made available to him supernaturally. Spare's visionary work resembles that of William Blake to some extent, although there are also Renaissance influences. In his case, the marked contrast between the artist's natural ability and his later occult sensitivity presents an interesting, and perhaps unique phenomenon. However, Angel's paintings reveal a pronounced Qabalistic content and may be accurately correlated with the energies and symbolic colors of the tree of life. Angel himself had no knowledge of the Qabalah; he spontaneously titled one of his works *The Tree of Life*, although ignorant of the fact that this title was a central motif in the Qabalistic mysteries.

In later decades in the United States, particularly during the "psychedelic" phase, when hallucinatory substances were used to find new access to the occult regions of the mind, a novel pattern of cosmic art emerged. The mandalas of José and Miriam Arguelles, Dion Wright and Roberto Matiello were examples. The psychedelic work of Abdul Mati Klarwein also attracted considerable attention. Vivid and tantric, like that of Spare it revealed both a Qabalistic leaning and a marked sexuality.

OCCULT LITERATURE

Occult literature can be divided into two major categories: works of fiction that are clearly influenced by the occult; and works of "fact," often containing esoteric wisdom allegedly written by supernatural authors, but more usually written by known practitioners of the occult arts.

Of the latter category, the ancient *Hermetica* (said to have been written by Hermes Trismegistus) has had the most profound influence on the occult, although the works of more recent occultists, such as Eliphas Lévi, Gerald Gardner and Aleister Crowley, are also important. One of the most fascinating recent examples of occult literature is *The Urantia Book*, published by the Urantia Foundation in 1955. Alleged to have been communicated to the world (possibly by means of channeling) by supernatural beings between 1934 and 1935, the

Left: The American writer Edgar Allan Poe (1809–49), whose tales and poems of horror and the occult profoundly influenced the Symbolist movement. Baudelaire was a particular admirer of Poe; he translated Poe's work into French.

Right: Charles Baudelaire (1821–67), the leading French Symbolist writer and Décadent, *was the author of* Les Fleurs du Mal *("The Flowers of Evil"), a work that celebrated the beauty he saw as inherent in the morbid and perverse.*

196 chapters of *The Urantia Book* make up a complex account of the structure and history of the universe, the creation of humankind and the story of Jesus Christ. According to the book, Earth (Urantia) belongs to the local universe of Nebadon, part of the superuniverse of Orvonton, itself one of the seven that make up the "grand universe" that is governed by a supreme being. Paralleling the biblical Old Testament's account of the evolution of the world and the New Testament stories of Christ (renamed Michael of Nebadon), briefly summarized, the duty of humans is to strive to be perfect, as is God.

The flowering of occult fiction first occurred in the nineteenth century, partly a product of the Romantic movement, and partly the result of writers' indulgence in such consciousness-enhancing substances as opium.

It was the English writers of Gothic novels who founded today's horror genre. The first Gothic novel— *The Castle of Otranto* (1764) — by Horace Walpole (1717–97), led to a stream of spine-chilling tales concerning the supernatural, most notably Mary Wollstonecraft Shelley's (1707–1851) *Frankenstein, or the Modern Prometheus* (1818) and Bram Stoker's (1847–1912) *Dracula* (1897).

As in art, the Symbolist movement also played an important part in the development of occult literature. A hero of the movement was the American writer Edgar Allan Poe (1809–49),

whose tales of horror, such as *The Murders in the Rue Morgue* (1841), were greatly admired. One of Poe's strongest followers was the French poet Charles Baudelaire (1821–67), author of *Les Fleurs du Mal* (1857), which sought beauty in the perverse. Other leading writers of the French Symbolist school included student of the occult Arthur Rimbaud (1854–91), Paul Verlaine (1844–96) and Stéphane Mallarmé (1842–98). Closely related to the French Symbolists were the early twentieth-century Italian "twilight poets," *I Crespuscolari*, whose members included Giosuè Carducci (1835–1907), author of the 1863 *L'Inno a Satana* ("The Hymn to Satan"); Gabriele D'Annunzio (1836–1938); Giovanni Pascoli (1855–1912); and Guido Gozzano (1883–1916). Interestingly, this Italian literary movement is also known as hermeticism, on account of its extensive use of occult symbolism.

With the exception of mystical novels of psychological disintegration, such as *Der Steppenwolf* (1927) by the German author Hermann Hesse (1877–1962), the occult fiction of the twentieth century has been dominated by the horror genre. Numerous Dracula and Frankenstein movies and such cinematic classics as *Rosemary's Baby* and *The Omen* movies have reinforced popular interest in, and knowledge of, the occult, as have Anne Rice's *Interview with the Vampire* and television series like "The X Files." The popular imagination has been awakened like never before, and this trend looks set to increase.

MYSTICAL MUSIC

Throughout history, all societies have recognized the consciousness-enhancing and healing powers of sound and music. In ancient times, for example, the Chinese believed that the universe was created by music, while in Hinduism and Buddhism, "Om" is the sound of perfection and the root of all things.

Because sound, including chanting, can result in an altered state of consciousness (which can be equated with ecstasy or mystical communion), it is a universal feature of the worlds' religions. Shamans, for instance, have an armory of magical chants and "power songs" at their disposal. They go into trances to the accompaniment of drumbeats or rattles, while the chanting of mantras, or "names of power," of Eastern faiths is not only an aid to meditation, but is additionally believed to send out cosmic vibrations. Many cultures—for example, the Native Americans of the Southwest, whose practices include lengthy chantway ceremonies—believe that music can summon magical powers. In the occult, chanting is demonstrated in the age-old incantation of spells, while twentieth-century Wiccans and neo-pagans employ chants to raise a "cone of power," a force that peaks to release psychic energy that performs a directed function.

The examples given above of music and musical chanting incorporate elements of a heritage specific to the musician's or chanter's culture. In recent decades, there have been countless commercially successful artists whose music is strongly influenced by such tradition: Clannad, for example, celebrate their Irish heritage; Yanni recalls Greek tradition; numerous groups perform the music of Hildegard of Bingen and the Gregorian chants; many African and Latin musicians have attracted a worldwide following.

Another important aspect of music is its healing function—a property especially cherished by Sufis and Native Americans—from ancient healing songs to modern musicians like Brook Medicine Eagle. In the West, however, music therapy has only become widely appreciated in the twentieth century, partly through the work of the American musician and therapist Helen L. Bonny. Jeffrey Thompson, composer of the synthesizer work "Isle of Skye," believes that music can soothe, inspire and heal through the stimulation of alpha and theta waves in the brain.

In as much as music is a potent a tool for relaxation and meditation (by lowering the pulse rate and affecting brain waves), it can be a powerful stimulant. For example, it can stimulate the release of the body's endorphins to alleviate pain. It can also provide a focus for self-exploration; the inner realm has been widely explored through a combination of such music and potentially dangerous mind-altering substances, especially during the 1960s and '70s, and during the "rave" phenomenon of the 1990s. Certain types of music (notoriously "heavy-metal" rock music) can cause aggressive behavior. Numerous rock and progressive-rock musicians have developed these experimental features within their music: The Beatles' *Sergeant Pepper's Lonely Hearts Club Band* was a work of exploration, as was the music created by Jefferson Airplane and The Grateful Dead. The "cosmic rock" of Pink Floyd, Tangerine Dream and King Crimson extended these ideas in rock music, and the works of progressive musicians including Mike Oldfield and Steve Hillage incorporate similar ideas within another, diffently focused musical direction.

New Age practitioners use music to promote positive feelings and emotional well-being. Often inspired by the chants and songs of ancient cultures or such natural sounds as the songs of whales or a steadily beating heart, this music is intended to evoke peaceful emotions and promote a feeling of harmony with the natural world. Voices, traditional instruments and melodies, electronic elements and recordings of sounds from nature are freely blended to produce the fluid sounds of "space music," the increasingly popular New Age genre exemplified by the work of musicians including Vangelis and Kitaro.

Left: The Sanskrit sacred syllable "Om" (or "Aum") is believed to be the sound of creation and perfection. When chanted, it helps the believer attain a higher level of consciousness and is thought to radiate cosmic vibrations.

Below: New Age music embraces natural sounds, such as the peaceful lapping of waves against the shore, to evoke feelings of peace, harmony and a sense of union with nature. The conch shell has particular significance within Eastern religions, because its sound resembles the sacred syllable "Om."

WHO'S WHO IN THE OCCULT

• Cornelius Agrippa (1486–1535)
Henry Cornelius Agrippa Von Nettesheims was born of noble parentage in Cologne. From an early age he encountered mystics and Rosicrucians and became vitally interested in the Qabalah and Hermeticism. His famous work *De Occulta Philosopha* was very influential in its day as a key magical text and deals especially with divine names, natural magic and cosmology.

• Albertus Magnus (1205–80)
Albertus, called "the Great," was born in the town of Larvigen on the Danube. Regarded by his contemporaries as a major alchemist and theologian, he attributed much of his vitality to visionary inspiration from the Virgin Mary. He became Bishop of Ratisbon, but was not an orthodox cleric. Some of his colleagues claimed that he communicated with the devil, and he himself claimed to have magical control over the weather. He is best known as an adept who discovered the Philosopher's Stone, and stated in his work *De Rebus Metallis et Mineralibus* that he had conducted tests on alchemical gold. Several other books on magic, love philtres and curious superstitions have been wrongly ascribed to him.

• Sri Aurobindo (1872–1950)
An Indian mystic, philosopher and poet. His philosophy, known as "integral yoga" is followed by many converts throughout the world. He began his career with a classics degree from Cambridge. Returning to India, he became the leader of the extremist faction of the nationalists, advocating armed revolt, and was eventually jailed. Turning from politics to mysticism, he studied the traditional forms of yoga and eventually synthesized them into his new philosophy of *purna* (integral) yoga. He developed a community of disciples at Pondicherry, and after his death the community built a new city, Auroville, on the Bay of Bengal. Mira Richard, the wife of a French diplomat who met Aurobindo in 1914, took over the leadership after his death, supervising the building of Auroville and founding the Sri Aurobindo Society in 1960.

• Alice Bailey (1880–1949)
An English writer on Theosophy and mysticism, who founded the "Arcane School" in 1923. After a period of activity in the Theosophical Society, she left to pursue an independent course. Mrs. Bailey was a prolific author: today the twenty-four volumes of her writings are published by the Lucis Publishing Companies in the United States, England and Switzerland.

• Franz Bardon
Little known outside specialist circles, Austrian magician Franz Bardon has written three important books: *Initiation into Hermetics*, *The Practice of Magical Evocation* and *The Key to the True Quabalah*.

• Francis Barrett
Apart from the possibility that Francis Barrett may have been connected with Bulwer-Lytton, who was himself an initiate and occultist, little is known of Barrett's life and magical interests. In 1801 he published *The Magus*, complete with illustrations of devils like Theulus and Asmodeus, which was described as "The Celestial Intelligencer," a complete system of occult philosophy. His work encompasses symbolism, numerology, alchemy and Qabalistic magic.

• Alan Bennett (1872–1923)
Bennett, also known ias Frater Iehi Aour, was Aleister Crowley's tutor in the magical arts. Bennett was originally absorbed in ceremonial magic and wrote the powerful evocation of *Taphthartharath*, used for man-

ifesting a spirit of Mercury. He also compiled part of the exhaustive magical reference system *777*, later published by Crowley. Eventually, Bennett tired of magic, and in 1900 he left England for Ceylon, where he became a worshipper of Shiva and assumed the title Bhikku Ananda Metteya. Later he joined a Buddhist monastery.

• Annie Besant (1847–1933)
An English Theosophist and social reformer who became the second President of the Theosophical Society in 1891. She was actively involved in various social movements throughout her life, ranging from feminist causes and the advocacy of birth control to the Fabian Society, Home Rule for India and the Boy Scout movement. Originally an outspoken atheist, she was converted to the Theosophical view by Madame Blavatsky (*qv*) in 1889 and rose rapidly in the Society, achieving a widespread reputation as a lecturer and author. She was closely associated with Charles Leadbeater (*qv*) in the sponsoring of Jiddu Krishnamurti (*qv*) as the new world teacher, and was involved in the Order of the Star in the East, which propagated that claim. Dr. Besant was also a leader of the Co-Masonic movement, a group of Freemasons originating in France and admitting women as well as men. She wrote prolifically, her most important Theosophical work being *The Ancient Wisdom* (1897).

• William Blake (1757–1827)
Blake experienced visions from an early age, and these informed his art and poetry, as did his interest in the Swedish mystic Emanuel Swedenborg. He came to believe that the universal truths lay in the human imagination and spent much of his time in meditation. After studying at the Royal Academy of Art in London, he became an engraver, developing in 1788 a technique he called "Illumined Printing," which combined his illustrations and his poetry. His best-known works include the poetic collection *Songs of Experience* (1794), *Milton* (1804–08), and *Jerusalem* (1804–20) and his brilliant mystical illustrations for the Biblical Book of Job and Dante's *Divine Comedy*.

• Helena Petrovna Blavatsky (1831–91)
A Russian mystic and adventuress, who founded the Theosophical Society in 1875. After a life of adventure and travel, she claimed to have been contacted by "Mahatmas," or "Masters," who inspired her to found the Society and to write several books laying the foundations of Theosophy. Her main works were *Isis Unveiled* (1877) and *The Secret Doctrine* (1888), and she also wrote a series of smaller books. Probably more than any other figure, this enigmatic and mysterious woman has influenced contemporary occultism, albeit in indirect ways; there is no doubt that she was a powerful medium and possessed psychic powers. She sought to synthesize Eastern and Western philosophy and religion, and science and religion, but her rather ponderous style and the incredible detail of her two main books makes their analysis extremely difficult. Madame Blavatsky was involved in a number of other occult movements, including an unorthodox branch of Freemasonry.

• Raymond Buckland (b. 1934)
An American witch, who has claimed the leadership of eighteen American Gardnerian covens and operated a witchcraft museum. Buckland claims the degree of Doctor of Philosophy and is often stated to be an anthropologist, although he reportedly works as a travel-brochure editor for an airline. His publications include: *Witchcraft…The Religion*, 1966; *Witchcraft*

from the Inside, 1971; *The Tree: The Complete Book of Saxon Witchcraft*, 1974; *Practical Color Magick*, 1983; and *Buckland's Complete Book of Witchcraft*, 1986.

• Edward Bulwer-Lytton (1803–73)
Best known for his book *The Last Days of Pompeii*, Bulwer-Lytton considered his most significant books to be those with a strong occult theme. These included *Zanoni*, a novel modeled on the Comte de Saint Germain, and *A Strange Story*. He studied at Cambridge and on several occasions entertained the French magician Eliphas Lévi at Knebworth, his family residence. Bulwer-Lytton was at one time the honorary Grand Patron of the Societies Rosicruciana in Anglia, a predecessor of the Golden Dawn.

• W.E. Butler (1898–1978)
A leading English authority on magic and the occult, who trained as a member of Dion Fortune's (*qv*) "Fraternity of the Inner Light," and studied under the English psychic Robert King. Butler wroteextensively on the Western magical tradition, acquiring a reputation as a highly skilled lecturer and teacher. His books include: *Magic, its ritual, purpose and power*; *The Magician, his training and work*; *Apprenticed to Magic*; *Magic and the Qabalah*. Butler established the magical order of the Servants of the Light (S.O.L.) in Jersey, which became noted for its practice of "pathworkings."

• Alessandro Di Cagliostro (1743–95)
Regarded by Carlyle as "The Prince of Quacks," Cagliostro, whose real name was Guiseppe Balsamo, was a traveler and something of a occult poseur. He gained something of a reputation as an alchemist in the courts of Europe at a time when princes and kings were keen to keep extra gold in their coffers. He later returned to London and was initiated into Freemasonry. Cagliostro was infatuated with the Egyptian origins of Freemasonry and he continued traveling around Europe as a occultist and resident magician-cum-faith healer. He spent the last few years of his life in prison.

• Paul Foster Case (d. 1954)
An American occultist and magician who founded the "Builders of the Adytum," centered in California and deriving from the traditions of the Order of the Golden Dawn; it centered largely on the Tarot Cards. Case was the author of several books, including *Highlights of the Tarot*, *The Tarot* and *The Book of Tokens*.

• Carlos Castaneda (b. 1925)
While studying at the University of California, Carlos Castaneda made the acquaintance of an old Yaqui Indian named Don Juan Matus. Don Juan allowed Castaneda to become his pupil in shamanism and sorcery, and Castaneda's books are a remarkably lucid account of Don Juan's ritual practices and philosophy of perception. Castaneda's first book, *The Teachings of Don Juan* (1968), attracted considerable attention in America, partly because of its vivid descriptions of hallucinogenic states of awareness. Castaneda now regards his apprenticeship in sorcery as most significantly providing a new vision for perceiving the ordinary world. His other books include *A Separate Reality*, *Journey to Ixtlan*, *Tales of Power* and *The Second Ring of Power*. They represent perhaps one of the most significant encounters of alien intellects in the history of anthropology.

• Edgar Cayce (1877–1945)
An American psychic and healer, born in Kentucky the son of a farmer, Cayce received a limited educa-

tion, but found later in his life that he could go into a trance and diagnose other people's illnesses, and prescribe treatment. He also claimed to recall former incarnations, and thus came to hold, contrary to his religious upbringing, the theory of reincarnation. His readings, given while in trance, have been recorded and kept, and in 1931 the Association for Research and Enlightenment was formed to collate and utilize them. Although Cayce wrote comparatively little himself, numerous volumes have been written about him and compiled from his readings.

• "Cheiro"
Count Louis Harmon, one of the world's most famous palmists and occultists, achieved a reputation among the rich and the notable, who flocked to him for readings. His reputation was enhanced by his prolific writing, and his books include: *You and Your Hand*, *Language of the Hand* and his memoirs, *Confessions of a Modern Seer*.

After he was orphaned at the age of twelve, Chinmoy Kumar Ghose lived at Sri Aurobindo's ashram at Pondicherry, where, a few years after his arrival, he attained the highest state of consciousness, the *nirvikalpa samadhi*. He remained in contemplation and study at Pondicherry until 1964, when he moved to New York to spread his message. He became known in the West as an inspirational teacher of Raja yoga and meditation, as well as a gifted musician.

• Grace Cooke (1892–1979)
According to the Englishwoman Grace Cooke, the spirit of the native American White Eagle of the Great White Brotherhood first appeared to her as a child. After becoming a Spiritualist medium in 1913, she received a vision from White Eagle asking her to encourage an international community of brotherly love (1936). As a result, she established the White Eagle Brotherhood. The organization became known worldwide through its channeling, healing and meditational practices, which were popularized through her books. Subsequently renamed White Eagle Lodge, the organization proclaims White Eagle's teachings: opportunity, correspondence, equilibrium and balance, karma, and reincarnation.

• Aleister Crowley (1875–1947)
See pages 41–43.

• Sir Francis Dashwood (1708–81)
Dashwood, one time Chancellor of the Exchequer, is best known for his notorious "Hell-Fire" club, at Medmenham Abbey in Buckinghamshire. His monks and nuns traveled by boat to the abbey and made use of a series of underground passages beneath it that were supposed to imitate the entrance to Hell. Their rituals combined sexual orgy and drunken revelry with a parody of the Mass.

• Andrew Jackson Davis (1826–1910)
Known as the "seer of Poughkeepsie," Davis was an American psychic and healer. He was heavily influenced by both Swedenborg and Mesmerism (*qv*), and wrote extensively on the basis of his clairvoyant visions, becoming one of the leading theorists of the young American spiritualist movement. His main work was *The Principles of Nature* (1847).

• Dr. John Dee (1527–1608)
Classical scholar, philosopher, mathematician and astrologer, John Dee began his career as an academic at Cambridge and traveled widely in Europe. Following a meeting with one Jerome Cardan in England in 1552, he became interested in the conjuration of spirits, and when Elizabeth I came to the throne, he was invited to calculate the most beneficial astrological date for her coronation. Dee's magical career really began, however, in 1581, when he met Edward Kelley, who was both a medium and a "skryer." Kelley, who is said to have had his ears

cropped on account of committing forgery, possessed an alchemical manuscript and Dee was especially interested in Kelley's alchemical secrets. Dee and Kelley made use of wax tablets (called "almadels") engraved with magical symbols. The tablet for a given invocation was to be laid between four candles, and it was then that an angel would appear. Eventually the angels began to dictate the types of magical equipment to be used, and in 1582 Edward Kelley began to receive messages in a new angelic language called Enochian. A dictionary of Enochian was published in the United States by Israel Regardie.

• Jeane Dixon (1918–97)
An American psychic who achieved a great deal of publicity for her predictions of national and international events, she was a practicing Catholic who attended services regularly. She claimed to have predicted the assassinations of President John F. Kennedy, Martin Luther King and Senator Robert Kennedy. Mrs. Dixon used cards, a crystal ball, astrology and numerology as methods of divination.

• Florence Farr (1860–1917)
Actress and mistress to George Bernard Shaw, Florence Farr was introduced to magic by W. B. Yeats. She formed her own magical group, "The Sphere." Perhaps her most significant contribution to magic was a volume entitled *Egyptian Magic*.

• J. Arthur Findlay (1883–1964)
An English Spiritualist and author, founder of the Glasgow Society for Psychic Research, and co-founder of Psychic Press Ltd., which published *Psychic News*. He spent many years investigating spiritualist phenomena and wrote widely on the subject. His best-known book was *On the Edge of the Etheric*.

• Arthur Ford (1897–1971)
A well-known American Spiritualist and medium, member of the A.S.P.R. and an ordained minister of the Disciples of Christ from 1923. His psychic experiences began during World War I. Although he began his career through a meeting with Sir Arthur Conan Doyle, it was his association with Bishop James Pike that generated much of his fame. The bishop consulted Ford after the death of his son, Jim, and believed that Ford had made contact with the young man's spirit. Pike wrote a book, *The Other Side*, recounting his experiences with Ford.

• Dion Fortune (1891–1946)
Dion Fortune, whose real name was Violet Firth joined the Theosophical Society and took courses in psychoanalysis at a young age. In 1919 she became a member of the Order of the Golden Dawn and began to write occult fiction. In 1924 she established the Society of the Inner Light. Most of her writings present a clear common-sense approach to the occult. Her book *The Mystical Qabalah* is regarded by many occultists as one of the best textbooks ever written on magic.

• Oliver Fox
Oliver Fox was one of the first pioneers in the area of controlled out-of-the-body experiences, or "astral projection." He considered one of the best methods of projection to be the "Dream of Knowledge," acquisition of consciousness in the dream state. His personal account of these practices was published in the *English Occult Review* in 1920, and in popular book form by University Books, New York, in 1962.

• Sigmund Freud (1856–1939)
The importance of the founder of psychoanalysis in the occult lies in his postulation of the human mind's unconscious. Although deeply interested in the occult, particularly in telepathy and possession, he denied the existence of paranormal phenomena.

• Fulcanelli (1877–1932)
A mysterious and semi-legendary alchemist, Fulcanelli

(Jean-Julian Champagne) is said to be one of the only serious researchers to pursue the *magnum opus*, or Philosopher's Stone, in this century. During the early 1920s, a French student of alchemy named Eugene Canseliet was given a manuscript by his mentor, the man now known as Fulcanelli. Published as *The Mystery of the Cathedrals*, the book caused a sensation in 1926, when it appeared in Paris. Basically, it expounded the alchemical symbolism carved in the decorative motifs on the Gothic cathedrals in Bourges, Amiens and Paris. Fulcanelli disappeared suddenly and for many years seemed to have vanished. Canseliet claims, however, that he saw him briefly years later, when he should have been around 100 years old, and "he looked not older than I was myself" (around 50). Some believe that Fulcanelli found the great alchemical secret of eternal youth.

• Gerald Brousseau Gardner (1884–1964)
See page 39.

• Uri Geller (b.1946)
A young Israeli psychic, Uri Geller became famous for his strange faculty for bending forks and stopping watches at will. Geller claims that his power derives from an extraterrestrial source. According to Andrija Puharich, who compiled the first biography on Geller, the ESP power comes from nine UFO entities "whose souls have transformed into computer." These computer beings are said to be using him as a mouthpiece until they commence an invasion of the planet, and to select him they undertook a computer analysis of the whole of mankind.

• Karl Germer (1885–1962)
German-born Karl Germer became the head of the Ordo Templi Orientis following the death of Aleister Crowley in 1947. Germer was responsible for publishing some of Crowley's obscure works, like *Magick Without Tears*. His magical name was Frater Saturnus.

• Joan Grant (b. 1907)
An English writer on reincarnation, who claims the ability to recall her former incarnations—a process she refers to as "far memory." She has written a series of semi-fictional works recounting in detail individual previous incarnations, from the Egyptian period to the Middle Ages and pre-Colombian America.

• Kenneth Grant (b. 1924)
Following the death of Aleister Crowley, Kenneth Grant continued as a devotee of Crowley's Law of Thelema and in 1955 set up his own Isis Lodge in England. Grant follows the form of magic pursued by Crowley after the latter's Egyptian initiation. Much of Grant's interest focuses on sex magic—the ritual union of opposites. He is also an authority on the great trance artist-magician Austin Spare.

• Celia Green (b. 1935)
As Director of the Institute of Psychophysical Research, Oxford, Celia Green was largely responsible for the revival of interest among British psychologists in out-of-the-body states of consciousness and "lucid dreams." The documented evidence in her book *Out of the body Experiences* continued the view of pioneers like Oliver Fox and Sylvan Muldoon—that "astral projection" was a natural function of the mind and could be achieved at will.

• Stanislas de Guaita (1861–97)
De Guaita, born of a distinguished Lombard family, was one of the main figures behind the fashionable Rosicrucian revival in the salons of Paris in the 1890s. Together with Sar Peladan, he founded the "Ordre de la Rose-Croix Kaballistique." De Guaita was a published poet and a student of law, but after reading the works of Eliphas Lévi he devoted himself completely to ritual and the occult.

• Georgei Ivanovich Gurdjieff (1866–1949)
Gurdjieff was a controversial figure, claimed as a great

mystic by some, and denigrated as a fraud by others. He developed a complicated cosmology based on the belief that humans exist in a state of unconsciousness, which must be overcome in order to obtain true consciousness. Around 1914 he established his first school in Moscow, devoted to the attainment of self-realization under the tutelage of "Men Who Know." As his method developed, he espoused such "shock" tactics as physical labor and dance, to break down learned and artificial perceptions.

• **Manly Palmer Hall (b. 1901)**
An American student of the occult, he founded the Philosophical Research Society in Los Angeles in 1936. He is a prolific writer on many aspects of occultism and the esoteric tradition. His books include: *The Secret Teachings of All Ages; Man, the Grand Symbol of the Mysteries;* and *Twelve World Teachers.*

• **Franz Hartmann (1838–1912)**
A German occultist, theosophist and physician. His books include: *Magic Black and White, Occult Science and Medicine, Life of Paracelsus, Life of Jehoshua.* Hartmann was the founder of the "Order of the Esoteric Rose Croix" and was connected with Engel's "Order of the Illuminati," and with John Yarker's Masonic group. He was also involved with Reuss (*qv*) and another German named Klein in the occult group that developed into the Ordo Templi Orientis.

• **Max Heindel (1865–1919)**
The pseudonym of Max Grashof, who was a member of that group of Theosophists in the United States led by Katherine Tingley. He claimed he had been initiated into the traditional Rosicrucian Order in Germany, and as a result founded the Rosicrucian Fellowship in California and published numerous books, including *The Rosicrucian Cosmo-conception.*

• **Adolf Hitler (1889–1945)**
It is claimed by many theorists that Hitler was deeply involved in the occult, and could have been a "front man" for an inner occult group which actually controlled the Nazi Party. Various authors have also suggested that Hitler's power was based at least in part on his possession of occult gifts. A number of occult and magical groups were operating in Germany at the time, and links with Hitler and other high-ranking officials of the Party have been established.

• **Harry Houdini (1874–1926)**
The famous stage magician and escape artist who, highly critical of Spiritualism, took part in a number of investigations of alleged "phenomena."

• **Lafayette Ronald Hubbard (1911–86)**
The founder and leader of Scientology and author of numerous books on that subject. Hubbard began his career as a science fiction author, but eventually discovered a technique which he called "Dianetics," later developed into the philosophy called "Scientology." The resulting movement eventually spread throughout the world. Hubbard claimed to possess a wide range of extrasensory powers through which he gained the information used in Dianetics and Scientology, including details of the reincarnational history of man, the nature of mental illness, its causes and treatment, and the development of vastly increased intellectual powers.

• **William James (1842–1910)**
A founding member of the A.S.P.R., the philosopher William James was the brother of the novelist Henry James. In 1871 he became a teacher of psychology, physiology, and philosophy at Harvard University. Fascinated by the paranormal, he collaborated with the British Society for Psychical Research in 1882 and helped found the A.S.P.R. (in 1885).

• **Allen Kardek (1804–69)**
The pseudonym of Hyppolyte Leon Denizard Rivail, a French Spiritualist and physician who had great influence on the Spiritualist movement (generally known as "spiritism") in South America. His books are: *The Book of Mediums, The Book of the Spirits* and *The Gospels According to Spiritism.*

• **Karl Kellner (d. 1935)**
While traveling through India and the Middle East in 1896, Karl Kellner, a German businessman, claimed to have come into contact with three adepts, two of whom were Arabs and the other a Hindu. On the basis of the sexual-yogic techniques that he learnt from them, he decided to establish an occult society, the Order of the Oriental Templars, or OTO.

• **Semyon Davidovich Kirlian**
A Russian electrical technician who developed the technique now known as "Kirlian photography" (1970–75) for photographing aura and energy fields.

• **J.Z. Knight (b. 1946)**
Knight is best known as the channeler of the 35,000-year-old "Ramtha, the Enlightened One." Unlike many channelers, Knight had no paranormal experiences until she was thirty-one, when Ramtha appeared to her as she was handling a model pyramid. Ramtha claimed that Knight was the reincarnation of his daughter Ramaya, and said that through channeling his wisdom she would "become a light unto the world," which her adherents indeed claim that she is.

• **Jiddu Krishnamurti (1895–1986)**
At the age of fourteen, Krishnamurti was identified by Charles W. Leadbeater and Annie Besant as the messianic Maitreya (the final manifestation of Buddha). After studying in England, he was initiated into the Esoteric Section of the Theosophical Society, and into the mystical Great White Brotherhood in 1910. In 1911 he became head of the theosophical Order of the Star of the East, but he became disenchanted with the teachings of theosophy and disbanded the order in 1929. From California, the headquarters of the Krishnamurti Foundation, he taught that religions are "obstacles preventing spiritual self-fulfillment, for they are mere refuges"; truth, he believed, comes from inside.

• **Anton Szandor La Vey**
The founder and leader of the Church of Satan in the United States. After a varied career, which included playing in an orchestra, working with a circus, assisting in hypnotism shows and being a police photographer, La Vey began holding an occult study group, which included Kenneth Anger (*qv*), the underground film-maker. Eventually, in 1966, he set up the Church of Satan. La Vey is the author of *The Satanic Bible* and *Satanic Rituals.*

• **Charles Webster Leadbeater (1847–1934)**
An English Theosophist and author, who left the Church of England, in which he was a minister, to follow Madam Blavatsky (*qv*) in her Theosophical work. Eventually, he became the leading colleague of Annie Besant (*qv*), and one of the major influences on Krishnamurti (*qv*). He lectured and wrote extensively on Theosophy, and divided his time largely between Adyar, the TS Headquarters, and Sydney, Australia, where he headed a commune of students of Theosophy. He became a Bishop in the Liberal Catholic Church, which he helped to found, and was its second Presiding Bishop. He also attained high rank in the Co-Masonic Order. Leadbeater was the subject of several scandals, and at one point resigned from the TS. He is alleged to have been a pedophile. His numerous books include: *The Masters and the Path, Man Visible and Invisible, The Hidden Side of Things, The Science of the Sacraments.* He also co-wrote several books with Annie Besant.

• **Sybil Leek (1923–83)**
Probably the best-known modern witch in America, Mrs. Leek came to the USA from England in 1964, and claimed to trace her witchcraft ancestry back to the twelfth century. Her books include *Diary of a Witch, The Sybil Leek Book of Fortune Telling* and *Cast Your Own Spell.*

• **Eliphas Lévi (1810–75)**
Baptized Alphonse-Louis Constant, Eliphas Lévi was born in Paris, the son of a poor shoemaker. He studied for the seminary but was obliged to leave because of his sexual behavior and his revolutionary political tendencies. Despite limited abilities as a graphic artist, he sketched political caricatures and moved for a time in select literary company. His marriage to Noemi Cadiot in 1846, when she was eighteen, was unsuccessful. Lévi turned to magical philosophy and produced a succession of works, the most important being *Le Dogme et Ritual de la Haute Magie, Histoire de la Magie* and *La Cle des Grandes Mystéres.* A.E. Waite, the occult authority who translated the first two titles, considered Levi's work important historically, but fraught with errors. However, Aleister Crowley considered himself Lévi's reincarnation and admired him unreservedly. Lévi's main contribution to modern occultism was his discovery that the twenty-two Major Tarot Trumps correlated exactly with the paths on the Tree of Life, making them an important key to magical consciousness.

• **Howard Phillips Lovecraft (1890–1917)**
An American author of some fifty-three stories and assorted fragments and collaborations, all of which are based upon a bizarre and terrifying occult mythology. They were originally written for the pulp horror magazines of his time, but have subsequently acquired a reputation for their powerful occult quality, resulting in Lovecraft's becoming something of a cult figure. He developed a mythology centering on "the dread Cthulu"—concentrated evil and powers of darkness struggling to break through and control the world. Lovecraft's life was unhappy, and he was plagued by frightening dreams and the presence of his own mythology. Lovecraft's stories have been collected into a number of volumes, including *The Tomb, At the Mountains of Madness, The Case of Charles Dexter Ward, The Haunter of the Dark, The Lurker at the Threshold* and *The Shuttered Room.*

• **Maharishi Mahesh Yogi (b. 1918)**
The Maharishi Mahesh Yogi became probably the best-known guru in the West through his teaching of transcendental meditation (T.M.), which he learned from Guru Dev, whose disciple he was for twelve years. T.M. involves chanting a personal mantra during meditation sessions. Eventually the meditator will achieve a state of transcendental consciousness, in which the true self will be discovered; the ultimate goal is the seventh state of consciousness, in which cosmic unity is achieved. After establishing the Spiritual Regeneration Movement (S.R.M.) in 1958, the Maharishi left India and traveled to the U.S.A. and Europe. During the next two decades, he founded the International Meditation Society (I.M.S.), the Students' International Meditation Society (S.I.M.S.), and the Maharishi International University, as well as the Foundation for the Science of Creative Intelligence. Various programs for world peace followed in the 1980s, and the movement is now known as the World Plan Executive Council.

• **Charles Manson (b. 1934)**
Currently serving a life sentence for his part in the Sharon Tate murders in August 1969, Charles Manson was a self-proclaimed messiah figure for his cult. He called himself "both God and Satan" and his gang "The Family." In California at that time occultism was beginning to entrench itself as a major philosophy of the subculture, and Manson's commune existed side by side with groups like the Process and

the O.T.O. Solar Lodge. Through the works of Aleister Crowley and L. Ron Hubbard, Manson believed that the end of the world was near. Manson's Satanic desire to kill increased to the point of multiple murder.

• **Samuel Liddell MacGregor Mathers (1854–1918)**
Samuel Mathers was undoubtedly one of the key figures in the realm of ritual magic and ceremonial, although he never became a popular cult figure like his rival Aleister Crowley. Nevertheless, he helped to found the Hermetic Order of the Golden Dawn. In 1887 Dr. Wynn Westcott (*qv*), who was a London coroner and Freemason, as well as a delver into the occult arts, showed some Rosicrucian papers to Mathers. Though written in cipher, they were interpreted as a series of rituals. Westcott asked Mathers to modify and embellish these so that they could be the basis of a new magical Order. Soon, however, Mathers claimed to be obtaining his inspiration from exclusive Secret Chiefs, and he began to wield autocratic authority over his fellow Order members. In particular, he demanded financial support while translating key occult texts in Paris. It was here that he located and translated a medieval grimoire, *The Sacred Magic of Abra-melin the Mage*, regarded by some as the most powerful magical document in the entire Western tradition. Mathers loved ancient mythology and occult lore, and among his other translations are the alchemical book *Splendor Solis* by Solomon Trismosin, and *The Kabbalah Unveiled*. He also wrote a short book on the Tarot.

• **Victor Neuburg (1883–1940)**
Neuburg was a poet, author, editor and magician. A literary inspiration to Pamela Hansford Johnson and Dylan Thomas, he was also a follower of Aleister Crowley in the days when the "Great Beast" practiced an obscure form of homosexual sex-magic. Neuburg accepted Crowley's claim that the perfect symbolic form of man was the heavenly androgyne—a figure containing both sexes—and he took part in the rites of the Argentinum Astrum as Crowley's magical partner. Neuburg avoided Crowley later in life, and moved away from the occult.

• **Nostradamus (1503–66)**
Nostradamus (Michel de Notre Dame) was Catherine de Medici's favorite astrologer. Conversant with French, Latin and Provençal, he dabbled in magic while maintaining that he was inspired by God alone. His book *The Centuries*, which has appeared in numerous editions since 1555, when it was first published, purports to include prophecies for the world up to its "end" in 1999.

• **Sar Péladan (1858–1918)**
Astrologer, magician, art critic and novelist, Joséphin Péladan became a fashionable dandy and aesthete in the Rosicrucian salons of Paris in the 1890s. Péladan took the title "La Sar Merodack" after the King of Babylon, and he sported a full Assyrian-style beard. He was fascinated by the symbol of the androgyne, and also contrived to establish decadence as a major art form. Péladan produced a cycle of novels entitled *La Decadence Latine*, which he hoped would counter the materialistic tendencies of France in his day. Influenced by de Sade, he was also a good friend and tutor in the magical arts to Stanislas de Guaita (*qv*), with whom he revived the Rosicrucian Mysteries.

• **Papus (1865–1916)**
Papus was the *nom de plume* of Gerard Encausse, a Spanish-born occult writer who trained originally for medicine. Influenced by Theosophy, he was impressed by the idea that all elements of the universe—mineral, vegetable and animal—evolve toward perfection in a sequence of struggles and sacrifice. He delved into hermetic and alchemical texts and found there a chemistry of the soul. Papus acquired

a reputation as a necromancer. He wrote a large number of books on the occult and was fascinated by the symbolic connections between the Tarot and Qabalah. His best-known work is *The Tarot of the Bohemians*.

• **Paracelsus (1493–1541)**
One of the most illustrious physicians and alchemists who ever sought the *prima materia*, the source of all life and virtue, Paracelsus was born Theophrast Bombast von Hohenheim, in Einsiedeln, Switzerland. He pursued medical studies under his father, who was a physician in Basle, and also delved into alchemy and occultism under the watchful care of Trimethius of Spanheim. Paracelsus traveled widely in Europe, seeking primarily a working basis on which to improve the poor medical standards of his day. His writings reveal a deep love of Christian mysticism, tinged with the pantheistic spirit common in alchemy. Paracelsus stressed the parallel between man, the *microcosm*, and the universe, or *macrocosm*, and considered that illness was a symptom of imbalance, nothing more. The three great principles of manifestation were sulfur (male), mercury (female) and salt (neutral), and the healthy person would combine these elements in harmony. He also believed in the magical creation of artificial creatures—Homunculi—a medieval precursor of test-tube babies. His alchemical and hermetic tracts include discourses on the planets, the elements and metals, and the relationship of alchemy to mysticism. His work marks the transition from alchemy as a crudely conceived pre-science for the transmutation of lead into gold, into a spiritual science of man.

• **Harry Price (1881–1948)**
A famous British psychic researcher, and one of the first people to establish the investigation of such phenomena on a scientific basis. From his background in stage conjuring, Price became expert at detecting fraud, although in later years some of his own investigations came under criticism. He established a massive library of works on the occult, spiritualism and psychic phenomena, which eventually became the National Library of Psychical Research. He was the author of *Fifty Years of Psychical Research* (1939), *Poltergeist Over England* (1945) and two studies of the Borley Rectory haunting, which he investigated.

• **Pascal Beverley Randolph (1825–71)**
An American occultist and the founder of numerous minor occult group. He had been a member of the Societas Rosicruciania in Anglia (a Masonic order), and claimed to have been initiated into a secret Syrian Order. He began his occult involvement as a medium, and eventually developed a special interest in sexual magic, on which he published several books, some of which led to charges in court. He committed suicide in 1871. It is generally believed that he had taught Kellner (*qv*) the theory and techniques of sexual magic later enshrined in the Ordo Templi Orientis, although his successor, Clymer (*qv*), denied all knowledge of such teachings. His principal works were: *Ravalette: The Rosicrucians' Story, Dealing with the Dead, Eulis: The History of Love*.

• **Israel Regardie (1907–85)**
Regardie was born in England, but lived most of his life in America, where he practiced as a Reichian psychotherapist. He is best known, however, as one of the major occult writers on magic, mythology and the rituals of the Golden Dawn. In 1928 he became Aleister Crowley's personal secretary, and in 1937 he published the first of four volumes providing full details of the magical rituals of the Golden Dawn and Stella Matutina occult societies. Many occultists felt that Regardie had broken an oath of secrecy, but his 4-volume work *The Golden Dawn* is a major source. Regardie's best writing was probably that in *The Tree*

of Life, which includes details of the mythology underlying modern magic, with special emphasis on Egyptian gods and the Hindu *tattvas*. His other key books include *The Middle Pillar*, which relates magic to Kundalini Yoga; *The Philosopher's Stone*, a study of alchemy and psychology, with a commentary on the *Coelum Terrae* of Thomas Vaughan; and *Roll Away The Stone*, which relates drugs to magic. His last publication was *Ceremonial Magic*, 1982. One of the last of a line of genuine occultists, Regardie was one of the greatest authorities on the Qabalah and ceremonial magic, and a popular counterculture figure.

• **Theodor Reuss (1855–1923)**
Reuss succeeded Karl Kellner as head of the tantric magic groups, the *Ordo Templi Orientis*, in 1905. It was he who invited Aleister Crowley to join their organization—accelerating The Great Beast's direction away from ceremonial ritual into the shady areas of sexual magic. After a stroke, Reuss resigned from his post as head of the OTO in 1922 and handed it over to Crowley, who endeavored to incorporate his own brand of occult lore. The OTO was suppressed by the Nazis in 1947.

• **Joseph B. Rhine (1895–1980)**
Dr. Rhine and his wife Louisa dominated scientific research programs into ESP for forty years. Rhine contacted William McDougall, professor of psychology at Harvard, after hearing a lecture on psychical research by Sir Arthur Conan Doyle. Both Rhine and McDougall later moved to Duke University, which has since become synonymous with research into telepathy, clairvoyance and psychokinesis. Rhine endeavored in the 1930s to give ESP scientific respectability by producing laboratory reports of subjects who appeared to show ESP ability far greater than chance. He worked with the well-known psychologists K.E. Zener (famous for his "Zener cards") and Dr. J.G. Pratt. Rhine's approach was mostly statistical, and his laboratory safeguards against fraudulence and error have been criticized. While Rhine paved the way for serious academic study of ESP, it is probable that the more exciting breakthroughs have occurred since his heyday, especially with regard to modern research into dream telepathy.

• **Jane Roberts (1929–84)**
It was not until 1963, when she received an automatic-writing communication, that the writer Jane Roberts had her first psychic experience. While subsequently experimenting with ouija boards, she made contact with the "energy personality essence" called Seth, whose channeler she would become. Seth claimed to have been born in Atlantis, and to have been reincarnated many times; he had known Roberts and her husband in their earlier lives in seventeenth-century Denmark. Although he communicated much information, including the coming of a messianic figure, in essence Seth's message was that humans, who are multidimensional, create their own reality.

• **Comte de Saint-Germain (1710–80)**
Popularly known as an aristocratic Freemason and Rosicrucian "who did not die," the comte was said to be the son of Prince Rakoczy of Transylvania. He grew up under the care of the last of the Medici, Gian Gastone, and was educated at the University of Siena. He had a penchant for grandiose titles, and during his mysterious career passed under the names of Comte Bellamarre, the Marquis de Montferrat and Chevalier Schoening, among others. The comte was said to have spoken Italian, German, English, Spanish, French, Greek, Arabic and Chinese. He was also a political envoy of repute and discoursed with figures as diverse as the Shah of Persia, Horace Walpole, Clive of India and Frederick the Great. It is said that Saint-Germain acquired wealth and immortality from his

discovery of the *Philosopher's Stone,* and that he demonstrated his alchemical prowess to the Marquis de Valbelle by transforming a silver coin into gold. Whatever the source of his knowledge and opulence, there is no doubt that Saint-Germain produced one of the most remarkable occult manuscripts ever in his *Most Holy Trinosophia,* a collection of alchemical/mystical visions.

• **Alex Sanders (1916–88)**
A contemporary English witch and leader of a worldwide movement in witchcraft, Sanders received considerable publicity for his claim that he was the "king of the witches." Sanders claimed origin from a family wherein witchcraft had been traditional for generations, and said he had been initiated at the age of seven when he accidentally discovered his grandmother performing rituals in her living room. Purportedly trained by his grandmother, he turned to black magic, through which he acquired a considerable fortune. He discovered the "left hand path" after the death of his sister and thereafter established himself as a teacher of witchcraft, heading a number of covens throughout England. Under these auspices, he married his wife, Maxine, who assisted him in his teaching as a High Priestess. He laid claim to a variety of titles and degrees.

• **David Spangler (b. 1945)**
When he was seven, Spangler had a profound mystical experience in which his past lives, and a feeling of unity with the universe, manifested themselves. After dropping out of university in 1965, he devoted himself to counseling and giving readings under the direction of John, a spirit being. In 1970 he joined Scotland's Findhorn Foundation Community as codirector, and the prophetic being Limitless Love and Truth began communicating with him. Spangler left Findhorn in 1973, after which he established the Lorian Association. His philosophy is based on the importance of humanity's development of a "planetary sensibility," or "Gaia mind," and he is thus regarded as one of the leading lights of the New Age movement.

• **Austin Spare (1888–1956)**
One of the most extraordinary artist/occultists who ever lived, Austin Osman Spare was hailed as a prodigy and won a scholarship to the Royal College of Art when he was only sixteen. Soon he came into contact with magic, Egyptian mythology and the teachings of Aleister Crowley and began to incorporate his mystical philosophy into his art. Spare believed in reincarnation, and claimed that all of his former lives, whether human or animal, were deeply embedded in the subconscious. The mystical purpose of man was to retrace those existences back to their source, which he called Kia. Spare believed this could be done in a state of trance, whereby one allowed oneself to be possessed by the atavists of former lives. He developed an interesting system of magical "sigils," which were symbols of meditation used for unleashing the potencies of the subconscious mind. Spare was undoubtedly one of England's finest illustrators, and some of his best work is contained in his *Book of Pleasure,* conceived when the artist was only twenty-two.

• **Rudolf Steiner (1861–1925)**
The German occultist, Theosophist and scholar who founded the Anthroposophical Society after breaking away from the Theosophical Society, largely over the issue of Krishnamurti (*qv*). Steiner acquired his Ph.D. for work on the German author Goethe, on whom he was an authority. Steiner, a clairvoyant, built up a complex philosophy and cosmology on the basis of his clairvoyant investigations, developing theories about subjects as diverse as farming and organic

gardening, Atlantis and Lemuria, the treatment of syphilis and cancer and the inner truths of Christianity. The Anthroposophical Society eventually spread throughout the world and developed a sub-group known as the Christian Community, in which members who sought a specifically Christian tradition could worship. Steiner's theories on education led to the development of "Steiner schools" throughout the world. Steiner was also connected with occult movements including the Ordo Templi Orientis, Engel's "Order of the Illuminati" and a group of Rosicrucians. A prolific author and lecturer, he published an astonishing amount of literature, including *Occult Science; an outline, Christianity as Mystical Fact,* and *Knowledge of the Higher World and its attainment.* His autobiography is titled *The Course of my Life.* Cf. *A Scientist of the Invisible* by A. Shepherd and *The Life and Work of Rudolf Steiner* by G. Wachsmuth.

• **Montague Summers (1880–1948)**
An English author of numerous books on Satanism, demonology, witchcraft and black magic, the value of which is disputed. He also translated a number of "classics" in those fields, including the *Malleus Maleficarum.* He was a believer, to the point of fanaticism, in the reality of the powers of evil, and advocated reintroduction of the death penalty for witchcraft. His books include: *The History of Witchcraft and Demonology, Werewolf, The Geography of Witchcraft.*

• **Richard Sutphen (b. 1937)**
Best known today as a hypnotist, Sutphen worked in advertising before his interest in the paranormal led him to study hypnosis. Past-life regression particularly interested him, for he believed that he had been a Mayan in a previous existence, and he developed something of a speciality in this area. He founded the short-lived Hypnosis Center in Scottsdale in 1973, and the subsequent Sutphen Corporation, which runs a successful seminar and publishing program. Reincarnationists, Inc., established in 1984, was less successful. A prolific author and lecturer, through his activities such as publicizing the power point of Sedona in Arizona, Sutphen has done much to bring aspects of mysticism into the public arena.

• **Emanuel Swedenborg (1688–1772)**
Swedenborg's brand of mysticism has had a profound effect on the beliefs of many esoteric societies, notably spiritualism and the New Age movements. After studying at the University of Uppsala, this son of a Lutheran bishop worked as a special assessor to the Swedish Royal College of Mines. Not until he was fifty-six did Swedenborg start having mystical trances, visions, and dreams, and he eventually came to believe that he had been chosen by God to instruct humanity on the content of his spiritual experiences, which were often dictated by "angels." Although deemed insane by many of his contemporaries, after his death a religion was formed around his beliefs called the Church of New Jerusalem (or New Church), and in 1810 the Swedenborg Society was founded to propagate his teachings. Simply expressed, according to Swedenborgianism, a spiritual world exists within the physical world, while the spirits of the dead are creations of individual human minds, which exist in a correspondingly self-created heaven or hell (his major work was entitled *Heaven and Hell.*)

• **Charles Tart (b. 1937)**
Professor Tart has become well known for his scientific research into trance, dreams, astral projection, out-of-the-body experiences and ESP. Tart is a researcher in Experimental Psychology at UCLA, Davis, and is one of a new line of scientists (which includes Claudio Naranjo, Paul Ornstein and John Lilly) who are endeavoring to close the gulf between

science and mysticism. Professor Tart's key work is his *Altered States of Consciousness* (1969).

• **Paul Twitchell (d.1971)**
The American founder of the "Eckankar" movements, which he led until his death, Twitchell claimed to have been taught the techniques of Eckankar by various masters, including the Tibetan "Rebazar Tarzs." He espoused the concept of out-of-the-body experience.

• **Arthur Edward Waite (1857–c. 1940)**
Toward the end of its day, the Golden Dawn magical society was headed by A.E. Waite. A reactionary against Theosophy, he detested the anti-Christian aspects of ritual magic and rewrote the ceremonial grades of the Order. Waite could not read Hebrew, but he produced three notable volumes on the Jewish Qabalah. The best of these was *The Holy Kabbalah,* which has since been republished. He wrote on nearly every aspect of the occult, and produced, with Pamela Coleman-Smith, a famous Tarot pack now known as the "Waite" or "Rider" pack. His other works include *The Occult Sciences, The Brotherhood of the Rosy Cross, The Mysteries of Magic* (a digest of Eliphas Lévi's teachings) and a fine mystical tract called *Azoth.* Waite also edited numerous alchemical and Masonic works, including the hermetic writings of Paracelsus.

• **Wynn Westcott (1848–1925)**
Dr. Westcott was a leading Freemason and coroner in London when a Rosicrucian manuscript in cipher came into his possession. MacGregor Mathers used the Rosicrucian rituals to form the basis of the Golden Dawn. After this, Westcott gradually lost significance in the Order, which he had hoped would rival the esoteric section of the Theosophical Society in London. He installed himself as a spiritual master of the Order, but his influence was slight.

• **Colin Wilson (b. 1931)**
When *The Outsider* was first published in 1956, it attracted widespread acclaim in literary circles as a treatment of the existential "loneliness" of visionaries, artists and creators. Wilson's view that such people have access to varying levels of inspiration and consciousness led him to compare two broad types of people: *murderers and criminals,* who have a type of negative intensity, and *mystics,* who could integrate these powerful, and sometimes transcendental, energies. Wilson's book *The Occult* was well received as an encyclopedic treatment of the influences underlying modern magic: alchemists, magicians, adepts and impostors, freemasons and witches—all were included. Wilson also advanced the view that man has an innate "magical capacity," which he called *Faculty X.* He argued that primitive man respected and applied this natural ability, but that civilized man gradually repressed and lost it.

• **Ambrose (1899–1972) and Olga Worrall (1906–85)**
The Worralls were gifted clairvoyants and healers, both of whom had experienced psychic phenomena, including visions of spirits and out-of-body experiences, since childhood, and who also demonstrated remarkable healing gifts from an early age. On the death of their infant twin sons in 1929, they decided to devote themselves to healing, often with spectacular success. They believed that their powers derived from "paraelectricity"—the universal life force.

• **W.B. Yeats (1865–1939)**
As a disciple of the Celtic mystery tradition, Yeats naturally gravitated toward the occult and founded a small group in Dublin called the Hermetic Students. A friend of "A.E.," the Irish mystic, Arthur Machen and MacGregor Mathers, he joined the Golden Dawn, and eventually became its leader at the turn of the century. Yeats became disillusioned with the Golden Dawn and left it, but magic continued to exercise an important influence on his poetry.

BIBLIOGRAPHY AND SOURCES

1: MAGIC

Franz Bardon, *The Practice of Magical Evocation,* Pravica, Graz-Puntigam, 1967.

J.H. Brennan, *Astral Doorways,* (1971); *Experimental Magic,* Aquarian Press, London, 1972.

C.A. Burland, *The Magical Arts,* Arthur Barker.

W.E. Butler, *Magic, Its Ritual, Purpose and Power* (1952) and *The Magician, His Training and Work* (1959) Aquarian Press, London.

Richard Cavendish, *The Black Arts,* Routledge & Kegan Paul, London, 1967.

W.B. Crow, *A History of Magic, Witchcraft and the Occult* (1968) and *The Occult Properties of Herbs* (1969) Aquarian Press, London.

Aleister Crowley, *Book Four,* Sangreal Foundation.

N. Drury, *The Path of the Chameleon,* Spearman.

Dion Fortune, *Psychic Self Defence,* Aquarian Press.

James Frazer, *The Golden Bough,* 1922 (various).

W. Gray, *Magical Ritual Methods,* Helios, Cheltenham, 1969; *The Inner Traditions of Magic,* Aquarian Press.

Rosemary Ellen Guiley, *Encyclopedia of Mystical and Paranormal Experience,* HarperCollins, 1991.

Douglas Hill and Pat Williams, *The Supernatural,* Bloomsbury Books, London, 1989.

E.O. James, *Prehistoric Religion,* Thames and Hudson.

Francis King, *Ritual Magic in England,* Spearman.

Gareth Knight, *The Practice of Ritual Magic,* Helios, Cheltenham, 1967.

L.W. De Laurance (ed.), *The Lesser Key of Solomon: Goetia, the Book of Evil Spirits,* De Laurance.

Eliphas Lévi, *The Ritual of Transcendental Magic,* 1856; *The History of Magic,* 1860; *A Key to the Grand Mysteries,* 1864 (various).

S.L. MacGregor Mathers (ed.), *The Sacred Magic of Abra-Melin the Mage* and *The Greater Key of Solomon,* De Laurance, Chicago, 1914.

Richard Marshall, *Witchcraft: The History and Mythology,* Saraband Inc., Rowayton, CT, 1995.

Ernest de Martino, *Magic Primitive and Modern,* Bay Books, Sydney, 1972.

Israel Regardie, *The Middle Pillar* (1970) and *The Golden Dawn* (1974) Llewellyn, St. Paul; *The Tree of Life: A Study of Magic* ,Weiser, N.Y., 1971.

Idries Shah, *The Secret Lore of Magic,* Abacus, London.

André and Lynette Singer, *Divine Magic: The World of the Supernatural,* Boxtree Ltd., London, 1995.

Guy Swanson, *The Birth of the Gods,* Univ. of Mich.

R.G. Torrens, *The Secret Rituals of the Golden Dawn,* Aquarian Press, Wellingborough, 1972.

Victor Turner, *The Ritual Process,* Penguin Books, Harmondsworth, 1974.

A.E. Waite, *The Book of Ceremonial Magic,* University Books, N.Y., 1961.

A.F.C. Wallace, *Religion, An Anthropological View,* Random House, N.Y., 1966.

Anton Szandor La Vey, *The Satanic Rituals,* Avon.

2: FORMS OF WITCHCRAFT

Marcus Bach, *Inside Voodoo,* New American Library.

Jack Bracelin, *Gerald Gardner, Witch,* Octagon.

Raymond Buckland, *Ancient and Modern Witchcraft,* H. C. Publishers, N.Y., 1970; *Witchcraft from the Inside,* Llewellyn, St. Paul, 1971.

Carlos Castenada, *The Teachings of Don Juan* (1968); *A Separate Reality* (1971); *Journey to Ixtlan* (1972); *Tales of Power* (1974); *The Second Ring of Power* (1977), Simon & Schuster, N.Y.

Richard Cavendish, *The Black Arts,* (see 1).

Aleister Crowley, *Magick in Theory and Practice,* 1929;

Book Four, (see 1); *The Qabalah of Aleister Crowley,* Weiser, N.Y., 1973; *The Vision and the Voice,* Sangreal Foundation, Dallas, 1972; *The Book of Lies,* Hayden Press, Ilfracombe, 1962; *The Book of Thoth,* 1944; *The Confessions of Aleister Crowley,* Hill & Wang, N.Y.; *The Magical Record of the Beast 666* (eds. John Symonds and Kenneth Grant), Duckworth, London, 1972; *Moonchild,* 1929; *Diary of a Drug Fiend,* 1922 (various).

Patricia Crowther, *Witch Blood,* House of Collectibles.

Scott Cunningham, *The Truth About Witchcraft Today,* Llewellyn Publications, St. Paul, 1988.

Nevill Drury, *Don Juan, Mescalito and Modern Magic: The Mythology of Inner Space,* Routledge & Kegan Paul, London, 1978.

Mircea Eliade, *Shamanism,* Bollingen, Princeton 1972.

Stewart Farrar, *What Witches Do,* Peter Davies.

John Fritscher, *Popular Witchcraft,* Citadel Press, NJ.

Gerald Gardner, *High Magick's Aid,* 1949; *Witchcraft Today,* 1954; *The Meaning of Witchcraft,* 1959.

Rosemary Goring (ed.), *The Wordsworth Dictionary of Beliefs and Religions,* Wordsworth Editions Ltd.

Kenneth Grant, *Aleister Crowley and the Hidden God.*

Rosemary Ellen Guiley, *Encyclopedia of Mystical and Paranormal Experience,* (see 1).

Peter Haining, *Anatomy of Witchcraft,* Souvenir.

Michael J. Harner (ed.), *Hallucinogens and Shamanism,* Oxford University Press, Oxford, 1973.

Christina Hole, *Witchcraft in England,* Fitzhouse Books, London, 1977.

Hans Holzer, *The New Pagan,* Doubleday, N.Y., 1972; *The Witchcraft Report,* Ace, N.Y., 1973.

Louise Huebner, *Power Through Witchcraft,* Bantam.

Pennethorne Hughes, *Witchcraft,* Penguin Books, Harmondsworth, 1952.

Francis Huxley, *The Invisibles,* Hart-Davis, London.

June Johns, *King of the Witches,* Peter Davies, London.

Francis King, *Ritual Magic in England,* (see 1).

H.C. Lea, *Materials Towards a History of Witchcraft* (2 vols.), Pennsylvania, 1939.

Lucy Mair, *Witchcraft,* World University Library, 1969.

Daniel Mannix, *The Hellfire Club,* New English Library, London, 1961.

Eric Maple, *The Dark World of Witches,* Pan, London, 1962; *Witchcraft,* Octopus, London, 1973.

Richard Marshall, *Witchcraft: The History and Mythology,* (see 1).

Leo Martello, *Weird Ways of Witchcraft,* H. C. Publishers, N.Y., 1969.

Max Marwick (ed.), *Witchcraft and Sorcery,* Penguin.

A. Metraux, *Voodoo in Haiti,* Deutsch, London, 1959.

Jason Michaels, *The Devil is Alive and Well and Living in America Today,* Award, N.Y., 1973.

Jules Michelet, *Satanism and Witchcraft,* Tandem.

Margaret Murray, *The Witch Cult in Western Europe,* 1921; *The God of the Witches,* 1933; *A Divine King of England* (various).

Geoffrey Parrinder, *Witchcraft,* Penguin Books, Harmondsworth, 1958.

Israel Regardie, *The Eye in the Triangle,* Llewellyn.

H.F.T. Rhodes, *The Satanic Mass,* Arrow, London.

R.H. Robbins, *Encyclopedia of Witchcraft and Demonology,* Crown, London, 1959.

Emile Schurmacher, *Witchcraft Today,* Tomorrow Publications, N.Y., 1963.

A.V. Sellwood and P. Haining, *Devil Worship in Britain,* Corgi, London, 1964.

André and Lynette Singer, *Divine Magic: The World of the Supernatural,* (see 1).

Frank Smyth, *Modern Witchcraft,* Macdonald.

Montague Summers, *The History of Witchcraft and Demonology,* 1926; *The Discovery of Witches,* 1928; *Witchcraft and Black Magic,* 1946 (various).

John Symonds, *The Great Beast,* Mayflower, St. Albans.

J. Tondriau and R. Villeneuve, *A Dictionary of Devils and Demons,* Bay Books, Sydney, 1972.

H.R. Trevor-Roper, *The European Witch Craze of the Sixteenth and Seventeenth Centuries,* Penguin Books, Harmondsworth, 1969.

Doreen Valiente, *Where Witchcraft Lives,* Aquarian Press, London.

Anton Szandor La Vey, *The Satanic Bible* (1969) and *The Satanic Rituals* (1969) Avon, N.Y.; *The Compleat Witch,* Lancer, N.Y., 1971.

J. Charles Wall, *Devils: Their Origins and History,* Studio Editions Ltd., London, 1992.

C.H. Wallace, *Witchcraft in the World Today,* Tandem.

Dennis Wheatley, *The Devil and All His Works,* Hutchinson Publishing Co., London, 1977.

3: SCHOOLS OF MYSTICAL BELIEF

Frater Achad, *Q. B. L.,* Weiser, N.Y., 1972.

Pagal Baba, *Temple of the Phallic King,* Simon & Schuster, N.Y., 1973.

Morey Bernstein, *The Search for Bridey Murphey,* Doubleday, N.Y., 1956.

The Bhagavad Gita, Penguin Books, London (published in various editions).

Helena Petrovna Blavatsky, *Isis Unveiled,* 1877; *The Secret Doctrine,* 1888; *The Key to Theosophy,* 1889.

J.H. Brennan, *Astral Doorways,* (see 1).

Buddhist Scriptures, Penguin Books, London.

W.E. Butler, *The Magician, His Training and Work* (1959) and *Apprenticed to Magic* (1962) Aquarian Press, London.

Arthur Conan Doyle, *The History of Spiritualism,* Doran, N.Y., 1926.

Baba Ram Dass, *Seed,* Lama Foundation-Crown Books, N.Y., 1973.

Martin Ebon (ed.), *Reincarnation in the Twentieth Century,* Signet Books, N.Y., 1970.

Nandor Fodor, *An Encyclopedia of Psychic Science,* University Books, N.Y., 1966.

Adolphe Franck, *The Kabbalah,* 1843 (various).

Eileen Garrett, *Many Voices: The Autobiography of a Medium,* Putnams, N.Y., 1968.

Clare Gibson, *Signs and Symbols,* Saraband Inc., Rowayton, CT, 1996.

Rosemary Goring (ed.), *The Wordsworth Dictionary of Beliefs and Religions,* (see 2).

Peter Grant, *Godmen of India,* Penguin Books, London.

William G. Gray, *The Ladder of Lights,* Helios.

Rosemary Ellen Guiley, *Encyclopedia of Mystical and Paranormal Experience,* (see 1).

Arthur Guirdham, *The Cathars and Reincarnation,* Spearman, London, 1970.

Z'ev Be Shimon Halevi, *Adam and the Kabbalistic Tree,* Rider, London, 1974.

H. Hart, *The Enigma of Survival,* Rider, London, 1959.

Joseph Head and S. L. Cranston, *Reincarnation in World Thought,* Causeway Books, N.Y., 1970.

Douglas Hill, *Return from the Dead,* Macdonald, London, 1970; with Pat Williams, *The Supernatural.*

John R. Hinnells, *The Penguin Dictionary of Religions,* Penguin Books, London, 1984.

Geoffrey Hodson, *The Kingdom of the Gods,* The Theosophical Publishing House, Madras, 1952.

Ellic Howe, *The Magicians of the Golden Dawn,*

Routledge & Kegan Paul, London, 1972.

C. Humphreys, *Buddhism*, Penguin Books, London.

Christopher Isherwood, *Vedanta for the Western World*, Allen & Unwin (various).

Francis King, *Ritual Magic in England*, (see 1).

Gareth Knight, *A Practical Guide to Qabalistic Symbolism* (2 vols.), Helios, Cheltenham, 1965.

C.W. Leadbetter, *An Outline of Theosophy* (1963) and *A Textbook of Theosophy* (1971), The Theosophical Publishing House, Adyar.

S.L. MacGregor Mathers, *The Kabbalah Unveiled*, 1888.

Georgess McHargue, *Facts, Frauds and Phantasms*, Doubleday, N.Y., 1972.

Ralph Metzner, *Maps of Consciousness*, Collier, N.Y.

J. Needleman, *The New Religions*, Allen Lane, London.

G.K. Nelson, *Spritualism and Society*, Schocken, N.Y.

James Pike with Dianne Kennedy, *The Other Side*, Doubleday, N.Y., 1968.

Frank Podmore, *Mediums of the Nineteenth Century*, University Books, N.Y., 1963.

Charles Ponce, *Kabbalah*, Garnstone Press, London.

Josephine Ransom, *A Short History of the Theosophical Society, 1875–1937*, The Theosophical Publishing House, Adyar, 1938.

Israel Regardie, *The Golden Dawn*, (see 1); *The Art of True Healing*, Helios, Cheltenham, 1966; *The Garden of Pomegranates* (1970) and *The Middle Pillar* (see 1).

Leo Schaya, *The Universal Meaning of the Kabbalah*, University Books, N.Y., 1971.

Gershom G. Scholem, *Major Trends in Jewish Mysticism*, Schocken Books, N.Y., 1961.

P. Sen, *Hinduism*, Penguin Books, London (various).

Hugh Shearman, *Modern Theosophy*, The Theosophical Publishing House, Adyar, 1954.

André and Lynette Singer, *Divine Magic: The World of the Supernatural*, (see 1).

H. Sperling and M. Simon, *The Zohar*, Soncino Press.

W. Stainton Moses, *Spirit Teachings*, Spiritualist Press.

Ian Stevenson, *The Evidence for Survival from Claimed Memories of Former Incarnations*, Peto Publications, Tadworth, 1961; *Twenty Cases Suggestive of Reincarnation*, American Society for Psychical Research, N.Y., 1966.

William Stirling, *The Canon*, 1897 (various).

Carlo Suares, The *Cipher of Genesis*, Bantam Books.

R.G. Torrens, *The Secret Rituals of the Golden Dawn*.

Upanishads, Penguin Books, London (various).

A.E. Waite, *The Holy Kabbalah*, University Books.

E. Wood, *Yoga*, Penguin Books, London (various).

4: DIVINATION SYSTEMS

E.T. Bell, *The Magic of Numbers*, McGraw Hill, N.Y.

J. Blofeld, *The Book of Change*, Allen & Unwin.

C. Butler, *Number Symbolism*, Routledge & Kegan Paul, London, 1970.

Paul F. Case, *The Tarot*, Macoy, N.Y., 1947.

Richard Cavendish (ed.), *An Encyclopedia of the Unexplained*, Routledge & Kegan Paul, London.

C.W. Chearley, *Numerology*, Rider, London, 1926.

"Cheiro," *Language of the Hand*.

Aleister Crowley, *The Book of Thoth*, 1944 (various).

Alfred Douglas, *The Tarot*, Penguin Books, Harmondsworth, 1973.

Fred Gettings, *The Book of the Hand*, Hamlyn.

Clare Gibson, *Signs and Symbols*, (see 3).

R. Gleadow, *The Origins of the Zodiac*, Cape, London.

Rosemary Goring (ed.), *The Wordsworth Dictionary of Beliefs and Religions*, (see 2).

Rosemary Ellen Guiley, *Encyclopedia of Mystical and Paranormal Experience*, (see 1).

Douglas Hill & Pat Williams, *The Supernatural*, (see 1).

John R. Hinnells, *The Penguin Dictionary of Religions*.

E. Howe, *Urania's Children: The Strange World of the Astrologer*, Kimber, London, 1967.

Marc Edmund Jones, *Astrology: How and Why it Works*, 1945 (various).

Stuart R. Kaplan, *Tarot Classic*, 1972 (various).

Gareth Knight, *A Practical Guide to Qabalistic Symbolism* (see 3).

V. Lopez, *Numerology*, Citadel, N.Y., 1961.

C. McIntosh, *The Astrologers and Their Creed*, Hutchinson, London, 1969.

André and Lynette Singer, *Divine Magic: The World of the Supernatural*, (see 1).

J. Spier, *The Hands of Children*, Routledge & Kegan Paul, London, 1955.

A.E. Waite, *The Pictorial Key to the Tarot*, 1910.

J.A. West and J. G. Toonder, *The Case for Astrology*, Penguin Books, Harmondsworth, 1973.

Dennis Wheatley, *The Devil and All His Works*, (see 2).

R. Wilhelm, *I Ching*, Routledge & Kegan Paul.

5: INNER EXPERIENCE

Raymond de Becker, *The Meaning of Dreams*, Castle Books, N.Y.

W.E. Butler, *The Magician, His Training and Work*.

Robert Crookall, *The Jung Jaffe View of Out of the Body Experiences*, C.F.P.S.S., London, 1970.

Nevill Drury, *The Path of the Chameleon*, (see 1).

Martin Ebon (ed.), *Exorcism: Fact not Fiction*, Signet.

Harry Edwards, *Spirit Healing* and *The Power of Spiritual Healing*, Jenkins, London, 1963.

Oliver Fox, *Astral Projection: A Record of Out of the Body Experiences*, University Books, N.Y., 1962.

Angel Garma, *The Psychoanalysis of Dreams*, Pall Mall.

Celia Green, *Lucid Dreams* and *Out of the Body Experiences*, Hamish Hamilton, London, 1968.

Rosemary Ellen Guiley, *Encyclopedia of Mystical and Paranormal Experience*, (see 1).

C.E.M. Hansel, *E.S.P.: A Scientific Evaluation*, Scribners, N.Y., 1966.

William Johnstone, *Silent Music: The Science of Meditation*, Collins, London, 1974.

Carl Jung, *The Archetypes and the Collective Unconscious*, Routledge & Kegan Paul, London, 1959; *Man and His Symbols*, Dell, N.Y., 1968.

Marvin Karlins and Lewis Andrews, *Biofeedback*, Garnstone Press, London, 1973.

I.M. Lewis, *Ecstatic Religion*, Penguin Books, Harmondsworth, 1971.

Gay Gaer Luce and Julius Segal, *Sleep*, Heinemann.

R.E.L. Masters and Jean Houston, *Mind Games*, Turnstone Books, London, 1973.

Robert A. Monroe, *Journeys Out of the Body*, Doubleday Anchor, N.Y., 1973.

Sylvan Muldoon and Hereward Carrington, *The Projection of the Astral Body*, 1929 (various).

T.K. Oesterreich, *Possession, Demonaical and Other*, University Books, N.Y., 1961.

Sheila Ostrander and Lynn Schroeder, *Psychic Discoveries Behind the Iron Curtain*, Bantam Books.

J.J. van Pelt, *Medical Hypnosis: New Hope for Mankind*, Gollancz, London, 1953.

Dom Robert Petitpierre, *Exorcism*, S.P.C.K., London.

Guy Lyon Playfair, *If This Be Magic*, Cape, London.

Israel Regardie, *The Middle Pillar*, (see 1).

J.B. Rhine et al, *Extrasensory Perception After Sixty Years*, 1940 (various).

L. Rose, *Faith Healing*, Penguin Books.

William Sargant, *The Mind Possessed*, Heinemann.

Harold Sherman, *Wonder Healers of the Philippines*.

Françoise Strachan, *Casting out Devils*, Aquarian Press.

Charles Tart (ed.), *Altered States of Consciousness*, John Wiley, N.Y., 1969.

Montague Ullmann, Stanley Krippner and Alan Vaughan, *Dream Telepathy*, Turnstone Books.

Benjamin Walker, *Beyond the Body*, Routledge & Kegan Paul, London, 1973.

Leslie Weatherhead, *Psychology, Religion and Healing*, Hodder & Stoughton, London, 1963.

6: ESOTERIC CULTURE AND LORE

Soren Alexandrian, *Surrealist Art*, Thames and Hudson, London, 1970.

Jose and Miriam Arguelles, *Mandala*, Shambala, Berkeley and London, 1972.

Richard Barber and Anne Riches, *A Dictionary of Fabulous Beasts*, Walker, N.Y., 1971.

Dennis Bardens, *Ghosts and Hauntings*, Fontana.

Franz Bardon, *The Practice of Magical Evocation*.

William Rose Benét, *The Reader's Encyclopedia*, 3rd ed., Guild Publishing, London, 1988.

Patti Jean Birosik, *The New Age Music Guide*, Macmillan, N.Y., 1989.

Jorge Luis Borges, *The Book of Imaginary Beings*, Avon.

L. Sprague de Camp, *Lost Continents*, Dover, N.Y.

H. Carrington and N. Fodor, *The Poltergeist Down the Ages*, Rider, London, 1953.

J. Churchward, *The Lost Continent of Mu*, Paperback Library, N.Y., 1968.

Basil Cooper, *The Vampire in Legend, Fact and Art*, Robert Hale, London, 1973.

J.C. Cooper (ed.), *Brewer's Book of Myth and Legend*.

Aleister Crowley, *The Qabalah of Aleister Crowley*.

Gustav Davidson, *A Dictionary of Angels*, Free Press.

I. Donnelly and E. Sykes, *Atlantis*, Steiner, N.Y., 1970.

Nevill Drury, *The Textures of Vision: Explorations in Magical Consciousness*, Routledge & Kegan Paul, London, 1979; with Stephen Skinner, *The Search for Abraxas*, Spearman, London, 1972.

W.Y. Evans-Wentz (ed.), *The Tibetan Book of the Dead*, Oxford University Press, N.Y., 1960.

Christopher Frayling, *Vampyres: Lord Byron to Count Dracula*, Faber and Faber, London, 1991.

M. Gardner, *Fads and Fallacies in the Name of Science*.

Clare Gibson, *Signs and Symbols*, (see 3).

Walter Glover, *The Art of Rosaleen Norton*, Sydney.

Kenneth Grant, *Images and Oracles of Austin Osman Spare*, Muller, London, 1974.

Rosemary Ellen Guiley, *Encyclopedia of Mystical and Paranormal Experience*, (see 1).

Douglas Hill, *Return from the Dead*, MacDonald, London, 1970; with Pat Williams, *The Supernatural*.

Abdul Mati Klarwein, *Milk N' Honey* (1973) and *God Jokes* (1977), Harmony Books, N.Y.

David Larkin (ed.), *The Fantastic Kingdom*, Fantastic Art, Salvador Dalí, Pan Books, London, 1973.

T.C. Lethbridge, *Ghost and Ghoul*, Routledge & Kegan Paul, London, 1961.

J.V. Luce, *The End of Atlantis*, Thames and Hudson.

Eric Maple, *The Realm of Ghosts*, Pan, London, 1964.

Raymond T. McNally and Radu Florescu, *In Search of Dracula*, Warner, N.Y., 1974.

John Milner, *Symbolists and Decadents*, Studio Vista.

Maurice Nadea, *A History of Surrealism*, Cape.

Barrie Neville, "The Trance Art of Victor Angel," in N. Drury (ed.), *Frontiers of Consciousness*, Greenhouse Press, Melbourne, 1975.

John Pollard, *Wolves and Werewolves*, Robert Hale.

Gabriel Ronay, *The Dracula Myth*, W. H. Allen.

John Russell, *Max Ernst*, Thames and Hudson.

W. Scott-Elliot, *The Story of Atlantis and the Lost Lemuria* (various).

Austin O. Spare, *A Book of Automatic Drawings*, Catalpa Press, London, 1973.

Bram Stoker, *Dracula*, 1897; *Dracula's Guest and Other Weird Stories*, 1914 (various).

G.N.M. Tyrrell, *Apparitions* (various).

Ornella Volta, *The Vampire*, Tandem, London, 1965.

Patrick Waldberg, *Surrealism*, Thames and Hudson.

Paul Waldo-Schwartz, *Art and the Occult*, Braziller.

Index